A Brief Guide and Handbook

Forms of Writing

P9-DTT-168

Third Edition

Kay L. Stewart
University of Alberta

Marian E. Allen
Grant MacEwan Community College

Prentice
Hall

Toronto

Canadian Cataloguing in Publication Data

Stewart, Kay L. (Kay Latette), 1942-
   Forms of writing: a brief guide and handbook

3rd ed.
ISBN 0-13-014464-9

1. English language – Rhetoric. 2. English language – Rhetoric – Problems,
exercises, etc. I. Allen, Marian, 1945-   . II. Title.

PE1408.S762 2000   808'.042   C99-931862-4

© 2000 Prentice-Hall Canada Inc., Scarborough, Ontario
Pearson Education

Page 114 "Warren Pryor" from Under the Ice by Alden Nowlan 1961. By
permission of Claudine Nowlan.
Page 139 "The Case for Two-Tier Health" by Dian Francis as printed in the
Edmonton Journal, November 15, 1998. By Permission of the National Post.
Page 172 "After Surgery" by Alice J. Davis from *Her Soul Beneath the Bone:
Women's Poetry on Breast Cancer* ed. by Leatrice H. Lifshitz, 1988.
Page 128 copyright 1998, Douglas Rushkoff

ISBN 0-13-014464-9

Vice-President, Editorial Director: Michael Young
Acquisitions Editor: David Stover
Developmental Editor: Lisa Phillips
Copy Editor: Allyson Latta
Production Editor: Sarah Dann
Production Coordinator: Wendy Moran
Permissions/Photo Research: Susan Wallace-Cox
Art Director: Mary Opper
Cover Design: Julia Hall
Page Layout: B.J. Weckerle

6 7 8 04 03 02

Printed and bound in Canada

To our parents

Preface
to the Third Edition

Our Approach

Our approach in *Forms of Writing* rests on this assumption: good writing results when you know your purpose, your audience, your subject, and the conventions of your chosen form. We focus on three main purposes for writing—to explain, to persuade, and to share personal experience—and show how your purpose influences the strategies you choose in writing for a particular audience. This emphasis on purpose and audience gives you a basic orientation that helps you to understand the conventions of a wide variety of forms, such as personal essays, research papers, and business letters.

This book works well in communications courses, introductory and advanced writing courses, and English courses with a writing component. Many students keep the text as a reference for writing in other courses and on the job.

This edition retains the basic organization of the previous editions. We have, however, updated the material and revised sections to make the book easier to use.

Features of the Text

- An overview of the writing process

- An extensive section on developing writing strategies and the critical thinking that informs them

- Short chapters with easy-to-follow guidelines for many different types of writing, with samples

- Checklists for evaluating your own or your classmates' writing

- A section on Writing with Style that enables you to work independently to improve your word choice and sentence structure

- Explanations of sentence structure, grammar, punctuation, and mechanics with Exercises and Answer Keys.

Organization of the Text

- Part 1, The Writing Process, gives you an overview of all the steps in completing a writing assignment, from defining your purpose and audience to revising and proofreading.

- Part 2, Developing Your Writing Strategies, introduces you to principles of paragraph structure and methods of developing paragraphs—such as analysis, definition, and evaluation—that you may use in many forms of writing.

- Part 3, Writing Essays, provides guidelines for the types of writing you are most likely to do in college and university courses, including essays on literature and research papers.

- Part 4, Business Writing, covers the kinds of business writing that most people do, whatever their occupation—letters of application and résumés, brief reports, and promotional material.

- Part 5, Writing with Style, explains stylistic choices and accepted practices in grammar and punctuation so that you can meet your readers' expectations for clarity and precision in language.

- The Appendices cover material you may need to consult frequently: guidelines for using quotations, documenting sources, and formatting your writing. A Glossary of grammatical terms and Answer Keys for exercises are also included.

Changes in the Third Edition

For this edition, Part 4, Business Writing, has been substantially revised and new material added. It now includes the following:

- All material on job applications conveniently gathered in one chapter

- A case study approach to writing résumés and reports

- Guidelines for creating brochures and flyers

Other sections of the text have also been significantly revised.

- Part 2, Developing Your Writing Strategies, is now divided into chapters corresponding to the types of essays covered in Part 3

- Exercises in the handbook section have been replaced, and new exercises appear throughout
- Web Links and material on conducting computer-aided research have been updated
- New examples illustrate many different forms of writing

Other Resources

- *Forms of Writing Workbook* provides additional exercises on sentence structure, grammar, and punctuation.
- *Instructor's Manual* includes suggested course outlines, classroom activities and exercises, teaching tips, and suggestions for further reading.

Good writing!

Acknowledgments

We wish to thank again all those who contributed to the previous editions; this text also owes much to you.

Throughout, we have relied heavily on work done by students in various courses. Where we had permission to do so, we have named them. Named and nameless, we thank them all for entrusting their writing to us.

Special thanks go to Tatiana LoVerso, who not only allowed us to reshape her research paper, but also found new quotations for us.

Thanks also to Sue Paulson, who transformed the Business Writing section with a minimum of fuss and a maximum of creativity; and to Diane Ewan, who put her inexhaustible knowledge of writing conventions to work in producing the new exercises. Ilona Ryder also made helpful suggestions about business writing, and the staff of the Learning Resources Centre at Grant MacEwan Community College gave invaluable assistance. Marian would like to thank Barbara North, Chair of the English Department, and Allen Watson, Dean of Arts and Science at Grant MacEwan Community College, for their support and encouragement.

At Prentice Hall, our thanks to Developmental Editor Lisa Phillips for her patience and helpfulness; to Production Editor Sarah Dann for her timely encouragement; and to Copy Editor Allyson Latta for her meticulous attention to detail. Working with this team has been a pleasure.

To colleagues, friends, and family who have offered encouragement and endured neglect while we completed this project, our heartfelt appreciation.

Kay Stewart
Marian Allen

CONTENTS

PART 2: DEVELOPING YOUR WRITING STRATEGIES

PART 4: BUSINESS WRITING

15   Writing Letters, Reports, and Brochures

16   Getting a Job

PART 5: WRITING WITH STYLE

APPENDICES

Appendix A: Quotations

Appendix B: Documentation

Part 1

THE WRITING PROCESS
An Overview

As the Industrial Revolution marked the nineteenth century, so the Communication Revolution has marked the twentieth. We can pop a video into the VCR, download from a computer database, fax a document to its destination in seconds. These new technologies, far from reducing the need for good writing skills, have increased them. Someone, somewhere, must write the script for the video, the entries in the database, the important letter or report. In the twenty-first century, that person may be you.

You can more easily meet the varied and changing demands made on your writing skills if you understand the basic steps that many successful writers take in completing a piece of writing.

What we offer is a blueprint: you may find your writing process much less clearcut and tidy. You may discover that you spend more time and energy on some steps than on others, depending on the writing project and your creative style. The writing process is not a rigid structure for you to impose on your writing, but a general plan to help you shape an idea into a written piece. Use the steps to guide you; make the process your own.

CHECKLIST

The Writing Process

1. What is your **subject** for this piece of writing?

   _____

2. What is your **purpose**?
   To explain what/how/why _____
   To change readers' opinions about _____
   To persuade readers to _____
   To share personal experience about _____
3. Who is your **audience**?

   _____

4. What does your **reader profile** suggest about your audience's needs and expectations?

   _____

5. Which method(s) of **gathering material** have you used?

   _____

   Do you have enough material to achieve your purpose?

   _____

6. What **focus** have you chosen for your subject?

   _____

7. Have you written a **draft** to clarify your thoughts?

   _____

8. Have you used an **outline** to organize your material?

   _____

9. Have you **revised** your draft for content and organization?

   _____

10. Have you **proofread** your writing to improve your style?

    _____

11. Have you **proofread** your writing for errors?

    _____

12. Have you presented your writing in an appropriate **format**?

    _____

Chapter 1

Identifying Your Purpose and Audience

In most writing situations, you know the subject you are to write about, such as poverty in Canada, a decline in sales, a manufacturing defect in your car. You also know the form your writing should take: an essay on poverty, a report on sales, a letter about the defect. You may be less aware of the specific kinds of writing possible within these forms. This book will introduce you to a broad range of forms and the strategies for using them most effectively.

Every piece of writing, whatever its subject and form, is shaped by its purpose and audience. The first question to ask yourself is about your purpose: What do I want this piece of writing to do? The second is about your audience: Who am I writing it for?

1a Defining Your Purpose

In this book, we will focus on three broad purposes for writing: to explain, to persuade, and to share ideas and experiences. The first purpose leads to **expository writing**, the second to **persuasive writing**, and the third to **personal writing**. Your understanding of your purpose and audience will influence your choice of form and methods of development, your relationship to your readers, and your choice of language and style.

Writing to Explain

Your writing is expository whenever your main purpose is to provide information, to explain how something works or how something is done, or to explain the meaning of concepts, historical events, works of art, and so on. As these examples suggest, in expository writing your emphasis is on your subject, rather than on your audience or on you as a writer. You and your readers are like observers peering through a microscope and trying to see the same thing on the glass slide.

Writing to Persuade

The central question of all persuasive writing is, *What is good?*— good for one person, a group, a nation, humanity, or the planet. Your purpose is to convince others of your vision of what is good. You may want to persuade your readers to share your attitudes and beliefs, or to act on those beliefs. To accomplish this goal, you have to consider how to appeal to your audience. In the interplay among writer, subject, and audience, the emphasis in persuasive writing shifts toward the audience.

Writing to Share Personal Experience

Personal writing gives you the chance to discover what you think and how you feel about ideas and experiences, and to share these discoveries with others. However, your subject is not always something that happened to you—you may also write about your reactions to the world around you. Nor does personal writing always have to be the serious business of revealing your innermost thoughts and feelings. You, the writer, are on centre stage, and you may therefore choose to present yourself as comic or tragic, satiric or romantic, serious or slightly mad.

Examples

To illustrate differences in these types of writing, we will consider three paragraphs on the same subject: shoplifting. The first comes from an expository essay on what causes people to shoplift.

Sample Expository Writing
Purpose: To Explain Behaviour

The most basic question about shoplifting is this: Why do people steal? According to a security guard for Sears, the reason is not need: "In all the time I've worked here, and of all the arrests I've made, and I've made over 400 arrests, not once, not once was it out of need." Most shoplifters who are caught have more than enough money with them to pay for the item and many have credit cards as well. So why do they steal? According to Bill Cheung at The Bay, the peak seasons for shoplifting are September and January–February, when new school terms begin. Presumably, at the beginning of the term, students look at the clothes or toys their peers have and want them. Children and adolescents, it seems, shoplift to fit in.

—Amanda Thompson

This paragraph illustrates the principal features of much expository writing. The writer explains why some people shoplift without stating her opinion about the behaviour. She presents her information and analysis as objectively as possible, referring to shoplifters as *people* and *students*, for example, not as *thieves* and *juvenile delinquents*. In this way, she keeps the focus on her subject, not on her opinions about the subject or on her own personality.

Sample Persuasive Writing
Purpose: To Change Opinion or Behaviour

Contrary to the popular view, most shoplifters do not steal because they are poor. A longtime security guard for Sears, who has arrested more than 400 shoplifters, points out that "not once" had the person stolen out of need. Shoplifters usually have more than enough money with them to pay for the stolen goods, and they often have credit cards as well. They may tell themselves that the stores are so rich they will not miss this little eraser/tube of lipstick/makeup case/radio/stereo/jacket. But it is not the stores that pay; honest customers pay through higher prices. There is thus no reason to be lenient with shoplifters. They are as guilty of theft as the person who steals a wallet from a locker room or a tape deck from a car, and should be treated accordingly. If we turn a blind eye to shoplifting, we are not only condoning a crime, but also sentencing ourselves to pay the penalty.

Here the writer's purpose is not to explain some possible reasons for shoplifting, but to persuade readers to change their attitude, and possibly their behaviour, toward shoplifters. In contrast to the neutral language of the expository paragraph, the writer uses emotionally charged words and phrases (*honest, guilty, lenient, condoning, sentencing*). This language focuses attention on the attitude that the writer wants readers to adopt.

Sample Personal Writing
Purpose: To Share Personal Experience

I was thirteen at the time, in a new school, and desperate to make friends. For the first few weeks, everyone ignored me. Not that all my classmates were friends with each other. At lunch hour and after school they divided into groups and alternately ignored and insulted each other. I was afraid that if I didn't make friends soon, they would stop ignoring and start insulting me. So one day, I followed a gang of five or six into the mall at lunch. As they straggled through The Bay, I kept several feet behind, stopping every now and then to gaze intently at leather briefcases or umbrellas so they wouldn't think I was being pushy. When they clustered around the jewelry counter, I ducked down the next row. And there in front of me were bags and bags of candy, ready for Hallowe'en. Without thinking, I grabbed one and stuffed it under my jacket.

This writer invites us to share the isolation, fear, and desire to belong that led to shoplifting a bag of candy. The story carries us along and makes us part of the events. Even though we may disapprove of the theft, we are drawn into the writer's subjective experience.

The first question to ask yourself about any writing situation, then, is *What is my purpose?* In some writing situations, you may be free to choose your own purpose. If you wanted to write an article on grizzly bears for a general interest magazine, for instance, you could choose to explain the grizzly's habits, to argue for better protection for this endangered species, or to share your own adventures in grizzly country.

In many school and work situations, however, your purpose will be given or implied. An assignment that asks you to write a persuasive essay on capital punishment defines your purpose. A manager who asks you to write a report on the branch office assumes that you will explain the problems, not air your frustrations in trying to compile the data.

1b Defining Your Audience

Defining your purpose is the first step in writing; the second is defining your audience. Just as your style of speaking changes as you move from the poolroom to the classroom, so your style of writing changes with your audience. Are you writing for readers who already know a great deal about your subject, or for those who know nothing at all? For educated adults, or for elementary school children? Considering the needs of your audience will help you decide, for instance, how much background information to give and whether to use a formal or an informal style.

Making Reader Profiles

You can develop a clearer sense of your audience by asking yourself these questions.

1. **Who** will read this piece? A specific person, such as a supervisor? A group of people with similar interests, such as *Star Trek* fans? A group of people of varying ages and backgrounds, such as newspaper readers?

2. What **attitude** will my reader(s) probably bring to this piece of writing? Interest and enthusiasm? Hostility and defensiveness? Critical detachment?

3. How much **knowledge** will my reader(s) already have about my subject? What information do I need to provide?

4. What **expectations** will my reader(s) have about the way this piece is written? Is there a specific format I should follow?

Answering these questions will give you a **reader profile**: a general sense of your audience's needs and expectations. Keeping this reader profile in mind as you write or revise will help you communicate more effectively. If you give some thought to what a potential employer looks for in a letter of application, for example, you can tailor your application to match those expectations.

Exercise 1.1

Choose two of the following subjects. Using the example of writing articles on grizzly bears as a guide (see p. 6), show how each subject could be the basis for three pieces of writing with

7

different purposes: one expository, one persuasive, and one personal.

Example: Subject—bicycles

Expository: to explain how to choose a bike
Persuasive: to persuade cyclists to obey traffic regulations
Personal: to share my experience cycling from Jasper to Banff

- kayaking
- tuition fees
- affordable housing
- Canada's role as a peacekeeper
- doing volunteer work
- pop culture

Exercise 1.2

Choose one piece of writing from your response to Exercise 1.1 and make a reader profile for one of the audiences below.

- a magazine for elementary school children

- a newspaper

- an e-zine devoted to that subject

- a television newscast

- an instructor

- an employer

Exercise 1.3

Using the same piece of writing you chose for Exercise 1.2, make a reader profile for a different audience from the list above.

Exercise 1.4

Briefly explain the major similarities and differences in the way you would write the piece for the two audiences you have chosen, based on your reader profiles.

Chapter 2

Gathering Material

Good writing, whether it's a job application letter or a term paper, begins with strong content focused around a central point. The following techniques will help you generate ideas, collect information, and find a focus.

2a Brainstorming

Brainstorming allows you to capture your spontaneous responses to your subject. Put a key word from your writing task in the centre of a blank page. Allow yourself to free-associate—what ideas, examples, questions, memories, or feelings spring to mind? Surround your key word with notes, without rejecting anything. If you were preparing a report on the need for life skills courses in high school, for instance, you might end up with a brainstorming diagram something like this:

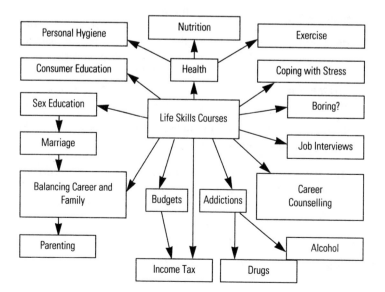

With so many ideas to consider, you can find a fresh angle on your subject or choose material of special interest to your readers. And brainstorming guarantees that you won't run out of things to say.

2b Freewriting

Many people discount their most creative ideas, intuitions, and memories before they start. To get around this internal censor, try **freewriting**. Write continuously about your subject for five or ten minutes, without stopping to correct or criticize. If you run out of things to say, write something like "I can't think of anything to say" and keep writing. Do not hesitate over words, make corrections, or stop to think. After ten minutes, look over what you've written and sum it up in a sentence. If your summary suggests new ideas, freewrite for another ten minutes.

2c Asking Discovery Questions

There are three ways to use this technique.

1. *Start with the journalist's five Ws and an H: Who, What, When, Where, Why, and How.*

   Answering these questions will give you information that your reader is likely to need in any situation. If you were writing a letter of complaint about a garment that had been damaged at the dry cleaners, for instance, you might ask these questions: What is the garment? Where did I take it? When did I take it in and pick it up? Who wrote up the order? What is the damage? How did the damage occur? What do I want the company to do?

   If you are writing on an unfamiliar topic, you may need to do research to answer even these basic questions.

2. *Ask questions based on methods of developing your ideas (see chapters 5, 6, and 7).* For an essay on drug addiction, for instance, you might ask questions such as these:

   • How is addiction defined?

   • What are the stages of addiction?

- What are the causes? the effects?

- Can I classify drug addicts?

- How does drug addiction compare with other kinds of addiction?

- Is there a story I could tell about drug addiction?

- How could I describe the behaviour typical of addicts?

- How do social factors contribute to drug addiction?

- What are the strengths and weaknesses of current drug treatment programs?

- What analogy would help to explain the difficulties in overcoming drug addiction?

- What examples would support my points?

3. *Ask questions specific to the appropriate academic discipline or area of inquiry* (for examples, see the questions for analyzing imaginative literature, p. 112, and the questions for evaluating an argument, p. 138).

2d Keeping a Journal

Keeping a **journal** can be an excellent way of gathering ideas and information for a long-term writing project. Use your journal entries to reflect on issues, respond to your reading, collect relevant newspaper or magazine items, note questions to pursue, and record your progress. When the time comes to write your essay, you will have lots of material and original insights.

2e Prewriting on the Computer

If you work on a computer, you can use it for gathering material long before you start to write your first draft. Brainstorming may be easier with pen and paper, but the computer is ideal for freewriting, asking discovery questions, and keeping a journal. For example, you can create a file (called *Notes,* for example) where you can keep notes on your reading, copy down quotations, compile references, and jot down ideas as they come to you. Print out and review this material before you start to write.

The computer can also help you avoid the temptation to correct typos or make other changes as you freewrite. Try darkening the monitor with the contrast control or covering the screen with a blanket or towel. (If you are working in a computer lab, you may get some odd looks, but the results should make it all worthwhile.)

2f Finding a Focus

You have defined your purpose and audience. You have gathered ideas and information about your subject. But you have so many ideas and so much information that you don't know what to include and what to leave out. You need a focus.

To define a focus for your writing, link your purpose and audience with one or more aspects of your subject. For a short piece, you may choose to discuss one aspect in detail. For a longer piece, you may include several. Suppose, for example, that your purpose is to explain some aspect of car auctions to newspaper readers. For a short piece, you could focus on what a car auction is. For a longer piece, you might also explain how cars are sold at auctions and why people buy or sell cars there.

Writing your focus at the top of your paper when you begin your draft will remind you of what you need to cover.

Exercise 2.1

Make a brainstorming diagram for one of the following subjects.

- music videos
- authority figures
- teens as consumers
- underemployment
- reproductive technologies
- horror movies

Exercise 2.2

Choose a different subject from the list above and generate material for an essay by freewriting or by asking discovery questions.

Exercise 2.3

Using the material you have generated in exercise 2.1 or 2.2, show how you could focus your material for five different purposes and audiences.

Example: Subject—Life skills courses
(see brainstorming diagram p. 9)

1. My purpose is to persuade teachers that preparing for job interviews by role-playing should be a part of every life skills course.

Finding a
Focus

Chapter 3

Drafting, Outlining, and Revising

3a

Fast-Drafting

Strategies for drafting and revising vary from form to form and writer to writer. For a brief letter, you may simply type out your request, proofread for mistakes, and seal it in the envelope. A letter of application, a report, or an essay will require a more careful consideration of content, organization, and style.

Strategies also vary among writers. Some writers discover their main point in the process of writing a draft, and then make substantial changes in content and organization. Others plan what they want to say, either in their minds or in an outline, so their first draft has a main point and a clear pattern of organization. Revision for these writers is largely a matter of smoothing out sentences and improving word choice.

We will illustrate both ways of getting started so that you can choose the method that best suits you and your writing task.

3a Fast-Drafting

If you decide to write a fast draft to help clarify your thinking, set a fixed period—usually an hour or two—and don't let yourself get bogged down. Write a complete draft within this time. If you have trouble with the introduction, for example, either leave some space and come back to it later, or write your statement of focus and go on from there.

When you reread, you may find that your main point has surfaced near the end and that you need to restructure. Making an outline of your draft will help you decide how to reorganize your material.

3b Making an Outline

An outline shows you at a glance the main divisions of your paper and the relationships among major points, minor points, and details. Making an outline thus helps you to classify your material and detect gaps in it.

There are several points in the process of drafting and revising at which you might find an outline useful. Some writers like to make an outline before they write a first draft. For this kind of preliminary outline, use your statement of focus as a guide to your main points. Under each main point, jot down the details you will need to include.

Other writers use a revision outline to clarify the organization of their ideas. After writing a draft, they make an outline showing the main point and supporting details in each paragraph. The outline will reveal problems in content and organization: paragraphs that need to be combined or divided, points that need further explanation, and topic sentences that could be improved, for example. You may find a revision outline useful for evaluating the structure and completeness of your piece.

You can also make a formal outline of your final version to accompany a lengthy report or research paper. Put your thesis—the main point of your piece—at the top of the page. List your major points with Roman numerals, your subpoints with capital letters, and details with Arabic numerals. The format of your outline should resemble the one below.

Sample Formal Outline

Thesis Because shoplifting has become so widespread, methods of identifying and apprehending shoplifters have changed.

- I. Extent of the problem
  - A. Type of goods stolen
    1. From novelty stores
    2. From department stores
  - B. Amount stolen annually
- II. Types of shoplifters
  - A. Professionals
  - B. Amateurs
- III. Some reasons for shoplifting
  - A. Need
  - B. Desire to fit in
  - C. Thrills

IV. Methods of detection
   A. Following suspects
   B. Using one-way mirrors and closed-circuit television

As you can see, each level of the outline (Roman numerals, capital letters, Arabic numerals) represents a division of the level below. For this reason, you should have at least two items at each level (if you have an A, you must have a B; if you have a 1, you must have a 2). Each item at a particular level must be an equivalent subdivision of the level above. For example, *Need*, *Desire to fit in*, and *Thrills* are equivalent items under *Some reasons for shoplifting*. This equivalence will be more obvious if you make items at each level grammatically parallel (see 18e, Faulty Parallelism).

3c Revising and Proofreading

Revision is one of the most important parts of the composing process, and often the most time-consuming. So give yourself plenty of time. When you have written a draft, evaluate it (or have someone else evaluate it) according to the appropriate checklist(s). For an overall view of the writing process, see p. 2; for paragraphs, p. 22; for essays, p. 70; for business writing, p. 178. Make any necessary revisions in content and organization.

Then read your work aloud to get a sense of how it sounds to another reader. If some sections seem wordy, monotonous, or stilted, see the checklist and pointers in Chapter 17, Improving Your Style.

Next, proofread carefully for typos, errors in grammar and punctuation, and misused words. For more information on these aspects of writing, see the checklist for Improving Your Style and Proofreading (p. 210) and the relevant sections of Part 5.

Finally, make sure that you have presented your work in the appropriate format. You will find examples in Appendix B, Documentation, and Appendix C, Proofreading and Format Conventions.

3d Drafting and Revising on the Computer

Most word-processing programs make drafting and revising on the computer quick and easy, allowing you more flexibility to experiment. You can insert, delete, and move text until you are satisfied with the result. If you and your classmates are linked by e-mail, you can share drafts of your work and post editing suggestions to one another electronically. E-mail also provides a forum for collaborative writing. You and others can log on simultaneously, and attempt to write or edit a document collectively. This process can provide you with insights into how others write, as well as give you helpful feedback on your own work.

Although you may make many changes on-screen as you write, it is a good idea to print hard copies to help you revise. One reason is that your monitor displays only a small section of your document. A hard copy will give you a better grasp of how well your material is organized and whether you've been enticed into wordiness by an empty screen. Another advantage is that you can circulate a hard copy to others for feedback.

To aid in editing, many word-processing packages include a built-in thesaurus, spell checker, and grammar and style checker. Although you may find these options helpful, you need to be aware of their limitations. A thesaurus, whether in print or on disk, cannot tell you whether a listed synonym is appropriate in a specific context. Spell checkers only recognize words that have been entered into their memories; they may tag as errors acceptable variations in the spelling of certain words (*analyse/analyze*, for example); and they will not catch properly spelled words used incorrectly (*there* for *their*, for example).

Grammar and style checkers have similar limitations. They may help you recognize grammatical and stylistic problems such as sentence fragments and convoluted sentences. But they cannot distinguish between an outright error and a choice you've made for stylistic or rhetorical effect. Like spell checkers, they are best used to supplement your own proofreading skills.

Word-Processing Guidelines

- Make backup copies. Always keep two copies of your work in electronic form (normally one on your hard drive and one on a disk) in case one gets lost or damaged. If your computer doesn't have a timed backup function, save your work every fifteen minutes or so.

- Don't wait until the night before your work is due to print out. Printers seem prone to last-minute glitches. Planning ahead is especially important if you are working with more than one system: systems may not be compatible; computer labs often don't allow disks to be brought in from the outside because of the danger of spreading viruses; or your instructor may not be able to read your e-mail attachment.

- Double space, using a readable, standard size font (10 or 12 characters per inch). Avoid condensed and ornate styles.

Exercise 3.1

Draft a paragraph on a subject of your choice and exchange drafts with a classmate. Use the Checklist for Paragraphs (p. 22) to make suggestions for revision.

Exercise 3.2

Exchange the paragraph you wrote in Exercise 3.1 with a different classmate. Use the Checklist for Improving Your Style and Proofreading (p. 210) to make suggestions for revision.

Exercise 3.3

Make a formal outline for an essay you have written. Use your thesis as a guide.

- Directory of Academic Internet Resources—listings of best Internet sites for each subject. For more on this site, see Conducting Computer-Aided Research, (14b).

  www.academicinfo.net/

- The Journal Writer—a monthly newsletter (subscriber paid). Includes guidelines and exercises for journal writing. Free online sample.

  www.rio.com/~wplace/journal.html

- York University Computer Assisted Writing Centre—an excellent resource that provides techniques and strategies for writing essays.

  www.yorku.ca/admin/cawa/strategies/contents.html

- Writers on the Net—classes, tutoring, mentoring, and writers' groups. Free newsletter.

  www.writers.com/

- Writer's Resources on the Web—extensive range of links

  www.inkspot.com/~ohi/www/writesource.html

- Canadian-Based Publications Online—articles and abstracts from newpapers, magazines, and trade journals.

  www.cs.cmu.edu/Web/Unofficial/Canadiana/Ca-zines. html#Magazines

Part 2

DEVELOPING YOUR WRITING STRATEGIES

CHECKLIST

Paragraphs

	OK	NEEDS WORK
1. Is your purpose clear?	☐	☐
2. Have you chosen an appropriate method of development?	☐	☐
3. Does the topic sentence state the main point?	☐	☐
4. Are the details adequate?	☐	☐
5. Are the details relevant?	☐	☐
6. Is the paragraph a readable length (not too long or too short)?	☐	☐
7. Have you used effective transitions?	☐	☐

Chapter 4

Writing Better Paragraphs

Paragraphs are the building blocks of writing. Introductory paragraphs lay the foundation; concluding paragraphs provide the capstone, or finishing touch. In between are the middle paragraphs, each one discussing one aspect of your subject (one point in an analysis, one step in a process, one event in a narrative). Each middle paragraph is thus both a self-contained piece of writing and a part of a larger structure. In this chapter we focus on general strategies for writing paragraphs.

You will find detailed guidelines for developing paragraphs for particular purposes in the following chapters: Chapter 5, Methods for Sharing Personal Experience; Chapter 6, Methods for Explaining; and Chapter 7, Methods for Persuading.

4a Topic Sentences

Good topic sentences serve as guideposts for your reader by making a point about your subject that you will discuss in greater detail in the rest of the paragraph. They also control the content of the paragraph by clearly defining its focus. Weak topic sentences define the focus of the paragraph but don't make a point. Statements of fact make poor topic sentences. They leave readers confused about both the focus and the point of the paragraph. Consider these examples:

> I took a summer school course. [statement of fact: does not make a point or establish a focus]

> Going to summer school affected my relationship with my children. [weak topic sentence: subject clearly focused but no point]

> Going to summer school forced me to make more conscious choices about the time I spent with my children. [good topic sentence: subject clearly focused, makes a point]

Exercise 4.1

Consider the following statements as possible topic sentences for a paragraph. Decide whether each one is a good topic sentence, a weak topic sentence, or a statement of fact. Rewrite weak topic sentences and statements of fact to make good topic sentences.

1. Last summer I climbed a mountain.

2. Hospitals can be bad for your health.

3. Canada is a member of NATO.

4. Watching a movie in a theatre is a more intense experience than watching it at home on television.

5. Nearly 20 percent of high school athletes take steroids.

6. There are many reasons couples divorce.

4b *The Body of the Paragraph*

As we have seen, topic sentences make a point that you can then develop through more specific points and details. If your paragraph lacks specific details, you will have trouble explaining your ideas and convincing your readers that the ideas are valid. Consider the following example.

> **Because most cyclists ignore the rules of the road, they are a danger to themselves and others.** Most motorists hate and fear cyclists. When I see how cyclists ride anywhere they want on the road, I wonder what they are protecting inside their helmets.

This paragraph consists of three generalizations that make the same point, rather than one topic sentence with general statements and specific details to support it. If you have trouble developing your ideas, you may need to clarify your purpose: Is your aim to explain something? to persuade your readers to change their opinion or behaviour? to share your experiences or perceptions? You can then choose an appropriate method (or methods) of development discussed in the next three chapters. The guidelines in these chapters will help you improve the content of your paragraphs.

Whichever method(s) of development you choose, you will probably need to provide examples to illustrate your main points. For suggestions on using examples more effectively, see (7a).

Exercise 4.2

List several examples you could use to illustrate each of the following ideas.

1. Many restaurants offer good food at reasonable prices.

2. My hometown's points of interest are waiting to be explored.

3. Many Canadian writers are highly regarded in other countries.

4c Paragraph Structure

There are two basic ways of organizing information in a paragraph. You can begin with your topic sentence and then fill in the reasons, examples, and other details that provide evidence to support it, or you can begin with these details and examples and gradually lead your reader to the main point you want to make about them. The first method places immediate emphasis on your main point, whereas the second emphasizes the process of thinking and feeling that led you to it. You can see the difference between these two basic ways of organizing information in the following examples.

Sample Paragraph: Topic-Sentence-First Arrangement

Working nights in a convenience store introduced me to a side of my neighbourhood I hadn't known before. One surprise was the discovery of neighbours who emerged from their homes only after midnight, but the night lives of people I had met before were also surprising. I discovered that old Mr. Moses, with whom I had exchanged perhaps twenty sentences in the past ten years, was a talkative insomniac, addicted to corned beef sandwiches at 3 a.m. He had been an intelligence agent with an amazing career, which he unfolded in successive nightly installments. And then there was Mrs. Anderson. I had always imagined her to be one half of a happily married older couple, but twice in the first month I worked at the store, Mrs. Anderson met a man (who was definitely not her husband) and disappeared into the night. I was beginning to see new meaning in the term "convenience store."

Sample Paragraph: Details-First Arrangement

Before I started working in one, a convenience store was just a place to go when you ran out of milk late at night. I hadn't realized that I had many nocturnal neighbours who emerged from their homes only after midnight. More surprising, however, were the night lives of people I knew. Old Mr. Moses, with whom I had exchanged perhaps twenty sentences in the past ten years, turned out to be a talkative insomniac, addicted to corned beef sandwiches at 3 a.m. In nightly installments he unfolded his amazing career as an intelligence agent. And then there was Mrs. Anderson. I had always thought of her as one half of a happily married older couple, but twice in the first month I worked at the store she met a man (who was definitely not her husband) and disappeared into the night. Working nights in a convenience store introduced me to a side of my neighbourhood I hadn't known before.

Note: Do not end a paragraph with the topic sentence for the next paragraph. While your intention may be to provide a transition, you will only confuse your readers.

4d Paragraph Divisions

By dividing your material into paragraphs, you signal that all the information in a particular paragraph relates to one aspect of your subject. In this way, you help your reader to understand how you have organized your material. Paragraph divisions that seem random—because paragraphs run on for pages or consist of only a sentence or two—will confuse your reader.

Readers find excessively long paragraphs difficult to understand and uninviting to read. Normally, you should be able to discuss one aspect of your subject adequately in about half a page. If you need more room to develop your ideas, subdivide your paragraph. Instead of trying to discuss several effects of taking a summer school course in one paragraph, for example, focus each paragraph on one effect, such as the effect on your relationship with your family.

You may occasionally use a one-sentence paragraph to signal a transition or to emphasize a point. But a series of short paragraphs can confuse readers; they lose the sense of how the paragraphs relate to each other and to the piece of writing as a whole. If several short paragraphs discuss only one aspect of your subject, you can simply combine them. More often, however, paragraphs are short because they do not provide enough reasons, details, and examples to explain one aspect of your subject. You will find many methods of developing paragraphs discussed in chapters 5, 6, and 7.

4e Transitions

Transitions are words and phrases (*on the other hand, for example, as a result, similarly*) that help a reader to move from one sentence to the next in your writing. If you compare the following paragraphs, you will see how transitions can dramatically increase the clarity of your ideas and the flow of your writing.

Transitions

Sample Draft Paragraph without Transitions

I had been working as a carpenter for five years. I injured my back. I needed to find a different sort of job. I had always been interested in starting my own business. I decided to take business courses at a community college. I was uneasy about taking college courses. My writing skills needed work. I got a D on my first essay. I was discouraged and considered dropping the course. My instructor asked me to speak with her. She explained how I could improve my essay and gave me a chance to revise it. I decided to stay in the course and pursue my dream of a new life.

Sample Revised Paragraph with Transitions

After working as a carpenter for five years, I injured my back. **As a result of this injury,** I needed a different kind of job. I had always wanted to start my own business, **so** I decided to take some business courses at a community college. I was, **however,** uneasy about taking college courses. English, **for example,** scared me **because** I knew my writing skills were weak. **When** I got a D on my first essay, I was discouraged and considered dropping the course. Then my instructor asked me to come in and speak with her. **During this interview,** she explained how I could improve my essay and gave me a chance to revise it. **Because of this encouragement,** I decided to stay in the course and pursue my dream of a new life.

In the revised paragraph, sentences are linked by transitions showing time relationships and causal connections. You will find information on transitions to use with a specific method of development in the appropriate section of chapters 5, 6, and 7. For more information on transitions, see Chapter 17, Improving Your Style.

Exercise 4.3

Write a paragraph on any subject that interests you. Begin with your topic sentence. Then rewrite the paragraph, putting the details first and ending with your topic sentence. Underline your topic sentences and circle all transitional words and phrases.

Transitions

Chapter 5

Methods of Sharing Personal Experience

As newspapers, magazines, and television networks have discovered, readers and viewers have a seemingly insatiable interest in others' personal lives. You too can enliven your writing by adding personal touches from your own or someone else's experience. In this chapter you will learn how to tell stories that illustrate your point; how to describe people, places, and things so that they come alive; and how to use analogies that convey your feelings and attitudes.

5a Telling a Story

Telling stories is one of the main ways we make sense of our lives for ourselves and share our world with others. Funny stories, heroic stories, romantic stories—they all have something to say about who we are. The stories we keep hidden—stories about our fears, our failures, our struggles—are often the ones that, when told, connect us to others. To see how you can develop these stories into personal essays, see Chapter 10.

Short personal narratives are often used to enliven other kinds of writing. An article criticizing cuts to health care, for instance, may begin with a story about a patient who died while awaiting surgery. It is these personal narratives we will focus on in this section. You will find examples of narration combined with analysis in the samples that illustrate causal analysis (6d), plot summaries (12c), and expository essays (11b).

Here are some suggestions for writing personal narratives.

• *Choose a single meaningful event with a definite beginning and end.*
The event may be part of a larger story that you could write about in a personal essay. For instance, you might write a narrative paragraph about one adventure with a friend that could

later form part of a longer essay exploring your relationship with this friend more fully.

- *Decide what point you want to make about this event.*

Did your adventure, for example, teach you something about taking risks or about taking precautions? about trust or about self-reliance? You could state this point explicitly in a topic sentence, or you could allow it to emerge implicitly from the way you tell the story.

- *Decide how to organize your paragraph.*

To heighten suspense, you can give events in chronological order, with your point emerging at the end. Or, if you want to emphasize your reflections on the incident, you could begin with your point and then tell the story.

- *Use transitions to help your reader follow the sequence of events.*

Show how events are related in time by using terms such as *first, next, then, last; in the beginning, in the end; soon, later, as soon as, meanwhile;* and by referring to specific times, days, months, seasons, and dates.

- *Select details that will create in readers a response similar to your own.*

Recording small details is one way to individualize your stories. In writing about a familiar situation such as attending a circus, for example, you might make the experience fresh for your readers by comparing the fake tears of a clown with the real tears of a child who drops an ice-cream cone.

- *Choose words that make the experience vivid for your reader and convey your attitude toward the event.*

For more on word choice, see Chapter 17, Improving Your Style.

- *Include your thoughts, feelings, and judgments about the event.*

Direct statements about thoughts, feelings, and judgments help readers understand the significance of details. For example, you might begin or end a series of seemingly random and contradictory ideas with the statement *I was confused.*

Sample Personal Narrative

This narrative paragraph creates suspense through its precise details, expressions of feeling, and chronological arrangement of events. The image in the last two sentences implicitly makes the writer's point about overcoming fear. These two sentences therefore serve as the topic sentence for the paragraph. A paragraph such as this would make a good introduction to a personal essay.

Others have ascended the incredibly high platform, seemingly thousands of feet above the pool. More than one has returned by the wet ladder, a sensible choice in my mind. Why then is my foot on the first rung? It is colder and slicker than would appear. My feet leave the safe ground and propel me towards the high roof of the pool. Partway up I consider turning back. Yes. But another below has decided to follow, and I must reach the top before turning around. Halfway up, I guess, but I dare not look down lest my arms and legs freeze in terror. I keep my eyes focused on the ladder, only inches from my nose. The last step comes into view. With dangerously stiff muscles and complete lack of grace or courage, I plant my feet on the concrete slab. I see my wet footprints and decide to look at nothing else. With the slap of feet an older boy makes his entrance onto this platform in the sky. He passes, grinning at me, and in one quick fluid motion he disappears over the edge. I hear nothing, nothing, then a faint splash. Something deep inside me snaps and I follow suit. Crazy. Stupid. Stop! I'm in the air, hand clasped tight over my nose as I shut my eyes. Dear God, I'm drowning. I must be at the bottom of the pool. Frantically kicking, I break the surface. It's hard to wipe this maniac smile off my face. Perhaps once more.

—Ken Miller

Exercise 5.1

Identify a quality you particularly like or dislike in yourself or someone else. Then write a narrative paragraph about an incident that reveals this quality.

Example: a roommate's stinginess—refusing to share nachos and pizza while we watched the Grey Cup.

Exercise 5.2

Choose a significant experience in your life (such as a birth, death, marriage, divorce, move, accident, achievement or failure). Use brainstorming to help you recall the small but meaningful incidents you associate with the experience (such as riding in an ambulance). Choose one of these incidents with a definite beginning and end, and write a narrative paragraph that shows its significance.

Example: Experience—changing schools in the middle of grade four. Event—failing a math test on my first day. Significance— always feeling an outsider at school.

5b Describing a Person, Place, or Thing

When you describe people, places, or things, you attempt to translate into words how they look, sound, feel, smell, move, or taste. The language you use to describe something will depend upon your purpose and audience. A geographer writing a scientific article about the Canadian Shield would describe Northern Ontario differently than would a real estate agent selling holiday properties. Someone writing a personal essay about growing up in the bush would offer a third perspective on the same landscape, one coloured by the intensity and selectivity of childhood memory.

In personal writing, you want your reader to share experiences—such as your father's delight in reading bedtime stories, your fear as you walk down a deserted street at night, your love–hate relationship with an unreliable car. As these examples suggest, descriptions are like snapshots of significant moments in which you capture your attitude toward a person, place, or thing. You convey your attitude by selecting details that work together to create a dominant impression of your subject. If you wanted to show your father's delight in bedtime reading, for example, you would ignore the note of exasperation that crept into his voice if you interrupted too often, and instead describe his excitement as he "became" different characters in *Peter Pan*.

Vivid descriptions of people, places, and things are central to most personal essays, as you can see from the sample essays in Chapter 10. Descriptive paragraphs also make good introductions for expository and persuasive essays. For example, you might begin a persuasive essay on the importance of parental involvement in children's learning to read with a paragraph describing your father reading. A descriptive paragraph like this adds human interest to discussions of general issues. For an example, see the sample expository essay on child poverty (11b).

Follow these guidelines for writing descriptive paragraphs:

- **Choose a subject that you are very familiar with or that you can observe while you write.**

It is surprisingly hard to remember the kinds of detail that will bring your paragraph to life—the colour of a friend's eyes, the sound of wind through trees, the smell of a school room. If you choose to describe something from memory, try closing your eyes and putting yourself into the scene before you write about it.

- **Decide what dominant impression you want to convey about your subject.**

A good description is not merely a catalogue of features: "My cat is a Siamese with the usual blue eyes and dark grey ears." It creates a *dominant impression* by giving details that convey a particular quality of your subject: a kitten's playfulness, an aunt's stubbornness, the peacefulness of a landscape.

- **Focus your paragraph.**

Describing a Person, Place, or Thing

For example, describe your subject at a particular time, or performing a particular action. This focus will help you to *describe* rather than give examples. For instance, you could vividly *describe* a kitten's playfulness—how it looks, moves, sounds—by focusing on how it acts in front of the mirror. Without this focal point, you might give many examples of a kitten's playful behaviour without describing any of them in enough detail to be interesting.

- **Select details that contribute to the dominant impression you want to convey.**

Include a broad range of sensory details—not just how something looks, but also how it sounds, feels, tastes, smells, moves.

- **Arrange the details in a spatial order with the most important detail last.**

Choose an arrangement that reflects how you as an observer would perceive your subject: in a panoramic sweep from left to right; from close up to farther away, or vice versa; or from the most obvious feature to the least obvious.

- **Show how objects are related in space.**

Use transitional words such as *nearer, farther; on the right, on the left; at the top, at the bottom; to the east, to the west.*

- **Begin or end with a point about the person, place, or thing you are describing.**

"My cat is very playful" is a descriptive generalization, but it is not an interesting point about the kitten's behaviour. You could make a more interesting point about the transitory nature of youth and playfulness. You could state this point explicitly in a topic sentence: "Watching my kitten play, I remember how I used to make faces at myself in the mirror, not realizing that the scowls of childhood would settle into the lines of middle age." Or you could let it emerge implicitly through your description: "Each day the kitten tires of the game more quickly, and soon we will both pass the mirror without a glance."

In the following paragraph from a personal essay, the writer tells us almost nothing about the physical appearance of a teacher who "shocked me so much that I experienced a marked change in my attitude towards school and the subject of English." Instead, he chooses details that show how Mr. Wellington's surroundings reflect his vulnerability, and then makes this point in a topic sentence at the end.

5b

Describing a Person, Place, or Thing

Sample Personal Description

Mr. Wellington was neither neat nor tidy. The chaos of his room seemed to echo the sound of someone saying, "Hang on, it's in here somewhere. I just put it down yesterday. I'll find it." The walls were covered from top to bottom with posters, but not a single one was hung straight. His desk was inhabited by masses of paper that had somehow gathered there as if attracted by a "paper magnet." Surrounding his desk was a whole herd of dictionaries, including a condensed version of the Oxford English Dictionary, which required a magnifying glass to peer into the depths of its compiled wisdom. He would frequently consult these books in efforts to stop the arguments waged against him about the meanings of words in the poems we analyzed in class. Throughout all this activity, his coffee cup was never to be seen detached from his hand. I cannot blame him for needing a cup of coffee to carry him through to the next period. It was his coffee cup that made him look human, vulnerable—not like the other teachers, who were not human but "teachers." Perhaps it was his vulnerability that inspired confidence, even though he was surrounded by what looked like ineptitude.

—*Steve Marsh*

Exercise 5.3

Make a list of the sensations you experience as you eat something, such as an ice-cream cone or a slice of pizza. Use all of your senses. Arrange your list so that a point emerges from your description.

Exercise 5.4

Write a descriptive paragraph about one of the following:

• a person who has had an impact on your life.

• a place where you feel safe (or unsafe).

• an ordinary object to which you have a strong attachment.

Exercise 5.5

Sit for half an hour in a public place—on a bus, in a mall, in church, at a hockey rink—and make notes about what you see, hear, and smell. Then write a descriptive paragraph about the place as a whole, one or more people in it, or a particular object. Be sure to select details that convey a dominant impression and make a point about your subject.

5c Using Analogies

Attitudes and emotions are difficult to describe without falling into clichés and generalities. Analogies allow you to translate inner experiences into vivid images that your readers can share. Consider, for example, the different attitudes suggested by these metaphors:

> Life is an exhilarating ride on a roller-coaster.

> Life is "a tale told by an idiot, full of sound and fury, signifying nothing" (*Macbeth*).

Each of these metaphors could be developed into an analogy by exploring the similarities it suggests. These analogies would tell us much more about the writer (or character) than would statements such as "Life is great" or "Life sucks."

To write an effective analogy, follow these steps:

- **_Make a list of metaphors or similes comparing your subject with a variety of things that are different in appearance, form, or kind but similar in behaviour._**

  Overcoming an addiction is like
  —salvaging a wrecked ship
  —weaning a baby
  —saying goodbye to an old friend

- **_Choose the metaphor or simile that best fits the attitude or experience you want to convey._**

  x—salvaging a wrecked ship [does not acknowledge the pleasurable aspects of the addiction]

  x—weaning a baby [suggests we "grow out of" addictions]

  ✓—saying goodbye to an old friend

- **_Develop your metaphor or simile into a paragraph by exploring the similarities it suggests._**

  What is it like to say goodbye to an old friend? There's the memory of good times and bad, the desire to hold on and the need to let go. This analogy, by emphasizing the positive aspects, may help readers who do not share the addiction to understand why it is hard to give up.

  In the following example, the writer helps readers understand the attractions of a disastrous marriage by creating an analogy to an ill-fated voyage.

Sample Analogy

In the beginning, being married to him was like taking a long-awaited voyage on a luxury liner. I had all the care, attention, and comforts I had dreamed of. I said to myself that I was on the best ship in the world and I felt lucky to be there. After a while, though, being married to him was more like being in the lifeboat with just enough rations for survival. But by that time, I had forgotten what life was like on the luxury liner. I said to myself that I was on the best lifeboat in the world and I felt lucky to be there. Finally, being married to him was like clinging to a paddle in the sea. But by that time, I had forgotten what life was like on the lifeboat, and I told myself that I had the best paddle in the world and felt lucky to be holding on to it.

Exercise 5.6

Complete each of the following similes.

1. Looking for a job is like _____ .

2. Finding your way around a big city is like _____ .

3. Visiting the dentist is like _____ .

4. Making a new friend is like _____ .

Exercise 5.7

Make a list of the similarities suggested by one of the following similes.

- Raising a large family is like running a business.

- A school (or family) reunion is like a gathering of aliens.

- Going to university is like travelling in a foreign country.

- Going on a blind date is like buying a lottery ticket.

Using
Analogies

Exercise 5.8

Choose one of the similes in exercises 5.6 or 5.7 above and write a paragraph developing that analogy.

Review Exercise 5.9

Write a paragraph about a hard-to-communicate experience or feeling, using two (or all) of the methods discussed in this chapter: narration, description, and analogy. For example, you might convey the intensity of your feelings about your first car by both describing the car and comparing it to Aladdin's magic carpet.

Chapter 6

Methods of Explaining

When your purpose is to explain, your focus is on your subject and what your readers need to know to understand your subject. In this chapter we will discuss four ways of explaining: **classifying**, which groups your material into manageable chunks; **comparing**, which highlights similarities and differences; **defining terms and concepts**, which lets your reader know what you are talking about; and **analyzing**, which shows how parts of your subject relate to the whole.

This chapter will give you practice in using these methods to explain a subject within a single paragraph. Paragraphs of explanation often occur within pieces of writing whose primary purpose is to persuade or to share personal experience. If you were writing a personal essay about a custom unfamiliar to many Canadian readers, for example, you might devote one or more paragraphs to explaining its history or its function within your culture. To see how to extend these methods into longer pieces of writing, see chapters 11 and 12.

6a Classifying

When you classify, you organize facts and ideas into categories and subcategories. That means you start with a general category, such as Customers, and divide the category into specific types or kinds. You might, for instance, divide Customers into these types: the impatient, the rude, the apologetic, the businesslike, the indecisive. These subcategories allow you to explain the general characteristics shared by many individual people. You can also classify abstract concepts. For example, you could divide the category Effects of Unemployment into subcategories such as economic effects, social effects, and psychological effects.

If you were writing an essay, you could make classification your principle of organization and devote a paragraph or more to each of your subcategories as shown in the following diagram.

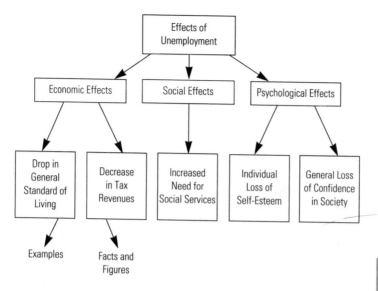

Classification can also provide a systematic method of organizing material as you move from generalizations to specific details in individual paragraphs. If your classification is easy to follow, you can present a great deal of information in a short space.

For this reason, classification paragraphs make good overviews of material you will then explain in more detail, and good summaries of material you have already covered. They are also handy for making humorous points and points that don't need much development, as in the sample paragraph that follows.

Here are suggestions for writing classification paragraphs:

- *Choose a general category that you know enough about to divide into two to four subcategories.* (For example: customers, coffee bars, musicals, Stephen King novels).

- *Decide on a principle of classification, and state this principle at the beginning of your paragraph.*

  A principle of classification tells you how to divide things into groups. For instance, you could group restaurant customers according to age groups, or attitudes toward staff, or eating habits. Each of these is a principle of classification.

- *Make a list of the types represented by your principle of classification.* If you chose "eating habits" as your principle of classification, for example, you might come up with types such as these: the bottomless pit, the doggie-bagger, the gushing gourmet, the constant complainer, the garbage collector, the reluctant sampler.

- **Describe two to four types, depending upon how much you need to say to explain each type.** Use actual examples (the man who made seven trips to the salad bar) or hypothetical examples (the kinds of complaints various customers make, all attributed to the constant complainer).
- **To signal your shift from one subcategory to another, use parallel sentence structure and/or transitions that indicate enumeration** (*first, second, next, finally*).
- **Begin or end your paragraph with the point you want to make.**

For example, "As you snicker or groan at the eating habits of others, consider how you appear to those who serve you when you go out to eat."

6a

Classifying

The following paragraph classifying people by the way they walk is taken from an essay on the importance of first impressions. The writer makes the point of the paragraph explicit in the topic sentence. Notice how she uses parallel sentence structure ("if" clauses) and transitions to guide readers through her four types of walkers.

Sample Classification

The way you walk tells others a lot about what type of person you are and how you feel about yourself. Fast-moving, hard-stepping, and arm-swinging, you look straight ahead and give the impression that you have something very important on your mind. It is an aggressive, no-nonsense, watch-out-world walk that usually signifies to others that you are quite confident (maybe too much so?). Your walk can intimi-date most mere mortals. If you are the "floater" walker, you take itsy-bitsy steps, barely hitting the ground, creating a kind of an airy flutter. You walk in a childlike, somewhat unconfident manner, which speaks of innocence, sweetness . . . and a touch of silliness if you are over age five. If you are a "shy" walker, you have little confidence. Your shoulders are slumped forward, your head is bowed down, your feet are turned in slightly, and you move quickly, almost noiselessly, hoping no one will notice you. The message is clear: please do not bother me, just let me be miserable in peace and quiet. Finally, you could be a person who walks with your shoulders back, chest high, spine stretched from the waist and straight, displaying comfortableness and confidence when you walk.

—*Brigitte Berube*

Exercise 6.1

Complete the following two diagrams with appropriate categories. What is the principle of classification for each subject? Can you figure out two other principles of classification for each subject?

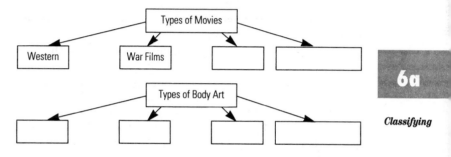

Exercise 6.2

Choose one of the following subjects and make a four-level diagram showing how you could divide your subject according to two different principles of classification. Use this model:

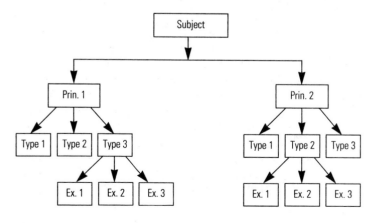

- music
- disabilities
- living accommodations
- pets
- crimes
- social problems

Exercise 6.3

Write a classification paragraph based on one of the principles of classification you developed for the diagram above.

6b Comparing

When you compare, you match similarities and differences in two or more subjects. **Comparison** may be your primary method of development in a piece of writing, as in the sample research paper, *"Tom Sawyer* and *Anne of Green Gables:* Two Models of Heroism" (14f). Or you may combine comparison with other methods of development.

To compare subjects effectively, you need a basis of comparison. A basis of comparison tells you which similarities and differences to focus on. For example, if you are asked on a biology exam to compare the fertilization process in mammals and amphibians, you have been given a basis of comparison: the fertilization process. In other writing situations, your purpose and audience will suggest an appropriate basis of comparison. If you are comparing two cars for your company, for instance, your basis of comparison will be determined by the purpose of the report. Is your company thinking of leasing one of the cars? Establishing a dealership? Paying insurance claims? Each of these purposes would lead you to choose a different basis of comparison, such as cost effectiveness, marketability, and amount of damage.

In other writing situations, the basis of your comparison may not be so obvious. Suppose you were writing an essay comparing the roles of the North West Mounted Police and the U.S. Cavalry in the settlement of the west. You would need to consider many facts and opinions about these forces before deciding on a general similarity or difference to use as a basis of comparison.

When your basis of comparison is not obvious, follow these steps.

List Similarities and Differences

Although making lists may seem time-consuming, you will discover that it is time well spent. Your lists will serve three purposes: they will ensure that you have lots of material, that you compare equivalent aspects of your subjects, and that you provide the same information about both. Let's take an example.

In writing about her trip to South America, one student wanted to make her impressions more vivid by comparing one aspect of life in Bolivia with its Canadian counterpart. Deciding to compare plumbing in the two countries, she compiled these lists:

Plumbing in Canada	**Plumbing in Bolivia**
—drinking water from kitchen tap	—water carried from square; boiled before drinking
—bath at any temperature	—water must be heated
—flush toilets	—often hole in backyard

Notice that the columns present matching points of contrast. These three differences provide material for a substantial paragraph.

Choose a Basis of Comparison

The next step is to decide what your similarities or differences have in common. From her lists comparing plumbing in the two countries, the student could have chosen any one of several points, such as health concerns, standards of hygiene, or availability of water. Each of these points would have provided a general difference that her examples would have illustrated. She chose to make the availability of water her basis of comparison.

Formulate a Main Idea

The crucial step, too often overlooked, is to decide what point to make about your basis of comparison. In an expository essay or report, your main idea might simply be a statement of your comparison: "In Bolivia, water is much less readily available than it is in Canada." In personal or persuasive writing, however, you want to convey your attitude toward the subjects you are comparing, not merely to report on their similarities or differences. Your reflections might lead you to a main idea such as the one the student traveller chose: because of its easy availability, Canadians may take water for granted, whereas for most Bolivians, water is a luxury.

43

Organize Your Comparison

Block Method

The simplest way of organizing a brief comparison is the **block method**. In this method, you mention both subjects in your topic sentence, but then say everything about one subject before saying anything more about the other. When you are ready to discuss the second subject, you signal the shift by a transitional word or phrase. Organizing her material on plumbing in Canada and Bolivia by the block method, the writer created the following paragraph.

Sample: Block Method

Although most Canadians take hot and cold running water at home for granted, indoor plumbing is a luxury for most Bolivians. When we want a drink, we merely turn on the faucet and fill our glasses. If we decide to have a bath, we just run the taps and adjust the water to whatever temperature we desire. We even have the comfort of toilets that flush. But few Bolivians have the luxury of indoor plumbing. Many have to stand in line at one tap in a central square at certain designated hours to fill their containers with water. This water must then be made to last for the remainder of the day. It must be boiled before it can be drunk and heated before it can be used for washing. A flush toilet is also not a feature in every Bolivian home. Toilet facilities usually consist of a hole dug in the back corner of the lot and often must be shared by several families.

—*Wendy Amy*

If the material is too long for one paragraph, you can easily start a new paragraph when you shift to your second subject.

Point-by-Point Method

The **point-by-point method**, in which you shift back and forth between subjects, is sometimes more effective than the block method when you are organizing a longer piece of writing (see Patterns for Comparison Essays, 9c). At the paragraph level, however, shifting between subjects can produce an annoying or confusing ping-pong effect, as you can see in this version of the previous example:

Comparing

Most Canadians take hot and cold running water at home for granted. Many Bolivians do not have the luxury of indoor plumbing. When we want a drink, we merely turn on the faucet and fill our glasses. Many Bolivians have to stand in line at one tap in a central square at designated hours to fill their containers with water. If we decide to have a bath, we just turn on the taps and adjust the water to whatever temperature we desire. Many Bolivians. . .

Normally, you would wish to avoid this rapid shifting back and forth between two subjects. Sometimes, however, a paragraph that ping-pongs may be effective for special emphasis or for humour.

Exercise 6.4

Choose two topics from the following and list the similarities and differences between the subjects being compared.

6b

- camping in a motor home and in a tent

- working full-time and working part-time

- watching a sport and playing a sport

Comparing

- an old friend and a new friend

- drawing and painting

- reading a novel or play and watching a movie made from the novel or play

- some aspect of life in Canada and the same aspect of life in another country

Exercise 6.5

Find a basis of comparison for each of the two topics that you chose in Exercise 6.4 above. Then decide what point you would make about each topic.

Exercise 6.6

Select a method of organization (block or point by point) and write a comparison paragraph based on one topic that you selected in Exercise 6.4.

6c Defining Terms and Concepts

"There's glory for you!"

"I don't know what you mean by 'glory,'" Alice said.

Humpty Dumpty smiled contemptuously. "Of course you don't—till I tell you. I meant 'there's a nice knock-down argument for you!'"

"But 'glory' doesn't mean 'a nice knock-down argument,'" Alice objected.

"When I use a word," Humpty Dumpty said in a rather scornful tone, "it means just what I choose it to mean—neither more nor less."

—From *Through the Looking Glass* by Lewis Carroll

Defining Terms and Concepts

Humpty Dumpty may get away with arbitrarily deciding what words mean, but most of us cannot. If we want to communicate, we have to use words in ways that others will understand. Thus when you use words unfamiliar to your readers, or use familiar words in an unfamiliar way, you need to provide **definitions**.

In examinations and other kinds of academic writing, you may be asked to define terms to show that you know what they mean. In most writing, however, you provide definitions not to demonstrate your own knowledge but to help your reader understand what you are talking about. Depending on what kind of information your reader needs, you may use a synonym, a class definition, an extended definition, or a restrictive definition.

Synonyms

A **synonym** is a word that means the same, or nearly the same, as another word. Use synonyms, set off by commas or enclosed in parentheses, to define slang expressions, specialized terms of trades and professions, regional and dialect usages, and foreign words and phrases. These examples illustrate how to integrate synonyms smoothly into a sentence:

At the heart of a microcomputer system is the central processing unit, or microprocessor, as it is also known.

—*Bernard Doering*

As we entered the Air India 747, the steward clasped his hands and said, "Namaste" ("Greetings to you").

—*Vijaya Rao*

46

Class Definitions

A **class definition** explains a term by saying what kind of thing it is (its class) and how it is different from other members of its class. Cats, for example, are a kind of feline (the class), but so are lions, tigers, cheetahs, leopards, and cougars. To distinguish cats from other felines, you might mention that cats are small and commonly kept as pets.

This is the standard form of the class definition:

An *X* is a member of the class *Y* with the characteristics *A*, *B*, *C* . . . .

A bailiff [term to be defined] is a person [class] who performs limited functions within a judicial system, such as having custody of prisoners in court, serving warrants, or serving as magistrate for minor offences [distinguishing characteristics].

Extended Definitions

Defining Terms and Concepts

When a synonym or class definition does not offer enough explanation, you will need to use an **extended definition**. Some writers take a paragraph, or even a whole essay, to define a term. In a persuasive essay, for example, you might give an extended definition of the word *violence* to show that it can legitimately be applied to the destruction of the environment.

Here are three ways to expand definitions.

1. Add examples.

2. Give negative examples—that is, words or things that might seem to be included in the class but are not.

3. Use an analogy to compare your term with something more familiar.

For instance, if you wanted to explain random sampling to readers who were not social scientists, you might use the analogy of pulling a handful of assorted candies from a jar. Or, if you wanted to make sure high school students understood the concept of random motion, you might use the following analogy.

Sample Extended Definition

The movement of molecules is referred to as random motion. Random motion is defined as "the movement of the smallest possible physical unit of an element or compound, composed of atoms." This definition may seem puzzling. However, if you think of a molecule as a billiard ball, and random motion as the movement of billiard balls, the meaning becomes much clearer. Picture in your mind the green top of a pool table with billiard balls scattered upon it. Each ball represents a molecule. If you close your eyes and push a single ball on the table with a strong degree of force, it will eventually hit another ball and send it into motion. This ball will strike another, and so on, with no set pattern or order. Just as billiard balls move within the boundary formed by the edges of the pool table, so molecules move within the boundaries of the element or compound of which they are a part. This is random motion.

—Kim Felske

6c

Defining Terms and Concepts

How often will an extended definition be needed? Don't insult your readers by defining words they know, but never assume your subject is as familiar to them as it is to you. Try to read what you've written with their eyes. Would a brief phrase explain basketball lingo for non-sports fans? Could you clarify what you mean by *oral literacy* by giving an example of storytelling in traditional Inuit families? Would an analogy help to explain the principle of indeterminacy to non-scientists?

Restrictive Definitions

Our understanding of words, especially of abstract terms such as *violence, loyalty, pornography,* and *censorship,* is shaped by our own experiences, and we bring these personal connotations to what we read. You can make sure that you and your readers are talking the same language by using a **restrictive definition**.

A restrictive definition specifies which meaning, from a range of possible meanings, a term will have within a particular context. Restrictive definitions thus allow you to limit your treatment of your subject. You may consider various meanings of the word *censorship,* for example, and then specify that you will use the word to mean the passage of laws designed to prevent the publication of certain material. Accordingly, your readers cannot expect you to discuss other actions that they might consider censorship, such as withdrawing books from libraries. As this example suggests, restrictive definitions are particularly necessary when the meaning of a term is controversial.

Because they establish common ground with readers and mark out the territory you will discuss, restrictive definitions make

48

good introductions. Suppose, for example, you were writing a research paper on the question of intelligence in chimpanzees. If you launched into an analysis of chimp behaviour without saying what you meant by *intelligence*, your readers might object to your argument on the grounds that intelligence in animals cannot be measured. You would therefore want to introduce your essay with a paragraph something like the one that follows.

Sample Restrictive Definition

Intelligence is sometimes defined as what intelligence tests measure. If we want to consider the question of intelligence in chimpanzees, we obviously cannot simply administer the Stanford Binet or other commonly used IQ tests. But we should be able to determine whether experiments with chimpanzees demonstrate elements of intelligence considered important by psychologists: the capacity for abstract thinking or reasoning, problem-solving, acquiring knowledge, and adapting to one's environment; memory, mental speed, and linguistic competence (Snyderman & Rothman, 1987).

By using this restrictive definition of intelligence as a thesis, you would establish a basis by which you and your readers could discuss the intelligence of chimpanzees according to specific behaviours.

Sources of Definitions

When you need to define a word, begin with a standard dictionary such as those published by Gage, Random House, and Oxford. For more detailed information about specialized meanings, changes in meaning over time, and current usage, consult works such as the following, found in the reference section of your library.

- **Unabridged dictionaries.** The *Oxford English Dictionary* provides a history of each word's use and changes in meaning.
- **Specialized dictionaries.** Available for many professions and academic disciplines. Examples: *Dictionary of Business and Economics, Dictionary of Philosophy, A Handbook to Literature.*

Exercise 6.7

Give a synonym or class definition that would explain each of these terms to readers unfamiliar with your subject.

1. rap music
2. black hole (or other scientific term)
3. hotdogging (or other slang expression)
4. winterize
5. blacksmith

Exercise 6.8

Write an extended definition of one of the following terms.

- powwow
- *samurai*
- sugaring off

- totem
- voodoo
- jock

- gender
- cross-dressing
- *film noir*

Exercise 6.9

Write a paragraph of restrictive definition for one of the following terms.

- literacy
- sexism
- equal opportunity

- mercy killing
- discrimination
- social justice

6d Analyzing: Dividing Your Subject into Parts

Analysis is a way of explaining a subject by dividing it into its parts and showing how the parts relate to the whole. We will discuss four types of analysis. **Systems analysis** shows the relation of parts in space; **process analysis** shows the sequence of parts in time; **causal analysis** shows the relationship between causes and effects; and **aesthetic analysis** shows how the parts of works of art relate to the whole.

By dividing up a complex or unfamiliar task, situation, or idea into smaller units, you can often make it easier for readers to grasp what you are saying about your subject. For particular writing assignments, you may use these four types of analysis alone or in combination. In writing a how-to article on making knives, for example, you would use process analysis to develop your material. But in writing an expository essay on knife-making, you might include sections on the process, on the effects of changes in technology, and on the marketing system consisting of suppliers, knife-makers, dealers, and collectors. Or in writing a review, you might discuss the process of making a film as well as analyze the final product. For examples of essays and other types of writing developed through analysis, see chapters 11 and 12.

Explaining Systems

We tend to think of a system as a physical object with working parts, such as a car engine or the body's immune system. But more abstract phenomena also operate as systems, such as systems of government and philosophy. When you explain how such abstract systems "work" by showing how the parts are related to the whole, you are also engaged in systems analysis.

A systems analysis is like a blueprint. You give an objective general description of your subject rather than a subjective particular description. If you were analyzing the functions of the Cabinet, for instance, you would discuss the role of the Minister of Defence, not the personality of the current minister.

Analyzing: Dividing Your Subject into Parts

Usually you begin by identifying the system and explaining its purpose in a topic sentence. Next you describe the most obvious or most important part of the system, such as the Prime Minister, and show how other parts function in relation to it. Then you explain the function of each part in relation to the whole. Use appropriate transitions to show how the parts are related.

Sample Systems Analysis

In the following example, the writer describes stereo systems in general (not his particular system with its scratches and coffee stains) and explains the function of each component.

A stereo system consists of a varying number of individual components, grouped in such a way as to give the audiophile a choice of musical reproduction. The heart of the system is the receiver, which takes the electronic impulses from the other components, amplifies them, and sends the signals on to the speakers. It is the job of the speakers to transfer these impulses back into sound, by means of an electromagnet. The original music may be recorded in a number of different ways, the most popular means being on record, tape, or compact disk. Each of these types of recording has a specific type of playback machine which, when hooked into the stereo system, allows for the reproduction of the original sound. To produce sound, the record turntable, cassette tape player, or compact disk player passes the vibrations or electronic pulses created by the recording on to the receiver for amplification and playback.

–Jim Griffin

Exercise 6.10

Write a paragraph explaining the parts of a system with which you are familiar and showing how these function as a whole. Here are some possible subjects.

- a computer system
- a camera
- the eye
- a tree
- a ballpoint pen
- a bicycle

Exercise 6.11

6d

*Analyzing:
Dividing
Your Subject
into Parts*

Write a paragraph explaining the parts of an abstract system with which you are familiar and showing how the system functions as a whole. Here are some possible subjects.

- a business
- an organization
- a family
- an economic system
- a set of beliefs (religious, philosophical, or political)
- a system of government (monarchy, parliamentary, etc.)

Explaining Processes

Process analysis has one of two purposes: to explain how something happens ("How Airplanes Fly") or to explain how to do something ("How to Fly an Airplane"). In each case, you emphasize what happens (or should happen) every time the process is repeated ("How to Develop Film"), rather than what happened during one particular instance ("How I Ruined My Sister's Wedding Pictures").

Begin with a topic sentence that identifies the process and its major stages. Then discuss the stages, and the steps within each stage, in the order in which they occur.

The amount of detail you include about each step will depend on your purpose and audience. When you explain how something is done but not how to do it, focus on the major stages so that your readers get a sense of the whole process; avoid giving detailed information about individual steps. On the other hand, when you give directions for readers to follow, discuss each step in detail, drawing your readers' attention to potential problems.

Use transitions indicating time relationships (*next*, *after*, *then*) or enumeration (*first*, *second*, *third*) to signal when you are moving from one stage or step to the next.

The following paragraph is designed to give readers a general understanding of the process of making Ukrainian-style Easter eggs. For an example of how to give more detailed instructions, see the sample how-to article, 12e.

Sample Process Analysis

The three major stages in creating an Easter egg are mixing the dyes, waxing, and dyeing. First, the dyes are prepared. Then, a special stylus with a cup-like reservoir is used to cover all the areas of the pencilled-in design that are to remain white in melted wax. The egg is then submerged in the lightest colour dye. After several minutes, the egg is removed with a spoon and wiped to remove any excess dye. All areas that are to remain yellow are then covered in wax, and the egg is placed in the next darker shade of dye. The waxing and dyeing process is repeated until the design is complete and all the desired colours have been used.

—*Laurel Kiehlbauch*

Exercise 6.12

Write a paragraph explaining a process. Choose your own topic or one of the following topics.

• how to operate a piece of equipment

• how to teach a child to tie shoes

• how to train your roommate to assume his or her share of the household responsibilities

• how to study for an exam

• how to say no

Explaining Causes and Effects

The analysis of causes and effects is basic to much of the writing you are likely to do in school or at work. You may write a research paper for a history course on the causes of the War of 1812; a lab report for botany on the effects of varying the amount of daylight received by tomato plants; or a letter to your insurance agent on the causes of a traffic accident.

Most actions or events worth writing about have multiple causes and effects. Brainstorming, asking discovery questions, and researching will help you avoid oversimplifying your analysis.

For a research paper on the effects of cutbacks in government spending on education, for instance, your first response might be to focus on the financial strain students are under because of higher tuition fees. You would gain a broader perspective, however, by brainstorming about other effects on students and reading about the effects on schools and post-secondary institutions. Your final essay might examine the effects of funding cuts on students, teachers, and institutions. For suggestions about the kinds of causes and effects you might consider, consult Asking Evaluative Questions (7b). For an example of an expository essay developed through causal analysis, see "The Effects of Child Poverty" (11b).

6d

Analyzing: Dividing Your Subject into Parts

If you are explaining causes or effects that are independent of each other, arrange your material in an order that suits your audience. You might discover, for example, that the three main causes of traffic accidents are poor road conditions, impaired driving, and mechanical failure. There is no causal connection among these three factors (drinking too much doesn't cause the roads to be icy or the car to break down). If you were writing an essay, you would decide which cause to emphasize, and discuss it last. If you were writing a report for the city transportation department, on the other hand, you would discuss the most important factor first.

If you are discussing a chain of causes and effects (A causes B, B causes C, C causes D), make sure that your topic sentence focuses on the most significant cause(s) and effect(s). Arrange your material in chronological order, but to make it clear that you are writing a causal analysis rather than a narrative, choose words and expressions that emphasize causal connections (*a major effect, a second cause, one consequence; caused, resulted, affected; as a result, because, consequently, moreover, therefore, thus*). Suppose you were writing an essay on the effects of the Riel Rebellion on federal politics. Your notes for one paragraph might read as follows:

1. Riel's execution **caused** a renewed demand for rights by French-speaking Québécois.

2. These demands alarmed the federal government; **as a result**, it abolished French language rights in Manitoba.

3. This action **resulted** in loss of support for the Conservative Party in Québec.

4. This decline in support **caused** the party to lose the next federal election.

5. Québec's pivotal role in federal politics is a continuing **effect** of its position as the sole defender of the rights of French-speaking Canadians.

In writing your paragraph, you would add a topic sentence emphasizing the most significant effect (the increased power of Quebec). You would also fill in additional details, while keeping the focus on the chain of causes and effects, as in the paragraph below.

Sample Analysis of Causes and Effects

Although the failure of the Riel Rebellion weakened the position of French-speaking Canadians in Manitoba, it had the enormously significant effect of strengthening the power of French-speaking Canadians in Québec. Before Riel was executed in 1885, Québec had ignored the struggle of the French-speaking Manitobans to maintain their cultural identity. As a result of his execution, Riel became a martyr to the cause of rights for all French Canadians and the focus for a renewed demand for French rights in Québec. Alarmed, the federal government abolished French education rights in Manitoba in 1890; Québec thus became the only province where provincial rights guaranteed the survival of French culture in Canada. The consequence of this action, it soon became obvious, was that no federal government could remain in power if it lacked Québec's support. The Conservative Party, weakened by MacDonald's death in 1891, lost the election in 1896 mostly because it had offended Québec by abolishing French rights in Manitoba; the Liberals, led by Wilfrid Laurier, gained power by securing a large majority in Québec. Since that time, no federal government has been able to ignore the French province.

Exercise 6.13

Write two separate lists of causes explaining why you will (or won't) be in debt when you graduate. Make one a list of independent causes; present the second list as a chain of causes and effects.

Explaining Works of Art

As you know from the discussion of systems analysis, you can analyze a functional object, such as a piece of machinery, by examining how its parts contribute to the operation of the whole. You can analyze aesthetic objects—works of art—in much the same way: by seeing how the various parts contribute to the effect created by the object as a whole. For instance, you might find that a certain song creates a mood of angry rebelliousness. To explain how the song creates this mood, you would consider elements such as lyrics, vocal style, instruments, and arrangement. We will use the term **aesthetic analysis** to refer to this method of explaining works of art.

Most often, you will use aesthetic analysis to explain creative works within "the arts"—such as music, dance, drama, film, literature, and the visual arts. There are various principles to consider in analyzing each art form. In Chapter 11, you will learn one way of analyzing works of imaginative literature (11c). For analyzing nonfiction, see Summaries (12c); for analyzing and evaluating an argument, see Position Papers (13d).

You can also consider a wide range of other objects and experiences, such as a landscape or a meal, from an aesthetic point of view. You do so when you focus on their artistic qualities rather than on their practical or scientific qualities. Practical and aesthetic considerations can be combined with evaluation (13h) in writing reviews of a wide range of products and services.

When you take courses in the arts, you are likely to write essays based on aesthetic analysis. On examinations, you may be asked to write a brief analysis of a work of art or to show how a specific part contributes to the whole. Follow these guidelines.

- Give all relevant information about the work, such as its title, date, creator, performer.

- Show that you understand the broader context of the work (such as other films made by this director) or the part you are analyzing (such as where this scene occurs in the film).
- Describe the most important features and explain how they contribute to the work as a whole.

The following example shows how you might respond to an exam question asking you to analyze a quotation from *Hamlet*.

Sample Literature Exam Question

Question
Explain the significance of the following excerpt in relation to the theme and structure of the work as a whole.

Excerpt
> Within a month,
> Ere yet the salt of most unrighteous tears
> Had left the flushing in her gallèd eyes,
> She married. O, most wicked speed, to post
> With such dexterity to incestuous sheets!
> It is not, nor it cannot come to good.
> But break my heart, for I must hold my tongue.

Superior Answer

This excerpt from Hamlet's soliloquy in Act 1, scene 2 of Shakespeare's play Hamlet provides our first insight into the Prince's state of mind. At this point, the ghost has not appeared to him, so he does not know that Claudius has murdered his father. Yet, even without this knowledge, he is deeply disillusioned by the hasty marriage of his mother to his uncle. He describes his mother's tears as "unrighteous" and condemns the marriage as incestuous, unnatural, an idea that echoes throughout the play in suggestions that Denmark is a diseased kingdom. He accuses his mother of lust and later generalizes this accusation to include all women, even Ophelia. We see his distress in the emphasis given to the words "She married" and in the exclamation "O, most wicked speed." His awareness that he cannot openly express his opposition to the marriage intensifies the pressure he is under and prepares us for the "antic disposition" he will later assume to disguise his feelings.

Exercise 6.14

Choose one of the following topics or a topic of your own and write a paragraph of aesthetic analysis.

- special effects in *Star Wars*
- an ad or a commercial
- a person's style of dressing
- a song
- a garden
- a poster or painting

Chapter 7

Methods of Persuading

Persuasion takes a wide variety of forms, from the snappy jingoes of television commercials to the carefully reasoned arguments of social critics. As these examples suggest, persuasive writing may appeal primarily to our emotions (television commercials) or primarily to our minds (logical arguments). Most persuasive writing—reviews, editorials, opinion pieces, political speeches—appeal to both.

Because the purpose of persuasive writing is to change readers' opinions or behaviour, the nature of your audience greatly influences the extent to which you appeal to your readers' intellect or emotions. Your audience for most writing in college and university will expect you to present carefully considered opinions and to support those opinions with evidence—such as facts, examples, and references to authorities on the subject. We will therefore focus on two strategies for making persuasive arguments: giving reasons and examples, and evaluating strengths and weaknesses. We will also demonstrate how you can give a persuasive edge to methods commonly used for explaining and sharing personal experience.

7a Giving Reasons and Examples

Whenever you state an opinion, your readers' first response is likely to be "Why do you think so?" Giving one or more reasons is the first step toward convincing your readers. The next step is giving examples—specific instances that show your reason(s) to be valid. For the argument to be strong, you must give reasons and examples that readers can verify independently. Consider these examples:

> This street is dangerous at night [opinion] because it is badly lit [verifiable reason]. In one four-block stretch, there is only one street lamp [verifiable example].

> This street is dangerous at night [opinion] because vampires hang out here [reason not verifiable]. Drops of blood on the corner show where there was a vampire attack [example not verifiable].

As you can see, both reasons and examples must have some basis in reality. That doesn't mean all readers will agree with you. They may not find your reasons convincing, or they may point to counter-examples. Nevertheless, by using sound reasons and good examples, you can persuade them that your opinion is worth considering. For guidelines on writing essays based on reasons and examples, see Opinion Piece (13b).

These guidelines will help you use examples effectively.

Guidelines for Effective Use of Examples

• *Include an example to support any important general point.*

Consider these two versions of a paragraph on the Marxist definition of violence. The first is a series of general statements.

> The Marxists maintain that an act of violence is quite different from a violent act. An act of violence is an act that causes harm and suffering whether or not it is done violently. This distinction between an act of violence and a violent act allows the Marxists to point out that acts of violence do not necessarily involve physical force.

In the second version, examples illustrate the main points.

> The Marxists maintain that an act of violence is quite different from a violent act. Stirring a cup of tea, for example, can be done violently and therefore could be described as a violent act. An act of violence, on the other hand, is an act that causes harm and suffering whether or not it is done violently. Such acts do not necessarily involve physical force. To illustrate this point, one need only envision a situation where urban terrorists poisoned the air, with the result that citizens died quietly in their sleep. No physical contact was made, but no one could say that violence did not occur.

Without the **examples**—the specific instances used to explain the general statements—it is difficult to grasp the distinction between an act of violence and a violent act.

• *Make sure your examples are typical.*

Suppose, for instance, you were arguing that mandatory retirement is unfair. You might want to support your position by giving the example of your mother, who was not eligible for a full pension, when she was forced to retire at sixty-five, because she did not begin to work full-time until she was forty. If you used only this example to support your argument, readers might object, saying that your mother's case was not typical and therefore was poor evidence. This example would be effective, however, if you could show that many women are in the same situation. You would also want to use examples of other people, such as those who change employers or careers.

- **Explain the meaning of your examples.**
An example seems puzzling when its relation to a general statement is unclear.

> Advertisements make life easier in some very basic ways. A good example is the commercials that play a few bars of many songs included on a tape.

How can playing snippets of songs "make life easier"? A sentence or two of explanation would make this connection clear.
Explain your point first and then give your example:

> Advertisements make life easier in some very basic ways. One way is by offering the consumer an opportunity to sample products before buying. A good example of this is the commercials for musical compilation tapes that play a few bars of many songs.

Where there are several steps in the argument, as here, add another sentence after the example to remind your reader of your main point. The paragraph on advertising ends with this sentence showing how the commercial makes life easier:

> These snippets give the consumer a fairly good idea of whether or not the tape suits his or her taste in music and is thus worth buying.

- **Integrate your examples smoothly.**
If you haven't had much practice using examples, you may be tempted to introduce them with awkward phrases such as *An example of this is when . . .* (see Mixed Constructions, 18g). You can integrate your examples more smoothly by using constructions such as these: *for example, a further example, is exemplified by, for instance, an instance is, such as, this point is illustrated in, an illustration of this point is.*

> Another instance of this government's indifference to the needs of ordinary people is the plan to tax basic foods and children's clothing.

> The adolescent's desire to conform is best exemplified by the popularity of a few kinds of designer jeans.

The half-hour line-ups in the cafeteria are further evidence of the need for more staff.

Exercise 7.1

Choose one of the following opinions and give three to five reasons you agree or disagree. List at least two examples to support each of your reasons.

1. *Maclean's* rankings of universities are useful (not useful).

2. Assisted suicide should (should not) be a criminal offence.

3. Young offenders should (should not) be given jail terms.

4. Human sexuality should (should not) be taught in schools.

5. High schools should (should not) offer training programs for specific jobs.

7b Evaluating Strengths and Weaknesses

To evaluate means to make judgments about the quality, worth, or importance of something. Since others may arrive at different judgments about the same thing, there is always an element of persuasion.

To arrive at a fair judgment, you must thoroughly understand the thing you are evaluating. The basis for evaluation is therefore analysis: dividing things into parts to determine how the parts contribute to the whole (see Analyzing, 6d). In evaluating, however, you take analysis one step farther: You ask not only "What is the function of this part?" but also "How well does this part fulfill its function?"

Asking Evaluative Questions

There are many perspectives from which to make judgments. Some depend upon the specialized knowledge of a profession (such as law or medicine) or academic discipline (such as economics). Others are more broadly applicable. You can make the basis of your own judgments clearer to your readers by identifying your own perspective(s). Are your objections to a film, for instance, aesthetic (the acting is bad) or moral (it glorifies violence), or both?

Here are questions to ask about your subject from four general perspectives.

Aesthetic

Is it aesthetically pleasing? What are its strengths and weaknesses? Do the parts make a satisfying whole? Is the form suited to the content or function? Is it well-made? Is it appealing to its intended audience or users? For an example of evaluation from the aesthetic perspective, see the sample review (13i).

Moral

Is it morally right or wrong? Why? Who does it help or harm? Is it ethical? Does it promote values I accept or reject? What are they? Why do I accept or reject them? For an example, see the sample opinion piece, "Why I Won't Buy a New Car" (13c).

Logical

Is it true? What are the arguments for and against it? Is the reasoning logical? Is the information accurate and complete? Does the evidence justify the conclusions or recommendations? For a more extended discussion of how to evaluate the logic of an argument, see Evaluating Logical and Emotional Appeals (13d).

Practical

Is it practical? What are its advantages and disadvantages? Will it work? Is it cost-effective? Is it useful?

You can clarify your thinking about your subject by considering each set of evaluative questions. You might use brainstorming diagrams or make parallel lists of good and bad points.

Suppose, for example, that you were writing a persuasive essay on whether pornography should be banned. You might begin with these points.

	Against Banning	**For Banning**
Aesthetic	Some "porno-graphic" works have literary and artistic merit	Most pornography is crude and boring
Moral	Right to freedom of expression	Contributes to violence against women and children
Logical	Difficulty of defining "pornography"	Research studies suggest social harm
Practical	Difficult to enforce	Protect children from sexual exploitation

Deciding Which Questions to Answer

Evaluating Strengths and Weaknesses

Often your subject or your form will limit the range of evaluative questions you answer. Truth may be irrelevant if you are reviewing a children's movie about talking dinosaurs. Your schedule and the availability of material will also determine how many questions you answer. If you are writing a short essay, it is better to consider one set of questions thoroughly than to skim through them all. For a longer essay, you may appeal to more readers and do more justice to your subject by considering two or three aspects—the aesthetic and moral dimensions of a book, for example, or the moral and practical issues facing the health professions.

Whether you consider both sides of a question or only one depends on your purpose and audience. You may emphasize either the good or the bad, but if your judgments are too one-sided, you are likely to bore or alienate your readers. Suppose, for instance, you were writing about hiking in the Laurentians. You could emphasize either the pleasures or the pains of hiking. But if the picture you paint is too rosy or too gloomy, readers may reject it as unrealistic.

Writing Evaluative Paragraphs

When you evaluate, you support your opinion by giving reasons, examples, and other kinds of evidence. This paragraph, taken from a research paper on acid rain, focuses on the economic benefits of reducing sulphur emissions.

Sample Evaluation

Curbing acid rain has advantages besides clean air. Recovering sulphur, rather than releasing it into the atmosphere, is economically beneficial. Sulphur has a world-wide market as a fertilizer. It has also been used as part of asphalt road fill. According to an industry report, stockpiles of sulphur will be depleted quickly if the current growth rate continues (Rankin and Rowland 1982). Some companies are actively searching for sour gas so that they can extract not only the natural gas but the sulphur, too. Plainly, more extensive sulphur recovery holds out the possibility of creating new jobs as well as cutting down on acid rain (Rankin and Rowland 1982).

7b

Exercise 7.2

On what grounds (aesthetic, moral, logical, practical) would you evaluate each of the following? Several of the topics can be approached from various perspectives.

Evaluating Strengths and Weaknesses

1. A city council decision to expand a major residential street to three lanes in each direction

2. A community theatre production of *West Side Story*

3. A school board decision to integrate special needs children (such as the hearing impaired) into regular classrooms

4. The exercise classes at a local health club

5. A proposal to designate a building as an historic site

6. A rap singer's latest recording

7. A proposal to raise the age for obtaining a driver's licence to 18

8. An educational institution's decision to raise admission standards

Exercise 7.3

State your position on one of the subjects in Exercise 7.2. List the arguments you would use to support your position.

Exercise 7.4

Write a paragraph based on your list of arguments in Exercise 7.3.

7c Using Other Methods to Persuade

As the three paragraphs on shoplifting in Chapter 1 demonstrate, you signal your purpose in a piece of writing partly through the language you use. You can give a persuasive edge to any of the strategies discussed in chapters 5 and 6 by using evaluative language in your topic sentences and throughout your paragraphs. Methods of explaining (classifying, comparing, defining terms and concepts, and analyzing) allow you to present a more logical, more carefully reasoned argument. Telling stories, describing people, places, and things, and using analogies—all these heighten the emotional appeal of your writing.

The following analogy between the behaviour of a rich family and the behaviour of rich nations, for example, makes a strong appeal to readers' emotions.

Using Other Methods to Persuade

Sample Analogy: Persuasive Writing

Picture a rich family living on a hill in splendid luxury. Look down on the plains around the hill and see the people in shacks, starving; hear the children cry. The rich family sends down a bit of food and clothing once a year, but otherwise they live as always. "We have the right to enjoy our wealth," they say. "We cannot feed and clothe and care for all those people," they explain as they add another foot of barbed wire to the fence around their property. Meanwhile the anger and frustration of the poor grow against them. The rich western nations are very much like this family. An early 1970s estimate numbered 420 million starving people on the plains of the world spread at our feet. Like the rich family, we send bits of food and clothing. Like the rich family, we make it harder and harder for the poor to get in. Meanwhile the anger and frustration of the poor grow against us.

—Ken Ainsworth

Here are two cautions about using analogies in persuasive writing:

1. Do not use analogies to make unfair emotional appeals—ones that arouse prejudice. For example, smearing an opponent's reputation by charging that "Voting for X would be like voting for the Devil" might appeal to some voters, but would likely alienate many more.

2. Analogies do not provide strong logical support for an argument. Because you are comparing things that are basically different, your analogy may break down if it is pushed too far. Readers who spot weaknesses in your analogy may reject your argument. See Position Papers, 13d.

Exercise 7.5
Write a persuasive analogy to illustrate one of the following subjects.

- the plight of refugees
- the disadvantages of a particular occupation
- the effects of smoking
- the problems of not being able to read
- a subject of your choice

Using Other Methods to Persuade

- Resources for Writers and Writing Instructors—a directory
  www.english.upenn.edu/~jlynch/writing.html

- University of Victoria—Excellent Writer's Guide
  www.uvic.ca/v4/academic.html

Part 3

WRITING ESSAYS

CHECKLIST

Essays

	OK	NEEDS WORK

Purpose and Audience

1. Does the essay have a clearly defined purpose (to explain, to persuade, to share your personal experience)? ☐ ☐

2. Does the essay meet the needs of your intended reader? ☐ ☐

Thesis

3. Does your thesis state a specific idea that the rest of the essay develops? ☐ ☐

Development

4. Is all the material in the essay relevant to your thesis? ☐ ☐

5. Are you satisfied that you have adequately supported your thesis? ☐ ☐

6. Are the connections among your ideas as clear as possible? ☐ ☐

Essays that Begin with the Thesis

7. Does the introduction identify your subject and the range of material you will cover? ☐ ☐

8. Does the introduction end with your thesis? ☐ ☐

9. Do your paragraph divisions indicate the major sections of your essay? ☐ ☐

10. Does each topic sentence clearly state the main point of the paragraph and show how the paragraph relates to the thesis? ☐ ☐

11. Do transitions help your reader to follow the connections among your ideas? ☐ ☐

12. Does the conclusion restate the thesis, sum up the main points, and suggest a broader context or the implications of your subject? ☐ ☐

Essays that Lead Up to the Thesis

13. Does the introduction identify your subject, arouse the reader's interest, and suggest the structure of your essay? ☐ ☐

14. Are your paragraphs arranged in order of increasing importance? ☐ ☐

15. Do transitions help your reader to follow the sequence of ideas, events, or details? ☐ ☐

16. Does the conclusion sum up the ideas, events, or details by stating or clearly implying your thesis? ☐ ☐

Comparison Essays

17. Have you effectively used either the block or point-by-point method of organization? ☐ ☐

Research Essays

18. In a research essay, have you included appropriate and correctly documented secondary sources? ☐ ☐

19. Is this material relevant to your thesis? ☐ ☐

20. Have you explained why you agree or disagree with this material? ☐ ☐

Chapter 8

The Key to Writing Essays: The Thesis

8a What Is an Essay?

"Write an essay," your instructor says. But what, exactly, is an essay? The term essay can be applied to a wide variety of nonfiction writing: light newspaper columns and impassioned letters to the editor; thoughtful magazine articles and scathing movie reviews; academic articles and the research papers you write in many of your courses. The common factor in all these types of writing is that they have a thesis, a main point to make about their subject.

8b What Is a Thesis?

A thesis states an opinion about a subject and presents one or more reasons to support it. In an **expository essay**, this opinion is the overall point you want to explain: "What this means is . . . " In a **persuasive essay**, this opinion is the argument you want to convince your readers to accept: "What you should think (or do) is . . . " In a **personal essay**, this opinion is a generalization based on your personal experience: "What this means to me is . . . "

A good thesis does more than state an opinion. It also gives one or more reasons to support the opinion: "You should do this for these three reasons . . . " As this example suggests, setting out your reasons allows you to control the content of the essay. Of all possible reasons for holding a particular opinion, you will discuss only those you have mentioned. Your thesis thus tells both you and your reader what you intend to cover.

You can formulate a better thesis if you follow these guidelines.

• *State an opinion rather than merely restating your subject or essay topic.*

Suppose, for example, that your subject is *group homes for the mentally disabled* and you have narrowed this subject to the

72

topic of *licensing regulations.* You will not have a thesis if you merely restate your subject: *This essay is about group homes for the mentally disabled.* Merely repeating your topic is no more useful: *This essay will discuss the licensing of group homes for the mentally disabled.* A thesis that states an opinion will give you a much clearer focus for your essay: *To prevent the exploitation of clients, social services should tighten regulations governing the licensing of group homes for the mentally disabled.*

- **State an opinion rather than a fact.**

Factual statements provide little focus or control over the content of the essay. You could turn a fact such as *Satellite dishes give Canadians access to hundreds of foreign television channels* into a thesis by stating your opinion of the effects of this situation: *By giving Canadian viewers access to hundreds of foreign channels, satellite dishes threaten the Canadian television industry.*

- **Make sure your thesis states your opinion, not the writer's.**

When you are analyzing a piece of writing, you will include the writer's main point about his or her subject somewhere in your analysis, but it will not be your thesis. Your thesis will explain *your* interpretation of the piece or evaluate its strengths and weaknesses. For example, the thesis of a newspaper editorial might be that Canadian judges should allow trials to be televised. After analyzing the editorial, you might arrive at a thesis stating that the writer's reliance on American examples weakens the argument.

- **Make the thesis as precise and specific as possible.**

If you state a well-defined opinion with one or more reasons to support it, you will know exactly what points to develop in the body of your essay. Avoid generalizations: *These stories have a lot in common* or *The Second World War had a big impact on Canada.* Instead, state the most important similarities in the stories or the most important social, political, or economic effect(s) of the war: *The diversification of manufacturing brought about by the Second World War transformed the Canadian economy.*

There is no one right thesis on a subject. Your thesis will reflect your unique way of looking at your material. It will be shaped by your purpose, your audience, your chosen essay form, and your methods of development.

Exercise 8.1

Consider the following sentences as thesis statements for an essay. If you think the sentence makes a clear point that would control the content of the essay, put **C** beside it. If you think it doesn't, explain how it could be improved.

1. There is at least one television set in 97 percent of Canadian homes.

2. Science fiction is popular because it gives readers the opportunity to explore new ideas.

3. This essay will analyze Canadian foreign policy during the 1950s.

4. Between 1950 and 1990 the depiction of women in films changed enormously.

5. In the essay "My Wood," E.M. Forster argues that owning property damages a person's moral and spiritual health.

8c Discovering Your Thesis

Normally you will need to gather some material or even write a first draft before you can figure out your thesis. In fact, if you formulate a thesis first and then look for information to support it, you are likely to distort your subject.

To figure out your thesis, follow these steps.

1. *Gather information about your subject. Use one or more of these methods—brainstorming, freewriting, asking discovery questions, keeping a journal, conducting interviews, or doing research.* See Part 1: The Writing Process: An Overview for more information on the first four of these. See Chapter 12 for information on interviews, and Chapter 14 for information on how to use research materials.

2. *Group this material into two or three categories.* For ideas on how to divide your material, see the sections in chapters 5, 6, and 7 on specific methods of development, such as classification, analysis, comparison, and evaluation.

3. *Formulate a thesis that focuses on the meaning of these broader categories.* Suppose, for example, that you have been asked to write an essay on your first job. If you

have come back to school after a career as a nurse, you might write a personal essay on the satisfactions and frustrations of nursing when you began work twenty years ago; an expository essay explaining working conditions then; or a persuasive essay arguing that working conditions for nurses have not improved much over the twenty years. Whatever your focus, you would begin by jotting down information about various aspects of your job.

Nursing Twenty Years Ago

1. Earned $275/month with reasonable rates for room, board, and laundry in nurses' residence
2. Advancement by seniority
3. Good job security
4. Not many chances to develop new skills
5. Performed menial and routine tasks, no clinical specialization
6. Worked 40-hour/five-day week; split shifts and short changes (e.g., work 3:30 p.m.–midnight, then 7:30 a.m.–4 p.m.); understaffed
7. Nurses supervised or administered; did little nurturing or ministering to patient
8. Nurses expected to follow doctor's orders, not to make independent decisions
9. Basic level of technology
10. Doctors viewed nurses as subordinate
11. Little interaction with management
12. Education required: basic three-year diploma; training based on practice

You would then group these aspects of nursing into more general categories, such as these:
- financial dimensions of employment (1,2,3,6)
- professional responsibilities (4,5,8,9,12)
- possibilities for emotional satisfaction (7,10,11)

Discovering Your Thesis

To work out an overall statement about nursing twenty years ago, you would first need to decide what point you could make about each of these dimensions of the job. You might choose the following points:

> Twenty years ago, nurses worked long hours with strenuous shift changes for low wages, but their jobs were relatively secure. Their opportunities to show initiative and develop new skills were quite limited. The emotional satisfactions of nursing were also limited by lack of direct contact with patients and their subordinate position to doctors and hospital administration.

The main message that seems to emerge is that twenty years ago nursing was a secure job but one with limited opportunities for intellectual growth and emotional satisfaction.

The way you formulate your thesis depends on the kind of essay you are writing and the emphasis you want to give to each of your points.

The Personal Thesis

8c

Discovering Your Thesis

Whether a personal essay is narrative, descriptive, or reflective, your thesis should make a point about what your experience *meant* to you. Often this is a point about what this experience taught you about yourself, about others, or about life itself.

> As a young woman seeking independence, I saw only the job security that nursing promised, not its limited opportunities for intellectual growth and personal satisfaction.

The Expository Thesis

The thesis for an expository essay is the generalization that emerges from your analysis of your material. The thesis explains the significance of your subject by telling your readers *what* its parts are, *how* it got that way, *why* it has the nature it has, or all three. This thesis explains *why* nursing twenty years ago was as it was.

> The relative abundance of health-care dollars meant that nursing jobs were secure; however, the hierarchical nature of the system meant that nursing provided limited opportunities for intellectual growth and emotional satisfaction.

The Persuasive Thesis

The thesis for a persuasive essay tells readers *what* they should think or do and *why*. You reach your thesis by evaluating the strengths and weaknesses of your subject (see Evaluating Strengths and Weaknesses, 7b). Your thesis may focus on strengths ("Nursing was a good career choice twenty years ago because of the job security it offered") or weaknesses ("Nursing was a bad career choice because of the limited opportunities for intellectual growth and emotional satisfaction"). On most issues, however, readers are more likely to be convinced by a thesis that gives a balanced perspective.

> Nursing twenty years ago bore little relation to the idealized notions invoked by critics of today's practitioners. Although jobs were secure, the profession offered few opportunities for intellectual growth or emotional satisfaction.

The Comparative Thesis

When you are comparing, whether in a personal, expository, or persuasive essay, your thesis should do more than state the most important similarities or differences in your subjects. It should also explain how or why they are similar or different. If you were comparing working conditions in nursing twenty years ago and today, for instance, you might discover that opportunities for intellectual growth and personal satisfaction have increased, but job security has decreased. Your thesis might explain the reasons for these differences in this way:

Discovering Your Thesis

> Changes in medical technology and in the structure of the health-care system make nursing more intellectually and emotionally satisfying than it was twenty years ago, but cuts in health-care spending make jobs less secure.

Exercise 8.2

Choose two of the following subjects. For each subject, develop a thesis for a personal, expository, persuasive, and comparative essay.

1. verbal abuse
2. student loans
3. professional sports
4. your favourite book, film, or television program
5. cultural differences

Chapter 9

Essay Structure

Essays, like houses, come in a variety of shapes, but they all have a structure—a principle of organization that binds the parts together. The structure serves two purposes: to show your readers how parts of your essay relate to each other and to create interest. Your choice of structure for a particular piece of writing will depend upon which of these purposes is more important.

The overall structure of your essay is determined by where you put your thesis—near the beginning or near the end. Since most essays for academic courses begin with the thesis, we will discuss this method in detail. Ending with the thesis is most effective for some kinds of personal and persuasive essays. You will find two patterns to follow when you choose this method.

Comparison essays present special problems of organization. We offer two possibilities, the block method and the point-by-point method. For suggestions about how to organize specific kinds of essays, see the appropriate section.

9a Beginning with Your Thesis

When you put your thesis in the introduction, it provides a framework for the rest of the essay. This pattern emphasizes the results of your thinking.

Advantages and Disadvantages

The main advantage of this method is its immediate clarity. By stating your main point first and then providing the evidence to support it, you never leave your reader wondering about the relevance or significance of your material. This method is particularly effective when you are discussing a complex or technical subject at some length, for most readers will have trouble following several pages of specific detail if they don't see how your evidence connects with your main point. For this reason, you will probably organize most of the essays you write for academic courses with the thesis first.

Beginning with your thesis may not be the best strategy, however, if you are writing on a controversial subject or on a topic that is unfamiliar to your readers. You may alienate readers who feel forced to agree or disagree with your conclusions before they have had time to consider the issue.

The Basic Components

Thesis and Topic Sentences

Your thesis, you will recall, gives your opinion about your subject and your reason(s) for holding that opinion. By giving your reasons in the order you plan to discuss them, you create a map to guide your readers through your essay. To show them where they are along the way, you use topic sentences that restate your reasons as points you will develop in your middle paragraphs.

In the following example, you can see how the thesis and topic sentences create a structure that focuses the reader's attention and controls the content of the essay.

Essay Topic Are fairy tales suitable for children? Write a 1000-word essay in which you defend your position.

Thesis By providing models of hope, courage, and determination, fairy tale heroes help children to see the value of developing these virtues in their own lives.

Topic Sentences

- From the story of Jack and the magic bean seeds, children learn that even seemingly foolish hopes can lead to success.

- Children who have felt abandoned like Hansel and Gretel can learn the value of courage in adversity from Gretel's brave rescue of her brother.

- Cinderella has been criticized recently for waiting passively for Prince Charming to rescue her, but a closer reading of this tale shows that she, too, uses hope, courage, and determination to solve her own problems.

Giving an essay such a clearly defined structure is not easy; you won't achieve a perfectly worded thesis and matching topic sentences on your first try. In the process of gathering material, you may discover a tentative thesis and major categories (such as courageous characters and hopeful characters). These categories—or the thesis—may change when you write an outline or a draft, since your ideas will usually become clearer, and so will your understanding of how they relate to each other. Then, when you revise, you can rewrite your thesis and topic sentences so that they provide a clear, logical framework.

The Introduction

In this type of essay structure, the opening sentences define the range of material you will cover and provide a context for the thesis, which ends the introduction. The opening sentences thus act like the framing shots of a movie, setting the scene and introducing the characters before the action begins.

Your introduction can be based on any of the methods of developing ideas discussed in chapters 5, 6, and 7. In academic essays, for example, you may classify the material you plan to discuss (such as types of fairy tales), define a key term from your thesis (such as autism), or sketch the development of a current situation (such as previous attempts to amend the Constitution). For a more general audience, you may want to create interest by giving a vivid example, telling a relevant anecdote, or describing a scene.

Whatever the method you use, be sure to give your readers all the background information they need, including authors and titles of works, and dates and places of events.

Remember the following points when you are writing your introduction:

9a

Beginning with Your Thesis

- ***Avoid making large claims that the rest of your essay does not support.*** Do not, for example, begin by saying "Children are not really frightened by fairy tales" unless you can (and will) provide hard evidence to support the generalization.

- ***State your thesis, not your topic.*** You do not need to include a sentence that merely repeats the assigned topic, such as *In this essay I will discuss the suitability of fairy tales for children.* The title of your essay should make the topic clear.

- ***Focus on the big picture, not the details.*** While you may choose to open with an example or incident that captures the essence of your argument, be wary of including detailed information that belongs in the body of the essay.

Sample Introduction

In the past, fairy tales were criticized as too unrealistic to provide suitable models for children. Recent critics are more likely to condemn fairy tales as too violent and/or too sexist. A closer examination of three popular fairy tales, *Jack and the Beanstalk, Hansel and Gretel,* and *Cinderella,* shows that this criticism is unjust, for these tales provide vivid examples of hopeful, courageous, determined characters who solve their own problems. Fairy tale heroes thus help children to see the value of developing these virtues in their own lives.

Middle Paragraphs

Sometimes, such as when you are tracing the development of a concept or analyzing a chain of causes and effects, your material will determine the order of your middle paragraphs. Usually, however, you will have to decide how to arrange your points. Consider how you can best keep your audience interested. You might begin with the point that your readers will find easiest to understand and end with the most difficult. Or you might build interest by beginning with your least important point and ending with the most important.

To see how you would decide which point is most important, consider the structure of the essay on fairy tales. The thesis and topic sentences suggest three blocks of material: Jack as a model of hope, Gretel as a model of courage, and Cinderella as a model of hope, courage, and determination. Because *Cinderella* has been most criticized (in *The Cinderella Complex,* for example) and there are more points to make in its favour, it makes sense to put this tale at the end.

You can't always cover a block of material in a single paragraph. To support the point about *Cinderella* with adequate examples, for instance, you would need several paragraphs. Whenever your discussion of a point takes up more than half a page (typed, single spaced), divide your material into subpoints, each with its own topic sentence. Use an umbrella topic sentence to tie the block of material together and show how it relates to the thesis.

9a

Beginning with Your Thesis

Sample Umbrella Topic Sentence

Cinderella has been criticized recently for waiting passively for Prince Charming to rescue her, but a closer reading of this tale shows that she, too, uses hope, courage, and determination to solve her own problems.

Topic Sentence [Subpoint 1]	Because Cinderella never stops hoping that she can go to the ball, she makes every effort to accomplish the difficult tasks her stepmother sets. [Examples]
Topic Sentence [Subpoint 2]	When she is returned to her rags and cinders, Cinderella is still brave enough to demand to see the Prince. [Examples]
Topic Sentence [Subpoint 3]	Far from waiting passively to be rescued, Cinderella makes a determined effort throughout the tale to solve her own problems. [Examples]

Conclusion

Your conclusion should draw together the evidence you have presented to reinforce the main idea of the essay as a whole. Instead of merely summarizing your main points, you emphasize their implications. While you don't want to raise new issues that should have been discussed earlier, you do want to show how your essay fits into a wider context. Your conclusion should have three basic components: a restatement of your thesis, a brief explanation of the significance of the major points, and a suggestion of the broader implications of the subject. You can present this last element in one of three ways:

Beginning with Your Thesis

- Move from the specific to the general to suggest that the material you have covered is part of a larger issue.

  Thus in a world too often disrupted by dislocation, divorce, and death, fairy tales offer children a hope of happiness.

- Compare your subject with another subject with which your reader is likely to be familiar.

  And, whatever the critics say, fairy tales are much less violent and sexist than the television programs most children watch every day.

- Stress the significance of your subject by emphasizing its causes or effects.

Children may learn these moral values elsewhere, but nowhere else will they experience so satisfying an entry into the magic of reading.

Sample Conclusion

Children, like adults, learn who they are and what they can be through the examples of others. The hope, courage, and determination modelled by Jack, Gretel, and Cinderella show children that these virtues can help them to create happier lives for themselves. In doing so, these tales add an ethical dimension to children's education, a dimension that is too often missing in modern life.

For examples of essays beginning with the thesis, see the sample essay analyzing literature (11d) and the sample literary research paper (14f).

9b Leading Up to the Thesis

If you choose this method, your thesis may appear in the middle of your essay or at the end, or it may be implied rather than stated directly. This pattern emphasizes the process of your thinking rather than your conclusions.

Advantages and Disadvantages

By delaying the presentation of your thesis, you can create suspense and interest. This approach is particularly effective in personal essays, in which you invite readers to share the process of coming to understand an experience. Leading up to your thesis is also useful in a persuasive essay when you want to convince your readers to consider a potentially controversial point of view or to think in new ways about an old problem.

The danger with this method is that you may end up with a lot of details but no main point. You can prevent this problem by structuring your essay according to one of the patterns discussed below.

Questions and Answers

In this pattern, you ask a question in your introduction that the rest of the essay will answer. You may consider and reject possible answers until you conclude with one that seems satisfactory; or you may give a series of partial answers that add up to a comprehensive one.

Introduction The introduction sets out the problem or issue and asks the question to be answered.

Middle Paragraphs In the body of your essay, you examine possible answers in detail. Each answer forms a major section of the essay, composed of one or more paragraphs. You can help your readers follow the structure of your essay by repeating key terms and using parallel sentence structure in each answer. Arrange your paragraphs in a sequence such as simplest to most complex or weakest answer to strongest answer.

Conclusion In the conclusion, you present the best or most comprehensive answer as your thesis. You can signal that you've reached your thesis by repeating the question from the introduction or by summarizing previous answers.

The following example demonstrates how the question and partial answers pattern can work.

Leading Up to the Thesis

Introduction [Question]	How can teachers help reduce violence in school?
Middle Paragraphs [Topic Sentences]	We can watch for signs . . . We can discuss the issue with students . . .
	We can also teach students ways of resolving arguments . . .
	Most important, we must model good problem-solving behaviour in our conflicts with students . . .
Conclusion [Thesis]	To reduce violence in schools, we must educate both ourselves and our students about the uses and misuses of power.

The sample non-literary research paper, "What Is Psychology?" (14g), displays elements of this pattern. Note that the question to be answered is raised in the title.

Specific Details to General Meaning

In this pattern, you begin with particular details and end with a thesis, either stated or implied, about the meaning of the experience as a whole.

Introduction The introduction plunges your reader into the subject of your essay and arouses interest through narrative or descriptive detail. It gives a sense of structure by suggesting the final event of the narrative (*We wouldn't rest until we found the lost treasure of the Incas*) or the scope of the description (*The old neighbourhood was unrecognizable*).

Middle Paragraphs In the body of the essay, fill in the specific details. As units of thought, your paragraphs will correspond to units of your narrative (*first week, next day, that afternoon, the moment had come*) or description (*the streets, the houses, our house*). Arrange your paragraphs in a chronological or spatial sequence that will lead naturally to the generalization in your conclusion. Foreshadow this generalization by references to thoughts and feelings (*I wondered whether we were on a fool's errand*) or by choice of diction (*narrow streets, cracked side-walks, shabby houses, our house shrunken and decayed*).

Conclusion In the conclusion, you sum up the meaning of the experience, either through explicit commentary (*The real treasures were those we had left behind: family, friends, and country*) or through an image that makes the point (*Staring back at me was the image of a white-haired old man, his face deeply creased by sorrow and worry. Several moments passed before I recognized my own reflection in the glass*).

For an example of this pattern, see the sample descriptive essay, "Smokey Mountain" (10d).

9c Patterns for Comparison Essays

You can use either the block or the point-by-point method to develop a comparison essay. We discussed both of these methods in detail in Chapter 6, when we described how to arrange material in paragraphs developed through comparison. Both methods have advantages and disadvantages.

Block Method

When you use the block method, you cover all the aspects of one subject before you discuss the other.

Advantages: Clarity and Simplicity

The block method gives you a chance to develop all your ideas on one subject before you turn to the other. It is therefore simple to work with when you don't have much time to organize an essay—in an exam, for instance. The block method can work well for short essays on familiar subjects, as in comparisons of places you have lived or people you have known. It is also effective when you are using a brief treatment of one subject as a basis for a more lengthy treatment of another. Finally, if you are comparing more than two subjects, you will probably need to use the block method to avoid fragmenting your material.

An important advantage of the block method is that you are less likely to distort your material by trying too hard to find similarities or by exaggerating the importance of one aspect of a subject. The sound patterns in one poem, for example, may contribute much less to the meaning than do the sound patterns in another.

Disadvantages: Repetition and Loss of Focus

One disadvantage of the block method is that readers may forget what you have said about your first subject by the time you make similar points about your second subject. For this reason, you may have to repeat points. Another danger is that you may lose your focus on the basis of your comparison: the common element you are discussing (such as the setting of the two stories or the economic effects of two policies). As a result, your reader may decide that you have discussed both subjects but never actually compared them. To avoid this problem, make sure your analysis focuses on the same element(s) of both subjects.

Sample Outline: Block Method

If you were using the block method to organize an essay comparing the advantages of working with the advantages of going to school, your outline might look like this.

I. The advantages of working
   A. Friendships with co-workers
   B. Money
   C. Free time
II. The advantages of going to school
   A. Friendships with other students
   B. Learning new ideas and skills
   C. Achieving goals
III. Working compared with going to school
   A. Friendships at work and school
   B. The immediate rewards of money and free time compared with the long-term rewards of learning and a sense of achievement

Notice that this structure leads naturally to putting your thesis at the end, where you draw together your comparisons.

Point-by-Point Method

Here you deal with one aspect of both subjects before moving on to another aspect of both subjects.

Advantages: Focus and Conciseness

An important advantage of the point-by-point method is that it helps your reader to grasp the most important similarities and differences by bringing specific points about your subjects closer together. It thus avoids one of the main disadvantages of the block method: repetition. This emphasis on points of similarity and difference also keeps you focused on the task of comparing. For these reasons, this method is often better for organizing a lengthy and complex comparison.

Disadvantages: Complexity and Fragmentation

With this method, you have to identify all the points of similarity and difference you plan to discuss before you begin writing. For this reason, it is difficult to use for in-class essays. Another disadvantage is that if you don't have much to say about each point, your essay may ping-pong rapidly from one subject to the other. You can correct this problem by gathering more material or by combining subpoints so that you can write separate paragraphs on each aspect of each subject, as illustrated in the outline below.

Sample Outline: Point-by-Point Method

Thesis Both myths and fairy tales can give us insights into cultural values, but fairy tales provide more useful role models for children because they portray more realistic characters who manage to solve their problems.

I. Cultural values in myths and fairy tales
  A. Cultural values in myths
  B. Cultural values in fairy tales

II. Characters as role models in myths and fairy tales
  A. Nature of characters
    1. Superhuman characters in myths
    2. Realistic characters in fairy tales
  B. Ability of characters to meet demands
    1. Failure of characters in myths
    2. Success of characters in fairy tales
  C. Fate of characters
    1. Unhappy endings of myths
    2. Happy endings of fairy tales

You will find an example of the point-by-point method of organizing a comparison in the sample literary research paper (14f).

*Patterns for
Comparison
Essays*

Chapter 10

Personal Essays

When you write personal essays, you share your thoughts, feelings, and experiences with your readers. But since you are writing an essay, your readers will also expect you to explain what your experience means. As we consider three kinds of personal essays (narrative, descriptive, and reflective), we will discuss how to fulfill your readers' expectations. Since most of your personal essays are likely to be based on events in your life, we will examine narrative essays most closely.

10a Narrative Essays

Like other essays, **narrative essays** must have a point, a main idea. To see why a main idea is important, let's consider an example.

Suppose you decide to write about "My Canoe Trip." The title, as you can see, doesn't suggest any point about the trip. It offers no principle to help you select which events to include and which to leave out, or how to arrange them effectively. So you might begin at the beginning, go on to the end, and stop. But would all the events of your trip, presented in that manner, interest anyone except your best friend?

Imagine, then, that you decide to focus on one incident and write about "A Frightening Canoe Trip." You would now have a way of deciding what to include in your essay, and you might even think about how to present your material—such as describing your nervousness as you approached a patch of white water and then flashing back to the events that led up to that moment. Readers interested in canoeing might find your experience thrilling to read about. But what about readers who never canoe and will never find themselves in a similar situation?

Think about your harrowing experience. What did you learn from it? There are many possible lessons that you might have learned—the dangers of overconfidence, for instance, or the

Narrative Essays

89

power of nature, or the joy of unexpected courage. Most of us learn these lessons at some time or another. A main point about what you learned, if it is true to your experience, will give your readers a second level of interest. They will not only find out what happened, but will also discover the meaning of the experience, both for you and for similar experiences in their own lives. This meaning will be the thesis that you state or imply through the telling of your story. It will give readers a new perspective on themselves or the world they live in.

What you have learned should not be a moral tacked on to the end—*From this incident I learned never to kill frogs.* It should emerge from the way you present the concrete details of the experience as well as the specific points you make. Writing *I was frightened* depicts your state of mind much less vividly than writing *Whenever I see little ripples in the river I think of the powerful currents beneath the surface, and my mouth goes dry with fear.* When you convey the unique quality of your experience through details such as these, your readers will understand more readily the meaning of the experience for you.

Writing Narrative Essays: The Process

Follow these guidelines when writing a narrative essay.

1. Focus on a single experience; you will then have room for the wealth of detail you need to make your essay interesting.

2. Make a central point about the meaning of this experience. You may discover this point in the process of writing.

3. Include only events and details relevant to the central point.

4. Provide enough specific details about *who, what, when, where, why*, and *how* for a reader to understand how events and actions relate to the central point.

5. Create interest through vivid, concrete diction (17c), figurative language (17d), varied sentence structure (17e), and other devices.

6. Put your thesis at the beginning, at the end, or at the point in the narrative where the meaning of events becomes clear to you.

7. Within this overall structure, arrange your material to create a specific effect, such as suspense, humour, or pathos.

10a

Narrative Essays

8. Make the sequence of events clear to readers by using transitional words and phrases (*the next morning, now that I look back*).

10b Sample Narrative Essay

Unwelcome Guest: The Case of the Snake

by Sydney Singh

In the backwater village in Guyana where I grew up, snakes were not uncommon. But they were rarely seen. They hid from humans, and for a very good reason: we killed them as routinely as we killed rats, mice, and other rodents. In my childhood, I may have killed a dozen snakes or so, but I do not recall the circumstances and details of any of the killings, except the last one. So fresh and vivid is my memory of this particular death that it would appear as if the event occurred only yesterday, and not forty years ago.

It was a very hot day in July, and I was home alone. I came out into the front yard, and there it was: a snake of unusual size, at the edge of the vegetable patch. For a moment I stood still, petrified with fear. The snake was unlike any I had seen before. It was brown as the earth, and larger than the common garden variety: about five feet long and two inches thick. Its head was held erect, a foot from the ground. There was dignity in its posture. Yet, my first impulse was to kill it. And I did.

Armed with a long, heavy piece of firewood, I struck. A sudden blow: a broken back. The snake immediately doubled up in a paroxysm of pain. As it writhed and thrashed in agony, I struck, again and again, savagely and unerringly. With each blow, its convulsive struggle grew less and less. Eventually it lay still. I poked its limp body with the end of the stick; it made no movement. The intruder was dead.

Gradually, the thumping of my heart subsided, and my initial fear vanished. I felt quite elated at my

10b

Sample Narrative Essay

daring feat, and could hardly wait for my father to come home so I could proudly show him the victim of my fearless courage. In the interim, I went inside to do some chores. A few minutes later, I came outside to glory in my act of bravery. Much to my horror, I saw another snake near the body of the dead one. I froze in my tracks. The newcomer was identical to the snake I had killed earlier, only slightly smaller. Even in my limited understanding, I recognized it was the female of the species, the mate of the dead snake.

My first thought was to kill her too. But I was arrested by her strange behaviour. She sniffed at the dead snake. Then she nudged him indifferently. When there was no response, she became more aggressive. She nudged him fiercely and frantically, urging him to move. Then realization seemed to dawn on her: her mate was dead. What followed was as incredible as it was fascinating. She threw herself on her mate; then she jumped high in the air and fell upon the body of her lifeless husband. She did this several times, wild with grief. Finally, wearied of her exertions, she gently rested her head on the dead body. After a little while, she slowly slithered into the thick grass and disappeared.

The spectacle of grief was not new to me. I had seen it in the exaggerated wailing of our women at funerals, and in the mournful cries of animals which had lost their young to sickness or starvation. But I had never seen such a display of genuine grief as that shown by the dead snake's companion. Child though I was, I was not without a moral sensibility. I realized, even then, what I had done, and my heart grew sick. It grew even sicker when my father musingly observed that the snakes were merely passing through our yard, on their way to some unknown destination. Later in life, I would refer to them as sojourners.

My father neither commended nor scolded me for my action. But in my guilty conscience I interpreted his words, "Dey was just passin' through," as a tacit expression of disapproval. That night I hardly slept at all. The dead snake and his disconsolate companion tormented my consciousness. I wondered where they came from, where they were going, and what would become of the widow. And then, for the first time, the enormity of my crime sank home: through my wanton act of cruelty, I had killed the husband, leaving the wife to continue, alone and lonely, on a journey they had begun together. There was no thrill in my victory, only a remorse sharper than a serpent's fang.

Many years passed before I realized that my aversion to snakes was associated with a myth that was part of my education. Snakes, we were taught both in school and in church, were our mortal enemies; it was the snake that was responsible for humanity's loss of paradise. According to the Bible, Satan, disguised as a snake, successfully tempted Eve to eat the forbidden fruit, and for his role in her disobedience, God pronounced a curse upon the serpent: "And I will put enmity between thee and the woman, and between thy seed and her seed; it shall bruise thy head, and thou shalt bruise his heel" (Genesis 3:15).

This curse has informed our relationship with the snake. Through the ages humans have systematically hunted the snake, and in many parts of the world decimated snake populations, to the detriment of our own survival. Yet there is no record that snakes have hunted men; few people in the world have died from snake bites. But perhaps more important, ever since that episode in the Garden of Eden the snake has been the archetypal symbol of evil. We associate it with deceit, cunning, and treachery. A person who betrays us, for example, is referred to as "a snake in the grass." A sly person has "beady snake's eyes." It is no exaggeration to say that the snake is perhaps the most maligned creature in the animal kingdom.

Many years ago, in an introductory literature course, I read a poem by D.H. Lawrence entitled "Snake." This poem did not lessen my loathing for snakes, but it gave me a whole new perspective and

Sample Narrative Essay

respect for these creatures, which inhabited the earth eighty million years before the appearance of humans. In the poem, the speaker tells of his encounter with a snake that has come to drink from his water-trough. His first instinct, like mine, is to kill the snake: "The voice of my education said to me, 'He must be killed'." But the speaker, much to his credit, resists the temptation; instead, he feels "honoured" that the snake should seek his hospitality. However, after the snake has drunk its fill and is about to return to the "horrid black hole" from whence it came, the speaker, overcome by "a sort of horror," picks up a log and throws it at the water-trough. He misses the snake, but is still racked with guilt:

> I thought how paltry, how vulgar, what a mean act!
> I despised myself and the voices of my accursed
>   human education.

The poem concludes with the speaker's regret at the departure of the snake; a wish for its return; and a realization that he has missed a rare opportunity:

> And so, I missed my chance with one of the lords
> Of life.
> And I have something to expiate;
> A pettiness.

> So do I.

Descriptive Essays

10c Descriptive Essays

If the unifying principle of narrative essays is *what happened to me*, the unifying principle of **descriptive essays** is *what I saw*. Keep this distinction in mind because narrative essays may include descriptions of people, places, and objects, and descriptive essays may include accounts of things happening. In a descriptive essay, however, the focus is on rendering your impressions of some part of the physical world and its meaning for you.

Subjects

You can write descriptive essays about places, people, or other animate and inanimate things. You might write, for example, about the town or neighbourhood in which you grew up to show that the community was either close-knit and friendly or alien and frightening. You might write a character sketch of a coach who taught you the importance of dedication, or you might focus on a family heirloom to explain its meaning in your life.

Image and Meaning

As in narrative essays, concrete images create meaning more effectively than do direct statements. Specific images of people, places, and objects allow your reader to see through your eyes and thus to understand the basis of your thoughts, feelings, and judgments. In the paragraph that follows, taken from the sample descriptive essay "Smokey Mountain" (10d), the writer uses repeated images of water, culminating in the reference to the hurricane, to convey his complex attitude toward the scene.

> These were the fringe dwellers of Manila, people who survive on an industry brutally isolated from the rest of the population. As I looked down from the safety of my perch high above the swarming crowd, the garbage appeared as faint streams spread across the valley. Bits of tin foil and splintered glass sparkled like breaking waves in the sunlight. The smear of black smoke rising out of spontaneous combustion appeared like thick steam from the water's surface. From where I stood, the whole scene had a certain beauty about it . . . but then, from the right distance, so does a raging hurricane.

This passage emphasizes the way a Canadian observer might feel safely distant from this scene of poverty and squalor. But it also conveys, in the image of the hurricane, the writer's recognition of the potential for violence and upheaval. Because we are encouraged to "see" this meaning for ourselves, the images are more effective than a direct statement of the author's reactions would be.

10c

Descriptive Essays

Organization

For short descriptive essays, such as "Smokey Mountain" (10d), it often works well to allow the meaning of the whole to emerge gradually from the accumulation of details. But to maintain readers' interest in longer descriptive essays, you may need to state your main point near the beginning and bring in other methods of development—such as a comparison of one person with another, or an analysis of the effects of a shifting population on a town.

Whatever overall structure you choose, you should arrange the parts of the essay by an appropriate principle of organization, usually spatial. This spatial organization may be literal (you could move from one part of the town to the next) or figurative (you could move from what is "easy to see" about a person to what is "hard to see"). Most important, your method of organization should culminate in an image that conveys the dominant impression you want to create.

10d Sample Descriptive Essay

Smokey Mountain

by Bill Howe

The young boy struggled up the side of the hill. His legs were straining under the weight of the sack he had slung over his shoulders and his one arm was flailing to catch his balance as he teetered over the narrow path. His shirt and trousers were soiled with sweat and dirt, and his legs were buried deep inside his oversized rubber boots. A floppy cap sagged over the side of his blackened face, hiding the scowl of dignified scorn he directed at the intruders. He quickly turned away and made off towards a sculpture of bed springs, tires, and scrap metal.

The hill I was standing on is known to the Filipinos as Smokey Mountain. It has been built up over many years from garbage deposits delivered from the streets of Metro Manila. Over eight million people contribute every day to this towering masterpiece, but its dismal appearance has not discouraged the poor who find their home within its refuge of waste. A population of some 15 000 squatters has developed into a thriving community, complete with a division of labour natural to such territory. There are people who sort through the garbage for cherished bits of plastic and metal, people who work in the distribution centres selling salvaged goods to local recycling plants, and people who go out into the streets at night to collect the garbage from the richer districts before it is diluted by the rest of the collection.

Most of the people migrated here to escape the hopeless life in the remote provinces, only to find the economic depression of their new surroundings worse than what they had left behind. The putrid smell of rotting debris wafting through the air continually reminds them of their own decay. The villagers are plagued with diseases contracted in their own backyard. On a good day, their labour might earn them only two or three dollars, but still they consider themselves fortunate to be able to earn money at all. The people appear proud and content with their life, and the children play in the garbage pile as if it were a giant sandbox filled with buried toys.

From where I stood, I had a panoramic view of the flow of garbage below. The convoy of tawny yellow dump trucks formed a brilliant streak which faded into the distant skyline of Manila. As the trucks dropped off their loads, people eagerly surrounded the untouched deposits, in hopes of discovering some carelessly discarded treasure to take home to their families. Tin cans, tires, wooden crates, plastic bottles, discarded clothing—nothing was overlooked for its value on the salvage market.

Attacking the hill from below was a huge bulldozer burrowing into the debris like a mechanical mole. As it lurched forward, it uncovered a trail of pristine spoil, its rutted tracks quickly filling with pools of mud freshly squeezed from the rubble below. The people followed the beast as though it was their master. As their bent frames waded slowly through the soggy mess, they seemed enslaved to the garbage beneath their feet, imprisoned by their own poverty.

These were the fringe dwellers of Manila, people who survive in an industry brutally isolated from the rest of the population. As I looked down from the safety of my perch high above the swarming

10d

Sample Descriptive Essay

crowd, the garbage appeared as faint streams spread across the valley. Bits of tin foil and splintered glass sparkled like breaking waves in the sunlight. The smear of black smoke rising out of spontaneous combustion appeared like thick steam from the water's surface. From where I stood, the whole scene had a certain beauty about it . . . but then, from the right distance, so does a raging hurricane.

One of the dump trucks passed me as I was leaving the smouldering mountain. I grinned to myself as I read the words inscribed across its side boards— "Manila on the Go!"

10e Reflective Essays

If narrative essays present a person acting, and descriptive essays present a person perceiving, **reflective essays** present a mind thinking and feeling about a particular subject. The emphasis shifts from the outer world to the inner world.

Subjects

Reflective essays allow you to explore the meaning of your experiences through methods other than narration and description. You might define what friendship means to you, for instance, by discussing the qualities and behaviour that characterize relations between friends. Or you might explore the meaning of friendship by classifying your friends, by comparing friends and acquaintances, or by developing an analogy such as "a friend is like a favourite pair of shoes." Or you might evaluate your own behaviour as a friend.

Another way of reflecting upon your experience is to focus upon causes and/or effects: what causes you to be a good or poor student or employee? what causes you to act outrageously or timidly? what are the effects in your life of being Native, White, Sikh, Asian, Black, French-Canadian? of being Catholic, atheist, Jewish, Muslim? of being an immigrant or Canadian-born? of growing up in a certain time, place, family, social class? of having your particular body, mind, temperament?

Organization

Because the emphasis in reflective essays is on thinking and feeling, you may find yourself shifting back and forth between making generalizations and giving specific details. To give the sense of a person thinking and feeling, you may allow the structure of your essay to mirror the sometimes unexpected movements of your mind. The trick is to find a balance between too loose a structure that lets the essay fall apart, and too tight a structure that stifles your personal voice. Try using one of the patterns for leading up to your thesis (9b), the block or point-by-point method of organizing comparisons (9c), or the weighing of alternatives characteristic of evaluation (7b).

10f Sample Reflective Essay

In this essay (a shortened version), the writer reflects upon the effects of living with—and without—a diagnosis of a disability. As she searches for a language for her experience, she moves back and forth between past and present. Transitions guide readers through these shifts in time.

A Language of My Own

by Camille Collett

I remember the day that I was diagnosed. Labelled. Legitimized. Before anyone had a name for my inability to function in normative situations (whatever those are), I was just different. *Extremely shy and withdrawn.* I was different and completely outside of the world that everyone else appeared implicitly to understand. *A good little girl—quiet and reserved.* These words described what others saw, but they did not describe the chaos of my inner world.

By the time I was old enough to understand that thinking was a process, I really believed that everyone else in the world thought the same way that I did. This meant that everyone had thousands of thoughts occurring simultaneously—like a wall of televisions all tuned to different channels blasting images and noise. The fixed volume on all the units made it difficult to differentiate one unit from another. Thinking, for me, was a process of focusing on one noise for a brief moment of absorption, without any retention, before, distracted, my thought pattern clicked onto a different television unit. As material became more detailed, my attention span diminished even further. As a consequence, I became a wealth of information that I could not organize or communicate except by impulsively blurting out facts which were unconnected and irrelevant to the events around me.

Eventually, life became too complicated to compensate for what was going on inside my head. At four, I could play piano sonatas by ear. But when I tried to learn to read music and consciously pay attention to what both hands were doing, I became frustrated and angry. No one would understand that the notes dancing off the page were art in and of themselves, engaging my curiosity. I became absorbed in a process of meaning that I didn't understand. Overwhelmed, I retreated and lived inside of myself. Inside I could make it calm and quiet.

After seventeen years of the qualified professionals asserting that I merely typified the shy, quiet young woman, someone heard me. Someone listened to my voice. The diagnosis validated the experiences that went unseen. Attention Deficit Disorder (ADD). Three small words became an identification number, indelible marks on my body: a woman with a behavioural and learning disability.

ADD, or ADHD (Attention Deficit Hyperactivity Disorder), as it is also called, results from developmental deficiencies that make it hard to inhibit, initiate, or sustain responses to tasks or stimuli, especially when there are few consequences. In other words, having weak internal mechanisms for regulating behaviour, children with ADD often act impulsively and have trouble concentrating on tasks unless their environment is highly structured. Although the medical community cannot agree on the actual cause of ADHD, recent research reported in the *Globe and Mail* suggests that ADHD may be linked to a deficit in a gene that regulates the body's use of thyroid hormone. According to the *Globe and Mail*, this is the first time that a "specific inborn flaw has been linked to a common behavioural problem." Inborn flaw. Flawed merchandise. Quality control down. The words "common behavioural problem" are inadequate. The words imply that all ill-mannered and rude children are the result of a bad gene pool. Simultaneously, words mean too much and not enough.

The signs had been there since I was born, but the medical community was blinded by expectation. I was a textbook case. My failure to thrive became a "milk allergy" and my refusal to eat was "normal." My nature came to be described as quiet and reserved (like a good little girl) rather than as withdrawn and removed. Except when people, uninvited, tried to invade my interior space, and then I would rage like a wild beast until I was left alone. Ambidextrous until I was eight, I was tested for brain dominance—not because I used both hands, but because it took me so long to decide which hand to use that I never did anything in school. The testing successfully determined that my right hand was dominant by 1%. Of course testing can only do so much and deciding which hand to use was replaced by which color crayon to use and later, in junior high school, by whether to use pen or pencil. I wanted to think but it hurt my head so I absorbed myself in books. Books became my reality and I lived inside them.

When I ventured outside the world of books and tried to talk about my frustration, I was invisible. I was white. I was blonde. I was the child of two highly educated individuals. According to the experts, I was merely the typically rebellious child of pushy parents. When I disagreed, I was told that girls don't have to do math and science. When I said I wanted to, I was told I couldn't know what I wanted because I was the child of pushy parents. When I said that the only person I was disappointing was myself, I was told that at fifteen I couldn't possibly have that kind of self-awareness.

Disability is one of those silent words that no one speaks. At least not around me. Feeling invisi-

Sample Reflective Essay

101

ble, I wait for someone to speak in a language that recognizes, even if it doesn't always understand, difference. A language that I can speak as a woman with a disability. Without that language, my head is filled with speaking silence. Awkward silence. The kind of silence that follows the disclosure of difference, eyes shifting away from the body that spoke. Yet I feel uncomfortable asserting my identification with disabled women because it reduces all of us to a common denominator. I am also afraid that the community I identify with the most will refuse to recognize the disability that cannot be seen. Medication is my only visible link to that community. I am afraid of being invisible.

Some people believe that I should rejoice in my invisibility, that I should consider it a luxury that I don't have to deal with the challenges of being visually or physically disabled in an abled world. They don't understand that access to the world is something I fight for every day, because unlike the stairs that exclude the crippled, the barriers that exclude a woman with learning disabilities are unseen.

Searching for a language true to my experience, I turn to writers who challenge this kind of unquestioned cultural authority. Women writers like Audre Lorde, Toni Morrison, and Adrienne Rich have found a language for their self-awareness. Donna Williams' *Nobody Nowhere*, which describes her experience growing up with autism, was a special gift, a validation from someone who understands unseen difference on her own individual terms.

The language that I await, the language that will allow me to bridge the gap between my inner world and the world outside, is beginning to come. Being disabled is a different life experience. It is a unique perspective in a world where perception is often taken for granted.

10f

Sample Reflective Essay

Chapter 11

Expository Essays

When you write an expository essay, your purpose is to explain something to a particular audience. Your subject might be a short story, an historical event, a current situation, a theory. To move beyond saying what your subject is to saying what it means, you need to use methods of development such as analysis, comparison, and definition. (For a reminder of these methods, see Chapter 6, Methods of Explaining.) The meaning you see in your subject—your interpretation of it—serves as the thesis for your essay.

11a Writing Expository Essays: The Process

Regardless of the subject of your expository essay, the steps in the process of formulating your thesis and organizing your material are the same.

Choosing a Primary Method of Development and a Focus

Some essay assignments state or imply a primary method of development and a focus (*Compare legislation governing impaired driving in Ontario and Quebec*). Others simply give a list of possible subjects (*Native land claims*), leaving you to choose your focus. If a primary method of development is not given or implied, make notes on what each method of explaining could contribute to your essay.

You might begin work on an expository essay on child poverty, for example, by making the following list.

Method of Development	Possible Material
Process Analysis	Not applicable?
Systems Analysis	How agencies dealing with the needs of poor children fit into the system of social services

103

Method of Development	Possible Material
Causal Analysis	What causes poverty among children
	How poverty affects children's short-term and long-term development
	How poverty among children affects society as a whole
Classification	Child poverty by region
	Child poverty by types of households
Comparison	Differences in the development of impoverished children and middle-class children
	Child poverty in Mexico and Canada
Definition	Meaning of poverty

From a list of possibilities such as that given above, you need to choose a focus for your essay. If you are writing for a newspaper or a magazine, you can let your own interests and your assumptions about the interests of your readers guide your choice. Suppose you were writing on child poverty for *Chatelaine*. Your reader profile might suggest that most of its readers were middle-class women with children. To appeal to their interests, you might decide to focus on differences in the development of middle-class children and impoverished children. Your primary method of development would therefore be comparison.

When you are writing an essay for a course, on the other hand, you are likely to choose a focus that reflects the concerns, objectives, or methodology of that field of study. Sociologists, for example, study the relationships between groups and society as a whole. For a sociology course, you might focus on what causes child poverty or how child welfare agencies fit into the system of social services. For these topics, analysis would be your primary method of development.

11a

*Writing
Expository
Essays:
The Process*

Gathering Material

There are many sources of material for expository essays. For subjects you are familiar with, brainstorming will often give you enough information. From working in restaurants, for example, you could write an essay explaining why staff turnovers are rapid or why some restaurants fail and others succeed. For course-related subjects, you may find material by asking systematic discovery questions (see Essays Analyzing Literature, 11c; Position Papers, 13d).

But sometimes you may have to gather information from other sources. You can conduct interviews (12a) and other types of field research for material on subjects of local interest. And of course there's a wealth of print material on most subjects (see Conducting Computer-Aided Research, 14b).

However you gather material, keep your focus and method of development in mind. They will help you decide what information is relevant to your essay.

Formulating a Thesis

Once you have gathered various bits of information, you need to ask yourself what they add up to. This process of synthesizing your material will lead you to a main idea, a thesis. A good thesis for an expository essay should **explain** some aspect of your subject: why one definition of a controversial term is better than another; how the setting in a short story contributes to the theme; what causes abusive relationships among family members. It should state an opinion about your subject and give reasons that set the limits of your discussion. A statement such as *Child poverty has many causes* does neither. In contrast, this thesis states an opinion and clearly defines the scope of the essay: *Child poverty has many causes: among them are parental lack of responsibility; scarcity of convenient, subsidized child-care facilities; inadequate social assistance programs; and an economy increasingly reliant on low-paying, part-time jobs in the service sector.*

Including Other Methods of Development

You can often write your first draft using only your primary method of development. When you revise, however, you may discover that to explain the meaning of your subject clearly and fully, you need to add definitions of terms (*poverty, adequate nutrition*), comparisons (*rates of language development in middle-class children and poor children*), or other material. To create interest, you may use the methods for sharing personal experience we discussed in Chapter 5. In writing about child poverty, for instance, you could tell a story about a child's visit to a food bank, describe the child's living conditions, or use an analogy such as "For a child, being poor is like living with a chronic and debilitating disease." The sample expository essay shows how you can bring a human dimension to an abstract concept such as child poverty. Readers—even most instructors!—will appreciate the human touch. If you are unsure whether this approach would be appropriate for a course-related essay, ask your instructor.

Organizing Your Essay

Expository essays written for college and university courses are usually organized with the thesis up front in the introduction, topic sentences showing how each middle paragraph relates to the thesis, and a restatement and extension of the thesis in the conclusion. This method of organization offers your instructor a well-defined framework and emphasizes what he or she is most interested in—your interpretation.

If you are writing in a different situation or for a different type of reader, you may want to consider leading readers through your explanation before you state your thesis in the conclusion. (For more information on both these methods of organization, see Chapter 9, Essay Structure.)

Let's consider the choices facing the writer of the sample expository essay, "The Effects of Child Poverty." This piece, based on interviews and firsthand observation, was intended for readers of a local newspaper. Since many readers would not have any direct experience of poverty and thus might not understand its grim realities, the writer begins with facts and details that lead gradually to the thesis.

11b Sample Expository Essay

The Effects of Child Poverty

Jimmy is a two-year-old living with his mother and baby sister in government-subsidized housing. The

complex is reasonably well maintained if you ignore
the rusting shopping carts abandoned here and there
and the mattresses soaking up rain in the disposals.
Today is a good day at Jimmy's place because there
is food in the fridge. A week from now the fridge
will be empty and it will be ten days before the
child tax credit comes through. It is now about two
o'clock and Jimmy has been staring at the soaps for
three hours. His mother feels she should turn off
the television and take him to the playground, but
he outgrew his rain boots a couple of months ago.
Not that the playground offers much for him to do:
two of the three swings are broken, the slide is
gritty, and the sand around it is pebbled with shards
of broken beer bottles. The local library has plenty
of books for children, but it's five kilometres away
and his mother has no money for bus fare. The relief
day care centre is closer and it has other children
for him to play with, but his mother is reluctant to
take his sister there because she has run out of baby
food and does not want anyone to know.

Jimmy's situation helps to define child poverty in
Canada. The problem is not just that Jimmy is missing out on the extras. His family fits the federal
government's definition of poverty: more than half
his mother's monthly income is spent on food, shelter, and clothing. Even so, the children are poorly
clothed and fed. Because most poor children in
Canada live in single-parent families headed by
women, Jimmy's situation is fairly typical.
According to the 1998 Campaign 2000 report on child
poverty, the number of poor children in Canada has
increased by 60 percent in the ten years since the
House of Commons unanimously passed a bill to end
child poverty in Canada by the year 2000 (Deanna
Shorten, "Children and Poverty," *Our Voice*, May
1999, p. 7). How is poverty affecting Jimmy? How
does poverty affect all children? How does poverty
affect our society?

Let's begin with the basic physical needs for
shelter, clothing, and food. Jimmy's need for shelter has been met by the subsidized housing his

11b

*Sample
Expository
Essay*

mother was lucky to get. The reduction in rent does not, however, give her more money to spend on food and clothing. The amount of the subsidy is just subtracted from her welfare cheque. At two, Jimmy doesn't worry about designer labels, but his mother worries about replacing the rain boots and snowsuit he's outgrown. Without appropriate clothing, Jimmy won't be able to attend a play group when he turns three. Jimmy's opportunities are thus limited by a scarcity of clothing.

Meanwhile, what happens if Jimmy doesn't get enough to eat? Children between one and three, according to nutritionists, need 4-5 servings of grain products, 4-5 servings of vegetables and fruits, 2 servings of meat or meat alternatives, and 3 servings of milk products every day. Of course, these servings are quite small (half an apple, one third of a cup of dry cereal), but a child needs food from all the food groups every day. Unlike adults, who can cope reasonably well with periodic food shortages, a child deprived of food will be stunted both physically and intellectually. After a week of crackers and bargain macaroni dinners, Jimmy is lethargic, uninterested in his toys, and only too willing to park himself in front of the television. He falls asleep when his mother tries to read to him. He is among the one in three children in Edmonton who, according to the Edmonton Social Planning Council, are malnourished (Shorten, p. 7). At two, going on three, most children can understand complex sentences and repeat simple ones. If they've been read to, they can identify a picture of an elephant or a farm. The effects of Jimmy's nutritional deficiencies show up in his inability to talk in sentences and the limitations in his vocabulary. He can't identify a picture of a horse or pick out a red crayon.

The widening gap between what Jimmy knows and what other children his age know means that he's likely to do poorly in grade one. Children who are tired, cold, and hungry can't learn much. Schools are increasingly called upon to provide children with a place to sleep, warm clothing, and food. In some schools, teachers spend much of their time trying to meet children's physical needs. Moreover, many children like Jimmy succeed in school only if they get extra instruction. But as schools try to do more with less money, helping some children often means depriving others. In Jimmy's neighbourhood school, funding for a teacher's aide was taken from money originally earmarked for library materials. As a result of the poverty of some children, educational opportunities for all children decline.

The broader effects of poverty are also visible in the current strains on the health care system. For example, inadequate nutrition for expectant mothers often results in low birth-weight babies. Research studies indicate that such babies not only need more hospital care at birth; they may also need more hospital care as adults. In a low birth-weight baby, organs such as the liver may not be fully functioning. The baby with the underdeveloped liver is more likely to need a coronary bypass as a middle-aged adult. Expensive, high-tech procedures that drive up health care costs are thus, in part, the effect of a diet of crackers and macaroni.

The costs of poverty extend far beyond welfare cheques and rent subsidies. Poverty creates a cycle of deprivation, failure, and despair. Children raised in poverty are more likely to become part of a permanent underclass of people who no longer believe they can break out of the poverty cycle. The effects of poverty, however, are not confined to the poor. Limitations in education and health care decrease the quality of life available to all citizens.

11c Essays Analyzing Literature

Purpose and Audience

When you write an essay on a piece of literature, your purpose is not to describe its content but to explain some part of its meaning (see Explaining Works of Art, 6d). By reading the piece carefully, you develop a general sense of its major themes, such as the theme "character is fate" that runs through

Thomas Hardy's novels. Then you analyze the work, or a portion of it, such as a scene of a play or the setting of a novel, by asking questions like those below. As a result of this analysis, you can refine your sense of theme and show how you arrived at your interpretation.

Since you are writing primarily for an instructor familiar with the work, you may be unsure of how much to say. You don't need to provide all the details you would for someone who had never read it, but you do need to use quotations and examples to show how you arrived at your interpretation.

Writing About Literature: The Process

When you analyze imaginative works of literature, you concentrate on their aesthetic qualities and moral implications. When you analyze works of nonfiction, such as essays, research articles, and proposals, you may focus more on the validity of the arguments they present. You will find suggestions about how to analyze and evaluate nonfiction in Summaries (12c) and Position Papers (13d).

You can write a more effective essay on imaginative works by following these steps.

1. ***Decide on a focus and a method of development.***
Most assignments in introductory literature courses give you a focus. You may be asked to explain how one or more elements, such as the setting, characterization, or title, relate to the theme of the work as a whole. The method of development for this type of literary criticism is **analysis**, the division of something into its parts in order to explain the whole more clearly. For example, you might analyze the structure and imagery of a poem to explain how they contribute to the theme.

In addition to analysis, some topics require **comparison:** *Compare the theme of initiation in stories X and Y.* Other topics will ask you to assess the strengths and weaknesses of a work: *Which film version of* Macbeth *presents a better interpretation of the thematic implications of Lady Macbeth's madness?* For this topic, in addition to analysis and comparison, you would use **evaluation** as a method to develop your ideas.

Topics such as these provide specific directions about what to focus on and how to develop your ideas. If your topic is more general, such as *Discuss three poems by Margaret Atwood,* use the discovery questions on page 112 to help you find a focus.

2. *Analyze the relevant element(s) or section(s) of the work.*

Use as a guide the discovery questions for imaginative literature given in the next section.

3. *Formulate a thesis.*

The thesis should make a point about the theme of the work and about how each element you have analyzed conveys that theme. Be sure that you have not merely restated the essay topic (for example, *This essay will analyze the use of landscape in a poem by Margaret Atwood*) or made a vague generalization (*Many poets use landscape to express a theme and mood in their poetry*). To direct your reader's attention to a specific use of landscape and thus to limit the content of the essay, you would need a thesis such as this one: *In Margaret Atwood's poem "Journey to the Interior," landscape depicts the struggle against depression.*

4. *Organize your essay.*

In your introduction, give the authors and titles of all the works you plan to discuss and establish the **focus** of your essay. Put your thesis at the end of your introduction.

In the body of your essay, keep your readers' attention focused on your subject by beginning each paragraph with a topic sentence that identifies one aspect of your subject. If you were writing an essay on colour symbolism in *The Great Gatsby*, for instance, each middle paragraph might begin with a topic sentence that stated the significance of a particular colour in the novel.

> White symbolizes Daisy's empty life and the dream Gatsby associates with her.
>
> Throughout the novel, gold symbolizes money.
>
> Red suggests both the glittering wealth of rubies and the blood of harsh reality.

Good topic sentences focus your reader's attention on the function of an element.

NOT	This poem has five stanzas. [descriptive summary]
NOT	In the first stanza, the speaker talks about . . . [narrative summary]
BUT	Each stanza of the poem represents a different stage of life. [analysis]

Give reasons, details, examples, and quotations to support each interpretative point that you make in your middle paragraphs. Be sure to clearly link the point and the supporting evidence.

In your conclusion, restate your thesis and summarize your most important points. If appropriate, suggest a broader context into which your interpretation fits (*The distrust of conventional values that we have seen is typical of the postwar period*).

Discovery Questions: Imaginative Literature

Subject What is this work about?

Genre What kind of work is this (descriptive essay, revenge tragedy, dramatic monologue)? What are the characteristics of this genre?

Setting What is the time, place, and social environment in which the work is set? (Alice Munro's *Lives of Girls and Women* is set among the working poor in rural Ontario in the late 1940s and 1950s.) What effect does the setting have on characters' lives? What values are associated with different times, places, or social environments? In drama and film, what do costumes, lighting, sets, and music contribute to the setting?

Structure How is the work put together?

Narrative/Dramatic Structure: What sets the plot in motion? What are the main events? Does the plot reach a crisis? How are the events arranged (chronologically, shifting from present to past, shifting from main plot to subplots)? What is the underlying issue or purpose that connects the events (a spiritual quest, a critique of society, a revelation of the main character's true nature)?

Poetic Structure: How are the thoughts and feelings organized? Why does the poem begin and end as it does? Does the structure follow the conventions of a particular kind of poem (an Italian sonnet, for example)?

Characterization What are the characters like? Is there a broad range of characters? How would you classify them? Are the characters given depth and complexity or are they stereotypes? What techniques are used to portray them (appearance, characteristic actions, speech, opinions of others, self-revelation)? Do characters change? What do we learn about the workings of race, class, gender, or other factors from the way characters live their lives?

11c

*Essays
Analyzing
Literature*

Point of View Whose eyes do we see through? Whose voice do we hear? In stories and novels, this voice is referred to as the narrator. Because you cannot be sure that the voice you hear in a poem is the poet's, it is customary to use the term *speaker* when you refer to the point of view in a poem.

Is the narrator (stories, novels) or the speaker (poetry) a participant, referring to himself or herself as "I"? How reliable is this narrator or speaker?

Is the narrator or speaker a non-participant, referring to the characters as *he*, *she*, or *they*? Is the narrator/speaker omniscient, seeing into the minds of all the characters? Does the narrator/speaker comment directly on the characters or the action?

Style (Diction and Sentence Structure) What are the effects of language level (formal, standard, informal) and word choice? Are there any unusual or especially effective words? In poetry, what effects are achieved through the sounds of words? How does word choice contribute to the characterization, setting, and theme? What are the effects of sentence patterns? Does the writer favour long, complex sentences or short, simple ones? Are sentence fragments used to create emphasis, excitement, informality? Is parallelism used distinctively? (For more information on the effects of variations in sentence structure, see Improving Your Sentence Structure, 17e). In poetry, how are lines and stanzas used? In films and plays, what are the effects of the pacing of dialogue and action? How do these elements of language contribute to characterization, setting, and theme?

Style (Imagery and Symbolism) Does the writer use any significant figures of speech (similes, metaphors, personification)? (For more information on figurative language, see Adding Interest, 17d). Do images and symbols create patterns of meaning? How do imagery and symbolism contribute to the characterization, setting, and theme?

Theme What is the central idea of the work?

Integrating Secondary Sources

If you wish to integrate other critics' interpretations into your essay, you will find help in Integrating Research Material (14e) and in the sample literary research paper, "*Tom Sawyer* and *Anne of Green Gables:* Two Models of Heroism" (14f). For information on how to cite your sources, see Appendix B, Documentation.

11d Sample Essay Analyzing Literature

The following sample essay demonstrates how you can analyze a piece of writing to show how the author develops a theme. Here is the poem the essay analyzes:

Warren Pryor

When every pencil meant a sacrifice
his parents boarded him in town
slaving to free him from the stony fields
the meager acreage that bore them down.

They blushed with pride when, at his graduation,
they watched him picking up the slender scroll,
his passport from the years of brutal toil
and lonely patience in a barren hole.

When he went in the Bank their cups ran over.
They marvelled how he wore a milk-white shirt
work days and jeans on Sundays. He was saved
from their thistle-strewn farm and its red dirt.

And he said nothing. Hard and serious
like a young bear inside his teller's cage,
his axe-hewn hands upon the paper bills
aching with empty strength and throttled rage.

—Alden Nowlan

Wasted Sacrifices in "Warren Pryor"

In his poem "Warren Pryor," Alden Nowlan explores the sad consequences of good intentions. Like most parents, Warren's parents want the best for him. Their vision of a good life for their son, however, is based on what they imagine he wants, not what he really wants. For this reason, their sacrifices create a trap of duty from which Warren cannot escape. Every element in this poem—structure, sound patterns, rhythm, diction, and imagery—reinforces the central irony: children who are forced to fulfill

their parents' dreams end up with lives as imprison-
ing as those their parents dreamed of escaping.

Nowlan develops the contrast between what Warren
wants and what his parents want for him through the
sequence of events and shift in point of view that
create the structure of the poem. The poem begins
with Warren's parents painfully scraping together
the money for their son to live in town and complete
high school. The second stanza is devoted to their
enormous pleasure and pride when he graduates and
gains "his passport from the years of brutal toil"
(1. 7). In the third stanza, when Warren gets a job
in a bank, his parents "marvel" that he now wears
his good clothes every day but Sunday. The final
lines of this stanza, which describe the parents'
triumph at rescuing their son from "their thistle-
strewn farm," mark the turning point of the poem.

In the fourth stanza, Nowlan abruptly shifts the
point of view and at last we see Warren himself:
caged, miserable, strangled by his parents'
sacrifices. The rigid structure of the poem
emphasizes the imprisonment Warren feels as he paces
in his teller's cage. Most of the lines have ten
syllables. Every stanza has four lines and the same
rhyme scheme: abcb. The rhythm of the lines,
especially in the first two stanzas, is mostly
regular iambic pentameter:

When every pencil meant a sacrifice
his parents boarded him in town

When the point of view shifts in the fourth stanza,
so does the rhythm: "And he said nothing." The extra
stressed syllables and the dramatic pause within the
line give us a vivid sense of Warren's agony.

Both the diction and imagery of "Warren Pryor"
emphasize the theme of wasted sacrifices. The words
describing the farm—"stony fields," "meager
acreage," "barren hole," "thistle-strewn"—make it
easy for us to see the hardships his parents have
endured. Surely his assistance would have made their
lives easier; instead, they "slaved" in "lonely

*Sample
Essay
Analyzing
Literature*

patience" to "free" their son. The allusion to the Twenty-Third Psalm in the comment "their cups ran over" suggests their complete happiness when Warren secures a job in a bank. Indeed, the cup of their contentment spills over the "milk-white shirt" he wears to work.

By comparing Warren to a "young bear," Nowlan suggests that the son is by nature unsuited for the job his parents delight in. The simile stresses his youth, power, wildness. He is both literally in a cage—the barred cubicle bank tellers used to work in—and figuratively imprisoned by his parents' expectations. The idea that Warren is trapped in a bank seems especially apt, for he will spend his life paying for the sacrifices his parents have made for him. The metaphors describing Warren's hands emphasize his sacrifices. His hands are "axe-hewn" (strong and roughly made), suggesting that he is better suited to wielding an axe than handling paper bills. His hands are "aching with empty strength" because, in the irony that concludes the poem, he longs to do exactly the work his parents' sacrifices have kept him from. As he strangles his frustration, he sacrifices his own desires so that his parents can keep their illusions.

Nowlan develops the real sadness of wasted sacrifices through every element of "Warren Pryor." Through the first three stanzas, we share the parents' pleasure in their own accomplishments. The central irony of the poem, of course, is that they have gained their happiness at the expense of their son's. Throughout the poem, Nowlan's skillful diction and imagery emphasize the sad reality of what their sacrifices have actually accomplished. While they congratulate themselves on rescuing him, Warren paces within the cage his parents' sacrifices have created for him. In a few short lines, Nowlan vividly captures the all-too-common conflict between parents' expectations and their child's fulfillment.

11d

Sample
Essay
Analyzing
Literature

Chapter 12

Other Types of Expository Writing

12a Interviews

When you are writing an expository essay, interviews can provide additional information and create interest. Conducting an interview, or a series of interviews, is often the best way to obtain information about local people, issues, and events. If you were writing an essay on the Cree Circle Dance for an anthropology class, for instance, you might supplement your reading by arranging to interview participants, spectators, and Cree elders about its significance. Interviews are also interesting as self-contained pieces of writing, because they allow readers to enter into another person's world.

Conducting a good interview takes planning. Here are some guidelines.

Preparing for the Interview

1. ***Choose your informant carefully.*** The most obvious choice is not always the best one. The drummer in a band, for instance, may have shrewder insights into the band's strengths and weaknesses than the lead singer. If possible, ask someone knowledgeable about your subject for names of people who would make good informants.

2. ***Make a list of questions that will give you the information you need.*** To help you both relax, start the interview with straightforward questions you already know the answer to. Limit your list to a small number of topics that will allow you to shape your material to suit your purpose. Alternate key questions with less relevant ones, so that you can finish your notes on important points while your informant answers the next question. Finally, avoid asking questions that can be

answered yes or no. Instead, ask open-ended questions that invite full responses: "How do you see the band developing over the next few years?"

3. ***Decide whether to take notes or to tape record the interview.*** Your choice will depend on how comfortable you and your informant feel with each method and how you plan to use the material. Transcribing an interview is quite time-consuming, so if you plan to use only a few direct quotes and paraphrase the rest of the material, taking notes should be sufficient. Tape the session if you want a lengthy first-hand account of the informant's experiences, or if you plan to present your material in a question-and-answer format. Taping is also wise if misquoting your informant could cause trouble. Test the equipment ahead of time so that you and your informant won't be distracted by technical problems.

4. ***When you request an interview, identify yourself and your project.*** Explain why the interview is important and how you will use the information. Give the person a sense of what you already know about the subject so that he or she will know how technical to be in response to your questions.

5. ***Arrange a convenient time and place for the interview and suggest how long you think the interview will take.***

Conducting the Interview

1. Express appreciation for the interview.

2. Tell the person again how you will use the information, and assure him or her that confidential information will remain confidential.

3. Refer to your list of questions as necessary, but don't stick to it so rigidly that the interview becomes boring.

4. Ask your informant to clarify, expand upon, or give examples of points. Specific details bring interviews to life.

5. If you are taking notes, don't try to write down everything your informant says. Jot down facts and opinions as you would

in taking notes for a course, using key words and ideas to help you remember the context (and write up your notes before you forget!). Take down a few direct quotations to capture the informant's personality and point of view. Before you end the interview, review your notes with your informant to make sure they are accurate and complete.

6. If appropriate, jot down details of the person's appearance, actions, manner of speaking, and the place so that you can include them in your piece.

Writing Up the Interview

You can present interview material in a variety of ways: in a question-and-answer format; as an edited transcript; or as an essay combining quotations, paraphrased material, background information, and a character description. You are probably most familiar with the question-and-answer format. This form, which works like a dialogue between you and your informant, is effective when you want to ask probing questions about a series of topics. The edited transcript, in contrast, allows your informant to tell a story without interruption, with you providing an introduction. Using the third method, you can select and arrange your descriptions and interview material to emphasize points you want to make.

Here are some guidelines for writing up your interview.

1. Use only the material that best suits the purpose of the piece you are writing.

2. Combine material from different parts of the interview if doing so allows you to explain a point more fully.

3. You may edit direct quotations to eliminate repetition, correct obvious mistakes, and so forth, as long as you do not distort the meaning or lose the flavour of the original.

4. If you discover that you need to check facts or fill in missing information, make a list of questions and call your informant. Try to call only once.

After the interview, write a brief letter to the person you interviewed, expressing your thanks. If possible, send the person a courtesy copy of the piece in which you used the information.

12b Sample Interview

The following piece illustrates an interview written in essay form. It gives a vivid sense of its subject, a young immigrant from India. See if you can figure out what questions the interviewer asked.

Conveniently Canadian

by Todd Babiak

"I guess the first thing I did was look at girls. Right off the plane."

Bobby Mehra squints his eyes and smiles, head bobbing to the Pearl Jam song. As he thinks of something to say, he spies on the skater kids who are crowded around the slushie machine.

"In India we didn't have that freedom. They say you're too young for that. Man, back there when you're fourteen, you don't even think about them, let alone look at them, you know, sexually. You deny a lot there. They say it's improper. Unless you're a poverty kid. Not to brag or anything, but my dad had a high job, eh. We were well off in India. We gave up a lot to come here, but I prefer the freedom. Not only to look at girls when you're fourteen, but other freedoms too. You know."

Bobby is seventeen. Since arriving in Canada four years ago, he has perfected his English, lost his Hindi accent, and forgotten how to write his native language. Every Saturday he works in the Mac's store his parents operate. Along with his convenience store shirt, he wears baggy green pants and Doc Martens with a two-inch sole. Carefully constructed sideburns highlight his amply gelled short hair.

"Here there is so much style. Back in India, the only magazines we ever read were comic books. What you look like is so important here. Another difference is the studies. Studies were way harder there. When you're young, and you're good middle class, you don't have parties, you don't drink, you don't smoke. You have to be twenty-one there to buy a pack of smokes, eh. I guess I still have a bit of that in me. Peer pressure doesn't do anything to me,

I've never taken a drink in my life. I've been everywhere, all the bars, but I don't drink. Basically, it's just so different to be young there. You don't get depressed about girls or working or money. You just work on your studies like crazy. Now I'm used to the Canadian way. I'm lazier."

Bobby turns up the radio when a U2 song comes on, his favourite group. As customers present him with bread, sour cream, super size Cokes and French Onion Sun Chips, he comments on the heat, the melting snow. *I can't believe how nice it is. Hope it stays this way.*

"My parents are the coolest people I know. I had my first girlfriend a year after I came here. They were like, *This is Canada.* My dad said, *You are completely independent, whatever you do you are still my son.* It's not like that with all brown kids. I mean I can't date a my-own-race girl. Once I tried. Basically, she was Muslim and we had to keep it a total secret. Not just because I'm Hindu but if you're from India, young girls don't date. She was pretty cool but we got nailed—her dad found out. It was awful. One thing about her I didn't like is that she was mad, disgusted, when she found out I'd had white girlfriends. She only dated brown guys. I hate that shit."

He replaces the coffee filters, checks prices on sour candies and wipes counters as he talks. He likes working. After he graduates from high school this summer, he plans to study Business Administration. He wants to work for a large corporation. Or a small bank. Two of his friends come in and they discuss tonight's plans. *A movie? This girl's party?*

"There's been a little bit of racial discrimination with my parents. I mean, my dad had a really high job in India. He comes here knowing English, with so much education, and he can't get an office job. Not even a file clerk. Everywhere he went, *You don't have any Canadian experience.* My dad would never call it discrimination, but . . . . All I know is it makes no sense.

"There is racism. This one guy in grade 8 said something racist, he called me a racist name. Basically I beat the shit out of him right in front of the teacher and got suspended for three days. In grade 10 I felt it a bit with a teacher. I'd never been late, I had good grades and I wasn't a shit in class. I'm late one day, by around eight minutes, and she kicked me out. My white friends were late all the time and she always let it go. I told her I felt like she was being racist and she got really mad. The principal got mad at me too. Oh well, I felt it, you know."

He tends to a bevy of customers.

"This is a good one. I just remembered it. Don't tell my father this one, don't tell him any of it. He just doesn't like to hear it. One night me and my buddies were in the McDonald's drive-through. And the girl at the speaker said they were closing. She asked us to tell the car behind us that they were closed. So I lean my head out the window and tell the guy behind us—a white guy in a taxi. About 25. The guy got out of the cab and called me a Paki. Said something like, *You should respect me more than that, Paki*. So we didn't order, we backed up and chased him. But we didn't get him. Don't tell my dad this, right. We saw him again a few weeks later, parked at the side of the street. Basically I asked him, eh, you know, why did you say that? So he starts to get out of the car, and he's putting on gloves. So some of my friends, big guys, showed up and he took off. I still hold anger against that, against him, against racist people. I'm young, I just want to go out there and finish it.

"Don't get me wrong. Most of my friends are white. Everyone is equal. When that guy said those things to me, it was my white friends who said, *Let's get him*. If I have a friend, I don't care what colour he is. I'm Canadian.

"I love learning about other cultures too. In the last few months I've been trying to get this Greek girl, eh. So I'm learning about her culture. It's great, you know. In India, there was so much religious tension. I was young but I remember the car bombings, the little wars. So much fighting. Even at school, with some kids whose parents taught them to fight Muslims or whatever. It's much better here for that. It's the exact reason my parents came here. For my future. I understand now, too, that even if I beat up that racist guy, it wouldn't fix anything. He'd just hate me more, he'd hate brown people more. He'd tell his family, his parents and eventually his kids about hating Indians. I guess that doesn't solve anything. I'm getting older. I'm not so young and stupid anymore, you know."

12c Summaries

A summary is a brief statement of the main points or events of a longer work, with enough detail to explain those points or events for a particular purpose and audience. A government committee, for instance, might publish a twenty-page summary of its 200-page report on the fishing industry, whereas television listings give two-sentence plot summaries of the week's movies. Summaries (also called abstracts, précis, synopses, briefs) abound in school and work-related writing.

Although writing a summary may seem easy, it isn't. In order to summarize something briefly and accurately, you have to understand it thoroughly. Before you can summarize, then, you must analyze the work—determine the meaning of the whole and how the parts contribute to that meaning.

Plot Summaries

Plot summaries tell your reader, in condensed form, what novels, films, and similar narratives are about. You will find plot summaries useful when you write reviews (13h) or essays and research papers analyzing narrative works (11c). Most plot summaries are a paragraph or two in length, depending on the amount of detail appropriate for your purpose and audience. Follow these steps.

1. Analyze the work (see Explaining Works of Art, 6d) to determine the issue that lies at its heart: Is it the conflict between good and evil? Or the misfortunes of "star-crossed lovers"? Or humans' inability to control the forces of nature?

State this issue in your topic sentence, along with the author or director and title of the work.

2. In the body of the paragraph, describe the main events of the plot that illustrate this issue. Make the causal connections among these events clear to your reader by emphasizing why an event occurred and by explaining its effects. If you are summarizing a long or complex work, you might want to set up a classification of events, such as the events in the main plot and events in the subplot. Present events in the same order as in the original unless you need to modify this order to fit your classification. Include other elements, such as characterization and setting, as necessary to explain the plot.

3. End your summary with the last major event in the original. Your concluding sentence should remind your reader of the main point about the work stated in your topic sentence.

Sample Plot Summary

We will illustrate these principles with a plot summary of L.M. Montgomery's *Anne of Green Gables*, one of the novels discussed in the sample literary research paper (14f).

In *Anne of Green Gables*, L. M. Montgomery creates the story of a young orphan girl whose task is to win a secure place in the community. Anne has been sent, by mistake, to the farm of an elderly brother and sister who had wanted a boy to help with the chores. Although an imaginative, talkative, hot-tempered girl was not at all what he had in mind, Matthew Cuthbert is quickly won over. His sister's acceptance of Anne is more conditional, and since Marilla is to have charge of the child's upbringing, Anne must continually prove her willingness to change behaviour that Marilla and other adults find unacceptable. Anne loses her temper when insulted by Marilla's friend and neighbour Mrs. Rachel Lynde; scandalizes churchgoers by appearing in Sunday School with wildflowers on her bonnet; is accused of losing Marilla's broach; refuses to attend school after being insulted by the teacher; makes her best friend, Diana, drunk on Marilla's homemade wine; unintentionally leaps into bed with Diana's imperious great-aunt; accidentally dyes her hair green; and almost brings disaster upon herself and her friends by her fanciful imagination. Gradually, however, Anne learns to curb her excesses. By the end of the novel she has made a place for herself in this small Prince Edward Island community and truly becomes Anne of Green Gables.

Summaries of Nonfiction Books and Articles

When you summarize a nonfiction book or an article from a newspaper, magazine, or scholarly journal, your purpose is to explain briefly what the work says, not to argue with it. Self-contained summaries appear in annotated bibliographies or as abstracts accompanying research papers, formal reports, and proposals. More often, you are likely to integrate your summary into a review (13h), position paper (13d), or research paper (14). Follow these guidelines for analyzing the work and writing the summary.

Analyzing Nonfiction

1. Write down complete bibliographical information for the article, chapter, or book. Use the format (MLA, APA, or other) appropriate to your audience (see Appendix B, Documentation).

2. Identify the writer's thesis. It is most likely to appear in the introduction or conclusion. To make sure you understand the thesis, restate it in your own words. If there is no explicitly stated thesis, formulate the main idea in your own words.

3. Identify the main sections. Look for guideposts: Does the thesis outline the structure of the piece? Do topic sentences or transitions indicate stages in development *(the first point, the second argument)*? Do headings or other typographical devices suggest the main divisions?

4. State the main idea of each section in your own words.

5. Locate and record subpoints and examples for the main idea of each section. Using point form will remind you not to merely paraphrase every sentence. Include brief quotations when the author's own words seem particularly important. Put quotation marks around any three or more consecutive words, and include the page reference.

12c

Summaries

6. Define all the key terms in your own words and include them in your summary. Pay special attention to words in italics or boldface. Look up any unfamiliar words.

7. Sum up by linking the writer's purpose and audience (if applicable) to the work's structure and focus (see Finding a Focus, 2f). Example: "This article explains [purpose] three methods [structure] consumers [audience] can use to protect themselves against fraud [focus]."

Writing the Summary

1. Give complete bibliographical information (author, title, place of publication, publisher, date), either as a heading or in the first sentence of your summary.

2. State your summing up and the writer's thesis in a sentence or two.

3. Explain the main idea of each section, with enough subpoints and examples to make the main idea clear. Show how these points connect with each other by using terms that emphasize the writer's purpose or methods of development, such as causal analysis, comparison, or classification: *This article explores two contrasting theories about the causes of breast cancer. The genetic theory holds that . . . The environmental theory holds that . . .*

4. Keep the material in the same order and proportion as in the original. Do not exaggerate the importance of a point you find especially interesting, or leave out a point that you find difficult to understand.

5. Use denotative (emotionally neutral) language, and focus on the article or chapter itself rather than your responses to it. Mention the writer frequently to make it clear that you are presenting his or her opinions on the subject, not your own. Remember to use quotation marks and to give page references for all quotations.

6. Do not mix your own ideas with the material you are summarizing; you may not be able to distinguish them a few days or weeks later. If you have been asked (or want) to include an evaluation of either the content or the style, put your evaluation, clearly indicated as such, in a separate paragraph.

Article to be Summarized

The opinion piece reprinted below takes several turns before the writer reaches his thesis. We have underlined key words and transitions so that you can more easily follow the process of analysis leading to the summary (p. 128).

Virtually Depressed? Welcome to Real Life

Maybe the news that <u>the Internet makes people depressed</u> shouldn't have taken us by surprise. It's what concerned <u>cyber-reactionaries</u> have been telling us since the beginning: The Internet renders us incapable of forming genuine relationships, isolates us in an empty electronic simulation and destroys family bonds. Now, the well-meaning <u>killjoys</u> have some science to back their conjecture.

As front-page new stories have announced to the world, <u>researchers</u> at Carnegie Mellon University <u>determined</u> that people who spend even a few hours a week on line experience higher levels of depression and loneliness than those who don't. <u>What makes the results particularly credible is t</u>hat the <u>two-year study's sponsors</u>—such companies as Intel, Hewlett-Packard and Apple Computer—have a vested interest in proving the opposite. The people promoting the Internet as a way of life (and commerce) for the 21st century surely didn't want their research to demonstrate any significant harmful effects to their coming reign.

<u>I pored over the study for gaps in reasoning. What sorts of on-line activitie</u>s were these test subjects engaging in? I know my own experiences in cyberspace were much more exhilarating when they were predominantly characterized by direct social interaction—communicating with people through newsgroups and bulletin boards. When I began struggling through the marketing-heavy pages of the World Wide Web, my joy diminished along with the opportunity to meet living human beings.

But <u>alas, the people in the study had been using the Internet's most communal features</u>: chat rooms, e-mail and discussion groups. In spite of the interpersonal nature of their activities, the subjects experienced an objective increase in depression and loneliness—a small but significant rise of about 1 percent as measured by standard psychological tests. Subjects also showed a marked decrease in time spent with families and in the size of their non-virtual social circles.

It would probably be too flip to suggest that these 169 people were merely suffering, as I so often do, with <u>complicated operating systems and dial-up adapters</u>. But this kind of thing <u>can't account for the overwhelming consistency of response</u> that this study indicates.

<u>The social scientists</u> who carried out the research have hypothesized that the Internet just doesn't provide the kinds of deep, emotionally supportive interaction afforded by the face-to-face encounters of real life. They believe that <u>virtual relationships can't substitute for real ones. Perhaps. But why, then, would the addition of electronic relationships into our lives make us more depressed</u> than we were to begin with? Is it just because on-line interaction cuts into the rest of our time, reducing our opportunity to interact with family and friends? If so, why would on-line interaction be so compelling? <u>Might it offer something that the real world, right now, does</u> not?

But <u>on the Internet's bulletin boards and chat groups we learn a lot more about the real world than we do from, say, the television shows</u> we have created to distract us from the depressing realities of modern life.

If the Internet gives us a temporary glimpse of what's really going on, we might best take a look—even if it turns out to be depressing.

—Douglas Rushkoff, *The Globe and Mail*, September 26, 1998, C11.

Sample Article Summary

In "Virtually Depressed? Welcome to Real Life" (*Globe and Mail*, September 26, 1998, C11), Douglas Rushkoff reflects upon the significance of a two-year study of the psychological effects of Internet use. The study, conducted by researchers at Carnegie Mellon University, showed that "people who spend even a few hours a week on line experience higher levels of depression and loneliness than those who don't." Conceding that the results can't be explained by sponsor bias, by the kinds of on-line activities the participants engaged in, or by frustrations in operating complicated equipment, Rushkoff nevertheless rejects the researchers' hypothesis that "virtual relationships simply can't substitute for real ones." Pointing out that on-line interactions must be compelling for people to engage in them, Rushkoff suggests an alternative explanation: chat rooms and bulletin boards give a more realistic, and

12c

Summaries

therefore more depressing, view of modern life than their users would otherwise be exposed to. [ca. 150 words]

12d How-To Articles

Books and articles telling how to do something fill the shelves of bookstores and the pages of newspapers and magazines. You can find advice on how to manage your money or your children, choose a doctor or a spouse, deal with anger or the plumbing. Since you probably have skills that other people would like to learn, you too can write how-to articles.

Although how-to articles cover a wide range of subjects, the method of development is basically the same: **process analysis.** In each piece of writing, you are explaining the steps in a process or procedure (see Process Analysis, 6d).

Writing How-To Articles: The Process

Follow these steps.

1. Choose a process or procedure that you can explain in five to ten steps. Sharpening a pencil is too simple; building a manned spacecraft is too long and complex.

2. Decide how much explanation and what level of language is appropriate for your intended audience. If you were telling children how to make cookies, for instance, you might say, "Put the mixing bowl in the refrigerator for an hour. Then take small pieces of dough and form them into balls about half the size of your fist." For experienced cooks, you would say, "Chill the dough and form into balls."

3. Write a short introduction pointing out the benefits of learning the procedure. Include a list of information as to any tools or materials required and where they can be obtained, if appropriate.

4. Describe the steps for your procedure in the order in which your reader will follow them. Number the steps or use transitional phrases that clearly identify them (*the first step, the next step, the third step*). Explain the purpose or reason for each step, and give enough detail for the reader to carry it out.

5. Mention any problems that your reader may have in carrying out the steps and suggest how to solve them.

6. Write a short conclusion emphasizing the desirable qualities of the finished product or the benefits of learning the procedure.

12e Sample How-To Article

Most how-to instructions are meant to be followed, but the form also lends itself to satire or humour, as in the example below.

How to Experience Treeplanting in the Comfort of Your Own Home

by Teresa Willman

Have you ever wanted to experience treeplanting but you did not know where to start? Well, here is how to experience a day in the life of a treeplanter without leaving your home. All you will need is a shower, some old clothes, a stairmaster or treadmill, peanut butter, and a lot of patience.

You will need to make a few preparations the night before. First you should place the clothes you will wear the next day in a bucket of muddy water. Next you should turn the heat off and open all the doors and windows. Then you should put the stairmaster or treadmill in the shower and put a backpack of rocks beside the shower. Finally you should set your alarm for five in the morning.

When your alarm goes off, press the snooze button. Keep doing this until 5:45 a.m. Then jump out of bed, quickly put on the wet clothes from the bucket and run to the kitchen. Grab a loaf of bread and the peanut butter and make five sandwiches. Eat one of the sandwiches now and put the rest in a plastic bag. If you know someone who has a pickup truck, have the person drive along a gravel road at high speed while you sit in the box. If not, sit on a washing machine during the spin cycle and hug a bag of ice.

12e

*Sample
How-to
Article*

After one hour go to the shower and turn on the cold water. Put the backpack of rocks on your back and get on the stairmaster or treadmill, setting it at the most difficult level. Stay on the stairmaster for two hours. Then you can eat one of your sandwiches but remain in the shower as you eat it (do not take longer than five minutes). Repeat this exercise for eight hours. It is helpful to sing mind-numbing songs such as the theme song to *The Brady Bunch* or *Flintstones*.

After eight hours you can turn off the shower, get back on the washing machine or truck and remain there for another hour. Turn the radio very loud and try to have a nap during this time.

Next, go to the kitchen, grab any food you can find and eat it as fast as you can. Make sure you eat until you are completely full. Next get yourself a warm beer, find some clean clothes and take a shower. Use dish soap to wash yourself and an old T-shirt to dry yourself. If you have enough energy, you can play an instrument or read a book before you go to bed.

There you have it: a day in the life of a treeplanter. This exercise is just a brief example of the physical endurance a treeplanter needs to survive an average day. If you want to experience the real thing, phone a local reforestation company. The manager will gladly sign you up.

12e

Sample How-to Article

Chapter 13

Persuasive Essays

13a Persuading Your Audience

In any form of persuasive writing, your purpose is to change or reinforce your readers' opinions and, in some cases, to encourage those readers to act. How can you make your writing persuasive? Persuasion, as we discussed in Chapter 7, rests on two principal kinds of appeals to readers: logical appeals and emotional appeals. **Logical appeals** are the reasons and evidence you present to support your position. Through logical appeals, you demonstrate your ability to think critically about an issue, to evaluate other points of view, to see connections between general principles and particular facts. **Emotional appeals** are the direct and indirect ways you engage readers' feelings: by referring to shared values, for instance, or by using emotionally charged language.

To choose an effective combination of appeals for a particular piece, you need to decide whether you are writing for a friendly audience, a hostile audience, or a neutral audience.

A friendly audience is one that shares your basic concerns but needs to be roused to action or renewed commitment. A parent speaking to community league members about building a new playground would be addressing a friendly audience, receptive to the idea but perhaps needing to be convinced that it was practical. For reviews, letters to the editor, or opinion pieces on noncontroversial topics, you can usually assume you are writing for a friendly audience.

At the other extreme is the hostile audience, actively opposed to your position. An employer trying to persuade workers to accept cutbacks in wages would face a hostile audience. For a hostile audience, you need to consider emotional appeals as well as logical appeals. Hostile workers, for example, might be more willing to accept lower wages from an employer who argued that "we're all in this together" than from one who seemed unconcerned about their welfare. When you write essays on controversial subjects, such as abortion and euthanasia, you will need to take special care not to alienate readers hostile to your position.

Most of the essays you write for courses are directed to a neutral audience—readers who expect a carefully reasoned argument and are skeptical of emotional appeals. These readers will pay more attention to persuasive pieces that do not take extreme positions, that consider the merits of different points of view, and that present extensive evidence to support their position. In Position Papers (13d), you will find a chart for evaluating logical and emotional appeals in works by other writers. You can use the same questions to test your own persuasive writing.

Organizing Persuasive Essays

How you arrange the parts of your essay will be determined by what your readers need to know and what you think they will find most convincing.

If you expect strong opposition, either because you are writing for an audience that you know is hostile or because you are taking an unpopular stand on a controversial issue, you may want to anticipate your readers' objections by discussing the merits and drawbacks of the counter-arguments first, before presenting your thesis and the arguments that support it. By the time you reach your conclusion, your opponents may be more willing to acknowledge the validity of your position than they would have been if your thesis had appeared in your introduction.

This type of organization also works well if you are writing for a friendly but perhaps complacent audience. To encourage readers to think more carefully about a position they may take for granted, you might begin with arguments upon which there is widespread agreement, and then raise the question of whether the situation is really as satisfactory as it appears. You will find an example of this strategy in the sample research essay "What Is Psychology?" (14g).

When you are writing for a neutral audience, it is usually best to state your position up front. Your readers will appreciate a clearly defined thesis in your introduction, topic sentences that indicate the stages of your argument, substantial paragraphs that show clear reasoning and a careful use of evidence to support your points, and a conclusion that summarizes and extends your argument.

Here you will find guidelines for four types of persuasive writing: opinion pieces, position papers, reviews, and letters to the editor. For an example of a persuasive research paper, see "What Is Psychology?" (14g).

13b Opinion Pieces

Opinion pieces are short persuasive essays, based on your own knowledge and experience, about an issue of interest to general readers. Columnists such as Ellen Goodman, Allan Fotheringham, and Barbara Amiel write opinion pieces for newspapers and magazines.

Many opinion pieces employ the strategy of giving reasons with examples as supporting evidence (see Giving Reasons and Examples, 7a). To create interest, they often begin with a personal anecdote. You will see this pattern in the sample opinion piece that follows. Notice that the writer gives partial reasons for not buying a new car, leading up to a complete statement of his thesis in the final paragraph.

13c Sample Opinion Piece

Why I Won't Buy a New Car
by Peter Banks

The third time my car broke down within a year, my friend Rebecca teased me, "Why don't you just buy a new one?" This advice was coming from someone whose parents gave her a Miata convertible for her sixteenth birthday. The carefree way she suggested I "just buy a new one" echoed through my mind for quite some time. I began to realize that in our throwaway society, many people are all too willing to "just buy a new one" regardless of any future consequences. However, an object that is more technologically advanced is not necessarily superior.

Many North Americans are deceived by the notion that acquiring the latest inventions will somehow bring them happiness. Although many new objects can

bring enjoyment, they do not make the consumer any
better as a person. The media prey on society's
search for material happiness. Automobiles are often
portrayed as the means to achieve power, success,
inner peace, and popularity. They are often shown as
the instant ticket to becoming a sex symbol. The one
thing that advertisements seem to neglect is that
these fancy machines are just that—fancy machines.
The driver of a red Lamborghini would still be the
same person if he or she were behind the wheel of a
rusty brown station wagon. However, the media continue to portray the acquisition of material possessions as the avenue through which goals such as
peace, good work, family stability, and personal
happiness can be achieved. Mini-van commercials are
loaded with images of loving families enjoying quality time together. Sports car advertisements attempt
to associate driving that particular car with popularity and sexual attractiveness.

While consumers are racing to keep up with the
latest in technology, many valuable resources are
needlessly wasted. Thousands of auto wrecking yards
across North America are filled with vehicles left
to rust into an ecological nightmare. Although some
are eventually crushed and recycled for future use,
these instances do not occur as often as they could.
Many of the mechanical components left in these
automobiles are still in perfect working order.
However, because the majority of modern engines are
composed of a tangled web of hoses and computer
chips, any working parts from the older cars are
completely incompatible. This makes re-using any of
the older parts impossible, thereby putting to waste
an entirely functional mechanism.

The needlessly complex mechanical designs of new
vehicles make it impossible for individuals to take
responsibility for even the most basic car maintenance. With consumers wholly dependent upon the
dealership's mechanical services, the dealership is
free to list exorbitant prices, to which customers
must agree. When the alternator of my 1981 Honda
Accord wore out, my dad and I simply rebuilt a part

from an auto wrecker and replaced it ourselves. The design of the engine compartment left every component easily identifiable and accessible. The entire job took just over an hour and we spent less than eighty dollars on it. The alternator on Rebecca's Miata, however, is buried far beneath the engine block. This particular part, which is prone to wear out with accumulated mileage, is positioned so that when it does have to be replaced, the entire engine must be removed. However, a regular garage will probably not have the necessary equipment to work on this particular vehicle. When her alternator does go, Rebecca will thus have to take her car to the Mazda dealership and pay whatever price is asked.

If I did buy a new car, it probably would not break down as often as the one that I am currently driving. But it might destroy my relationship with my dad. The easiest, most enjoyable times my dad and I spend together are while we work as a team, desperately trying to repair my car. I know that "I love you" has always been a hard thing for him to come out and say. But as I think back, nothing says it louder than the time we spent working in the garage last summer. I was shocked to find him using the old, crooked tool box that I made for him in grade 5. I almost broke into tears when I saw that crooked, unsymmetrical Father's Day present loaded up with tools, while Dad's numerous other boxes, which are much sturdier and more convenient, sat in the basement unused. Buying a new car would end the wonderful times my father and I spend together doing repairs, times that I have grown to cherish.

No, I won't buy a new car. It would cost too much—in the destruction of the environment, the waste of precious resources, the loss of self-reliance, and the loss of human contact.

13d Position Papers

In a **position paper,** your purpose is to present arguments showing why you agree or disagree with something you have read. Writing this kind of essay will help you develop your critical thinking skills, for it requires you to analyze, evaluate, and formulate your own opinion.

Writing Position Papers: The Process

Here are the main steps.

1. ***Summarize the piece you are responding to*** (see Summaries, 12c). Be sure to state the subject of the article and the author's thesis, describe the organization of ideas, and state the most important points in each section.

   Summarizing the article is a useful first step because it helps you to understand the author's ideas. Including a brief version of your summary in your position paper will help your readers understand your response.

2. ***Analyze and evaluate the author's logical and emotional appeals*** (see the chart, below). If you agree with the author, make a list of additional points and evidence to support the position; make a second list of opposing arguments, so that you can refute them. If you disagree or partially disagree, make a list of counter-arguments and evidence.

3. ***Identify the writer's basis of evaluation*** (see Evaluating Strengths and Weaknesses, 7b). Is the writer's position based on moral, practical, logical, or aesthetic criteria, or a combination of these perspectives?

4. ***Clarify your own basis of evaluation.*** Do the points you agree with reflect your moral position on the subject? Do you doubt the practical advantages of the author's position?

5. ***Formulate your thesis.*** It should present both your evaluation of the writer's point of view and your own opinion.

6. ***Organize your response to include opposing arguments.*** One way to do this is to briefly summarize other views about your subject and indicate why you agree or disagree before you develop your thesis in more detail. You might use this method if, for example, you wanted to argue that positions X, Y, and Z were all based on self-interest rather than on the common good.

   Another possible approach is to take up an opposing argument point by point, examining its strengths and weaknesses and pointing out alternatives. You might adopt this method if, for instance, you wanted to argue against a series of proposals contained in a speech or document. These two methods are examples of an evaluative or "pro–con" structure, that is, an organization based on arguments for (*pro*) and arguments against (*con*) your position.

Evaluating Logical and Emotional Appeals

Logical Appeals These questions test the validity of the author's reasoning and evidence.

- Does the author assume the truth of a point that needs to be argued?
- Does the author trivialize or distort opposing points of view?
- Does the author oversimplify an issue by reducing it to two extreme alternatives?
- Are causes and effects actual or hypothetical? Do predicted effects seem exaggerated or unlikely?
- Are faulty causal connections made? Watch for these problems with causal reasoning: (1) claiming that what is true in some instances is true in all instances; (2) claiming that something happening after an event was caused by it; (3) claiming a single cause or effect of something that may have multiple causes or effects.
- Does the author make sweeping generalizations that are difficult to prove or disprove?
- Do all the points support the thesis? Have important points not been taken into consideration?
- Are key terms defined (6c)?
- Do comparisons proceed from a common basis (6b)?
- Are examples used appropriately (7a)?
- Are facts and figures accurate, up to date, and taken from reliable and identified sources? Are they used appropriately (14a)?
- Are authorities cited within their field of expertise?
- Is the evidence sufficient to support the points made?

Emotional Appeals These questions help you define the author's values and attitudes.

- Does the author appeal to values he or she assumes readers share (such as patriotism, family values, concern for the environment)?

- Does the writer make personal attacks on those who hold different opinions or appeal to readers' prejudices against certain groups?

- What attitude toward the subject (such as anger, concern, sadness) does the writer convey through choices in diction, sentence structure, and other stylistic devices? What uses, if any, does the writer make of humour, wit, irony? (For suggestions about analyzing and evaluating style, see Chapter 17, Improving Your Style.)

- What relationship with the reader (friendly, hostile, expert) does the author establish through direct comments, choice of personal pronouns, or emotional appeals (13a)?

- Are emotional appeals appropriate to the purpose and the audience?

- How does the author's personality, as reflected in the piece, affect your response?

Sample Evaluation of an Article

Let's work through these steps for a position paper that responds to Diane Francis' article below ("The Case for Two-Tier Health," *Edmonton Journal*, Nov. 15, 1998.)

The Case for Two-Tier Health
There are Public and Private Schools: Why Not Hospitals?

DIANE FRANCIS

Canada's health-care system is deteriorating, but a painless cure exists if only Ottawa would understand what's required.

And the way to treat health care is not by infusing more money, which is what the federal Liberals are planning to do in the next budget.

All that's required is for the feds to change the Canada Health Act to let the health-care system operate in the same way as does education, the country's other important social service.

There were 5,002,114 students in public schools across Canada in 1993–94, according to Statistics Canada. These are the latest figures available.

That same year there were 265,275 pupils in private primary and secondary schools.

These parents paid $1.5 billion

in tuition fees for their children but also contributed, through income and other taxes, to the public schools their children were not using.

The cost of supporting primary and secondary public schools in 1993–94 was $33.4 billion or $6,680 a pupil.

If Ottawa imposed the same rules on education as it does on health care—that there must be one system for all—then parents wanting alternative education would have to send their children to the United States or elsewhere.

More significantly, most would not be able to afford to send their children to foreign boarding schools. They would be forced to enrol their children in public schools.

If all kids in private schools had been forced to do that in 1993–94, the public schools would have been faced with having to educate another 265,275 pupils without another dime of financial support.

The point is, the government saves huge amounts of money by allowing "two-tier" education.

At the same time, Canadian parents should have the right to alternative education if they pay for it themselves while still supporting public education.

This should also apply to health care. Instead, the Liberal prescription for what ails is to—you guessed it—spend our tax dollars. But without major

surgery, the system will continue to deteriorate as our population ages.

European countries have two-tier systems in both health and education. Canada has an unofficial two-tier health system; wealthy Canadians can go to the United States for quick or alternative services.

Another reform is to allow Canadian medical personnel and facilities to treat foreigners.

In education, Ottawa actually encourages foreign students to attend its private schools, colleges and universities. Tens of thousands do so annually, which economically benefits the country and institutions that usually hike tuition costs to foreigners.

Canadian universities, for instance, subsidize the cost of educating Canadian students by allowing foreigners in at sometimes four times the tuition.

Unlike educators, Canada's medical establishment is not allowed to do the same, allegedly out of concern that doctors and hospitals would favour foreign patients paying more for services over Canadian patients paying less.

This is foolishness and equivalent, in educational terms, to making it illegal for teachers and professors to teach foreign students.

But the benefits to schools are obvious and would be greater in health care.

Americans pay obscenely

higher fees for virtually every medical procedure and there is a great deal of money to be made in Canada by selling them our services. They would pay more than Canadians pay and it would still be less than is charged south of the border.

Cashing in on this huge bonanza could be accomplished by allowing surplus hospitals, slated for closure or already dormant, to be sold to private interests such as doctors or insurance companies, to treat foreigners.

Besides foreigners, well-heeled Canadians should be able to tap into this private system. This would be no different than licensing private schools.

Some would argue that the best and brightest medical personnel would switch to the private system, thus abandoning the public health-care system.

But that potential problem could be easily avoided by requiring Canadian-licensed doctors, nurses and technicians to put in a requisite number of years and/or hours per week in the public system. This is what many European countries require.

Americans would flood such a private network, thus reversing both the medical brain drain and the patient drain of wealthy Canadians south of the border.

A private health-care system would actually benefit the public system, by relieving the caseload burden, reducing waiting lists and postponing the rationing of care. This is the lesson learned as a result of the existence of private schools, which removed 265,275 students in 1993–94 from public school classrooms at a savings of $1.5 billion a year.

To simply throw more money at the current system because of an unwillingness to change is to perpetuate unnecessary costs on taxpayers and a brain drain.

Worst of all, status-quo thinking is to miss out on a golden opportunity to earn hundreds of millions, if not billions of dollars, by competing against the U.S.'s inefficient and expensive medical system.

Steps in Preparing Your Position Paper

1. ***Summarize the article you are responding to.***

For a summary of Francis' article, see the sample position paper.

2. *Analyze and evaluate the author's logical and emotional appeals.*

Strengths

- Francis addresses worries about the decline in public health care shared by many Canadians.

- Francis forces readers to think about the similarities and differences between health care and education as social services.

Weaknesses

- Francis oversimplifies complex issues to either-or alternatives: either "throw money" at the existing public health-care system or create a two-tier health-care system with private facilities and foreign patients.

- Francis' comparison between education and health care is actually an analogy that ignores important differences and presents only superficial similarities.

  Parents can choose not to educate their children, but people cannot choose not to become ill.

  Educational services are needed by a relatively small segment of the population for a limited period of time, but people need health-care services to be continuously available throughout their lifetimes.

  Education does not involve life and death issues; health care does.

- Francis makes faulty causal connections. Private health care will not improve services in public health care.

- Francis both distorts and trivializes the arguments against her position. "Status quo thinking" is not a fear of change but a desire to preserve the strengths of Canadian social services.

- Lack of specific examples weakens Francis' argument.

- Francis makes appeals to the readers' greed sound as if they are appeals to moral principles.

- Francis never addresses the fundamental moral issue: the right of all Canadians to equal health care services.

3. *Identify the writer's basis of evaluation (see Evaluating Strengths and Weaknesses, 7b).*

Francis' argument is based on both moral and practical grounds. She argues that Canadians have a moral right to use private health care facilities just as they have a moral right to use private schools. The combination of two-tier health care and foreign patients would have the practical benefit of saving and generating huge amounts of money.

4. ***Clarify the basis of your evaluation.***

I disagree with Francis' position on logical, practical, and moral grounds.

5. ***Formulate your thesis.***

Francis' argument for two-tier health care has serious logical, practical, and moral weaknesses. The solution to problems in public health care is not private facilities and foreign patients. Instead, we need to provide adequate funding for the public health system.

6. ***Organize your essay to include opposing arguments.***

You could begin by writing a paragraph or two taking up all the arguments against your position or you can address these arguments one by one throughout your essay. You can make the main points in the body of your essay much more obvious with strong topic sentences. In each topic sentence, make a point about some aspect of the writer's logic, evidence, or use of emotional appeals.

13e Sample Position Paper

```
        The Case Against Two-Tier Health Care
                   for Canadians

In "The Case for Two-Tier Health" (Edmonton Journal,
Nov. 15, 1998), Diane Francis argues that we can fix
all the problems with health care in Canada by doing
two things: creating private health care services
for Canadians who can afford them, and actively
recruiting foreign patients who will contribute a
"huge bonanza" of cash. Both proposals are based on
an analogy between health care and education, the
two most important social services provided by the
government to all Canadians. Having a legal right to
obtain private health care, Francis argues, is no
```

different from having a legal right to send children to private schools. Furthermore, just as Canadian colleges and universities profit from the higher tuition fees paid by foreign students, so private hospitals and clinics should be allowed to accept higher paying foreign patients. These proposals, Francis argues, will benefit all Canadians by providing the funds to improve health care for all patients. The only alternative to adopting a two-tier system, Francis concludes, is for governments to impose "unnecessary" taxes and provide worsening public health care for an aging population. Although Francis addresses an issue of great importance to many Canadians, her solutions have serious logical, practical, and moral weaknesses.

The logic of Francis' argument is flawed because public health care and public education are quite different social services. While we can choose private or public education for our children, we do not choose to have breast cancer, heart disease, or a broken arm. Furthermore, educational services are needed by a relatively small segment of the population for a limited period of time, but people need health-care services to be continuously available throughout their lifetimes. The educational opportunities offered by private schools are not essential in the way that medical treatment usually is. Finally, the costs of private education hardly compare to the costs of medical procedures, especially if these procedures are done at profit-making private facilities. How many Canadian, after all, could afford $100,000 for a week in the hospital?

The causal connections in Francis' argument are also flawed. She assumes that patients using private health care will free up more resources for patients using the public system. Francis thus ignores the fact that government funding for public hospitals depends on the number of procedures performed. As registered nurse Wendy Yule points out, "a hospital which performs 100 hip replacements in a given year receives less government funding the next year if only 90 hip replacements are done. Waiting time does not decrease, then, for public system users" (12).

Francis also bases her argument on effects that seem both exaggerated and unlikely. Perhaps Americans will "flood" to Canada for cheaper health care, but how will private Canadian families avoid charging what Francis describes as the "obscenely higher fees for virtually every medical procedure" (15) done in the United States? A crucial advantage of Canadian public health care is that we do not need to battle with the providers of private health-care insurance while making a profit for companies and shareholders in private health facilities. The absence of specific examples also weakens Francis' assertions about the benefits of two-tier health care. The reader is left wondering which "European" countries currently use a two-tier system and whether patients there actually receive better care in either public or private facilities than they currently do in Canada.

By oversimplifying complex issues to either-or alternatives, Francis distorts and trivializes the arguments against her position. She says that Canadians must choose *either* to "throw money" at public health, thereby creating an additional tax burden, deteriorating health care for an aging population, and incentives for highly skilled professionals to emigrate to better facilities in the United States *or* to allow private health care and actively recruit foreign patients. Those who support the first choice are "status-quo thinkers" who fear change. Many Canadians, however, would define the status quo as Canada remaining different from the United States. Support for this status quo means improved funding for a public health-care system that provides better services for all Canadians.

Francis' failure to address the fundamental moral issue in health care is glaringly obvious. The term "two-tier" suggests that private facilities are higher (better) than public ones, but most Canadians think that all of us are entitled to the same high quality of health care. One letter to the *Edmonton Journal* eloquently makes this point: "Our health care system is an important element in the framework of what constitutes our civil society. The creation of a two-tier health-care system would quickly erode, if not destroy it." Francis replaces a moral principle fundamental to Canadian society with repeated appeals to greed. Private health care and foreign patients will create "a great deal of money," a "huge bonanza," a "golden opportunity to earn hundreds of millions if not millions of dollars." Francis' vision of a Canadian health-care system which would profit from overcharging sick foreigners and reserve the best of our health-care resources for the wealthy is enough to sicken most Canadians.

Works Cited

Francis, Diane. "The Case for Two-Tier Health." *Edmonton Journal* 18 Nov. 1998: A 15.

Junk, Don. Letter to the Editor. *Edmonton Journal* 24 Nov. 1998: A 13.

Yule, Wendy. "Privatizing Health Care." *Alberta Views*, Spring 1999: 12–13.

13f Letters to the Editor

Most letters to the editor are intended to persuade readers that something is good or bad: the premier is doing a good job or a lousy job, park trails should or should not be paved, nurses should or should not have the right to strike. They are generally short, about 250–500 words. Paragraphs within the letter are also short because letters are usually printed in narrow columns. The following guidelines will help you make your point quickly and effectively.

1. ***Focus on a particular issue of interest to a number of readers, and, if possible, link that issue to a current situation.*** A general plea for world peace, for example, is less likely to hold your readers' attention than an argument against selling arms to warring countries. Identify the issue in your first paragraph.

2. *Explain why the issue concerns you.* Are you writing as a spokesperson for a relief organization? As a pacifist? As a citizen upholding the ideal of Canada as a peacekeeping nation?

3. *Instead of condemning people who hold other views, try to establish common ground with them.* Summarize their positions accurately and acknowledge the extent to which their point of view may be true or understandable. You might acknowledge a country's need to defend itself, for example, but point out that access to more powerful weapons increases the likelihood of bloodshed.

4. *State your own position and your reasons for holding it. Be brief but specific.*

5. *If possible, suggest a practical action that readers can take.* They can't ensure world peace; they can write a letter to an MP.

13g Sample Letter to the Editor

In this letter, the writer focuses on a local issue to raise public awareness and encourage appropriate action.

Like many Torontonians, I have often donated used clothing to Goodwill, the Salvation Army, and women's shelters in the belief that others would find useful what my family no longer needed. When I began doing volunteer work for one of these organizations, I realized that one category of clothing is desperately needed but rarely donated—underwear.

To the question "Who would want used underwear?", the answer is "Anyone who does not have any." Women and children, for example, often arrive at crisis shelters without any possessions or money. Sometimes they can collect their clothing after a few days, but often they are unable to return home. Until they can return home or go shopping, they are in desperate need of a change of clothing, including, of course, underwear.

So when you are bundling up clothing that you or your family no longer use, don't hesitate to include outgrown underwear. Or the next time you go shopping, pick up some on sale to donate. The women and children at crisis shelters, and those who use other clothing depots, will be very grateful.

—L.M. Hrychuk
North York

13h Reviews

You are probably most familiar with the brief reviews of books, films, television programs, and eating places printed in newspapers and general-interest magazines, such as *Maclean's* and *Saturday Night.* These reviews are intended to give casual readers some sense of whether a new movie is worth seeing or a new restaurant worth trying.

Longer reviews—often called **review articles** or **review essays**—are designed for readers with some knowledge of the subject. Car enthusiasts, for example, might read the reviews of all the new models in *Car and Driver,* even if they are not planning to buy a car. Academic journals often carry review articles on research in specific areas, such as intelligence testing. Because these reviews provide substantial background information and extensive commentary, they are useful sources of information for research papers.

We will focus on guidelines for writing brief reviews for a general audience. If you wish to expand your treatment of your subject into a review essay, you can do so by consulting appropriate sources of information: other reviews, other works by the same person or group, articles relevant to your subject, biographical dictionaries, newspaper files, and so forth.

Follow these guidelines when writing a brief review.

1. *Include identifying information somewhere in your review.* The most essential information (determined by your intended audience and type of publication) usually appears in a separate heading before your review or in your introduction. Here is what you should include:

   Book review author, title, publisher, price, type, length, hardcover or paper. As applicable: name of editor, translator, or other contributors; supplementary material provided (such as maps, illustrations, appendix, index); date of publication; edition.

   CD-ROM review title, publisher, price, system requirements.

   Computer software review product, manufacturer, price, system requirements. As applicable: other products in category, ordering information.

Film review title, director, distributor, type, principal actors. As applicable: date of release; length; suitability rating; other contributors (music, special effects, etc.).

Live performance review (as applicable) title, name of person or group, place, date(s), type, price.

Product review manufacturer, model, price. As applicable: availability, warranty, service record.

Record or compact disk review title, person or group, type, label, price.

Restaurant review name, address, type of food, business hours, price range, credit cards accepted, availability of alcoholic beverages, décor, service. As applicable: reservation requirement, dress code.

2. *Try for a lively introduction, one that will catch your readers' interest and convey your general opinion of what you are reviewing.*

3. *Give readers a sense of the whole through a brief summary or description.* Don't include so many details that you leave readers nothing to discover. Never give away surprise effects or the endings of films, plays, or novels.

4. *Discuss what you liked and disliked about what you are reviewing, with specific examples.* Try for a balanced view: even the aspects you like the most may appeal only to certain people. For suggestions about what to consider, see Evaluating Strengths and Weaknesses (7b).

5. *End with a snappy summary of your overall judgment.*

13i Sample Review

Here is a sample restaurant review, written for an alternative newspaper.

```
          Sublime Subs, Rapturous Wraps
In a hurry but tired of McMeals? For a fast, tasty,
and reasonably healthy alternative, try Badass
Jack's Subs and Wraps.
```

149

13i

Sample Review

Specializing in home-cooked meats and buns (no processed meats or frozen buns for these guys), Badass Jack's offers seven different subs on sourdough or multigrain buns with an array of fresh vegetables. Or let your friendly server create a wrap: a flavourful tortilla piled high with chicken, beef, or seafood; your choice of fresh and frozen vegetables; the whole thing topped with a zesty sauce (try Kathmandu Curry or Caribbean Jerk, or for the less adventurous, Tennessee BBQ and Texas Ranch). You can also ask for these sauces on chicken and beef subs. Beware: one of our party found the BBQ sauce overpowering.

Vegetarians take note: in addition to a vegetarian sub and wrap, BAJ's serves falafel and several salads.

An assortment of beverages, including Stewart's sodas, and modest desserts round out the menu.

BAJ's is a fast-growing local chain, and it's easy to see why. Good food, fast, friendly service, and a warm Southwestern decor that's a definite step up from pink molded plastic. And speaking of steps up—except for two chairs, seating is bar-table style, a drawback for people with disabilities or short legs. But you can fax ahead and eat at home in comfort.

Badass Jack's Subs and Wraps, with six locations in the Edmonton area; also in Calgary, Red Deer, Ft. McMurray, Saskatoon, Nanaimo, and Victoria. Hours 11 a.m.–11 p.m. weekdays, 11 a.m.–midnight Saturday, 11 a.m.–10 p.m. Sunday. Under $10.

Chapter 14

Research Papers

A **research paper** is an expository or persuasive essay in which you include facts and opinions from other sources to support your analysis or point of view. As you will see in the sample research papers, "*Tom Sawyer* and *Anne of Green Gables*: Two Models of Heroism" (14f) and "What Is Psychology?" (14g), those sources are usually published books and articles on the subject. But research material can also include interviews and other data that you gather yourself.

14a Purpose and Audience

The purpose of a research essay is to examine a subject in greater depth than would be possible on the basis of your own knowledge. In many cases, you may not have any prior knowledge to draw upon. How many of us, without using research material, could write an essay on the introduction of Buddhism into China, for example? Writing research essays is one of the best ways to extend your knowledge of a subject.

A research paper should not be merely a compilation of other people's ideas, however. To make sure it isn't, you need to have some idea of where you are going before you do research. You can use brainstorming or discovery questions (2a and 2c) to figure out the questions you will need to answer in your paper. Or, if you know something about your subject, you can write a draft first and then find research material to broaden or clarify your thinking.

As you carry out your research, you are likely to find unanswered questions and areas of disagreement among your sources. Writing a research paper will allow you to take part in the ongoing debate about your subject.

Research papers are written by specialists for other specialists. Citations and references allow specialist readers to evaluate the sources of facts and opinions and to follow up possible lines of investigation. As a student writing a research paper, you are learning to act like a specialist in a particular field. You will therefore present your material differently than you would for a general audience. You will use a more specialized vocabulary, maintain a slightly more formal tone, and assume your readers' general familiarity with the subject. (For example, a biologist would explain what DNA is for a general audience but not for other biologists.) Nevertheless, a research paper should not sound as though it has been compiled by a committee. The best research papers are those in which the style and tone reflect something of the writer: flashes of wit, clear thinking, depth of knowledge, sudden insights, and a feeling for language.

Guidelines for Doing Research

- Use the most up-to-date material available, especially for topics related to science, technology, and current issues and events.

- Don't depend too heavily upon one or two sources. If your material is too limited, you may get an inaccurate idea of the central issues about your subject. You may also find it hard to develop your own perspective.

  Six to eight references will usually give you enough material for a research paper in an introductory course. In advanced courses, you may be expected to have a more thorough knowledge of what has been written about your topic.

- To end up with six to eight usable references, you will need to start with a **working bibliography** two to three times longer (see Conducting Computer-Aided Research, 14b). This strategy will allow you to cross off material that turns out to be unavailable or irrelevant, without having to do another search.

- Include articles as well as books in your working bibliography. Articles are a little harder to track down if you don't have Internet access, but they are more current, and journals are less likely to be checked out when you need them.

- Take notes as you read (see Summaries, 12c). You will understand the material better and you will not lose track of where ideas and information came from. Put quotation marks around any three or more consecutive words you take directly from the source and indicate page references for each idea, item of information, and quotation. Make sure your notes include complete bibliographical information (see Appendix B, Documentation).

- As you write each draft, put the author and page number in parentheses after each item that you take from your notes. If there is any chance of confusion (authors with the same name, more than one work by the same author), add a short form of the title or the date of publication.

- In your final draft, make sure that these parenthetical references conform to the documentation format required for your essay. For detailed guidelines on MLA and APA documentation, see Appendix B, Documentation.

14b Conducting Computer-Aided Research

Your first step in gathering research material is to compile a working bibliography: a list of ten to twenty books, articles, and similar material on your topic. The best place to begin is your library's on-line catalogue.

Using the on-line catalogue, you can search for books relevant to your topic in three main ways: by keying in the name of the authors whose works you wish to find, the titles of books you are looking for, or the general subject headings pertaining to your area of research. Subject searches are often the most useful, allowing you to locate dozens of potentially valuable items in seconds. They can also be the most frustrating and time-consuming, however, if you do not choose appropriate search terms or if you fail to limit your search sufficiently. If you need help, consult a reference librarian.

In addition to the on-line catalogue, many libraries now offer Electronic Learning Resources (ELR), giving access to databases and a multitude of sources through the Internet. Two of the most valuable databases for doing research are AcademicSearch (book reviews and journal articles in humanities, education,

14c

*Using
Research
Materials to
Make a
Point*

social science, and general science, as well as general references) and MasterFILE (articles and pamphlets on topics in business, multiculturalism, and consumer health, as well as general reference). Both these databases contain the full text of more than a thousand journals and magazines published since January 1990. You can access these databases from library computers or, if you have a campus e-mail address, from a home computer.

Through the Internet you may also find material on your topic via a plethora of listservs and newsgroups. Be cautious, however, about the authenticity and credibility of information from these sources. Electronic publications that are available in print versions are more trustworthy than bulletin board postings. If you are unsure about the reliability of your sources, check with your instructor. For useful web sites created by academics and librarians, see the Web Links at the end of this chapter.

Bibliographies, indexes, and other reference materials are also stored on CD-ROM. CD-ROM searches are a quick and efficient way of locating books; articles in newspapers, magazines, and scholarly journals; and other sources, such as encyclopedias. Some databases, such as the *MLA International Bibliography*, will give you references to works on your topic, but you will have to check the on-line catalogue to see whether your library has the items you want. Other databases may contain the full texts of newspapers or scholarly journals.

By the end of your search, you should have references to many books and articles on your topic. Choose ten to twenty that seem relevant to your focus and are accessible through your library. These references make up your working bibliography. Some items won't be available, some won't address your topic after all, and some you won't use for other reasons; but you should end up with six to eight that you can cite in your research paper.

14c Using Research Material to Make a Point

A research paper, like other kinds of essays, must have a thesis. At earlier stages of your education, you may have collected information on a subject and presented it in an orderly fashion. When you write a full-fledged research paper, however, you must organize your research material to support a point.

In writing your paper, you may be concentrating so much on organizing your material that you lose track of your thesis. Suppose, for instance, that you were writing a research paper arguing that the education faculty should take steps to improve the status of teaching as a profession. Your first draft of a paragraph recommending higher admission standards might look like the following.

14c

*Using
Research
Materials to
Make a
Point*

Sample First Draft

Marleen C. Pugach of the University of Illinois has recommended these selection criteria for prospective Education students: 1) basic skills testing, consisting of entry-level tests in reading, mathematics, and written and oral communication; 2) a minimum grade point average; and 3) a structured interview to assess the applicant's personal qualities (161-63). At universities such as Oregon State and Northern Kentucky, students must successfully complete a two-tofive-day full-responsibility teaching experience prior to being accepted into a teacher training program. The number of drop-outs increased from approximately 5% to 25% (Edgar 96).

This draft paragraph serves the writer's need to gather together information from a variety of sources. However, it does not serve the reader's need to understand the significance of this information because the point of the paragraph gets lost among the examples.

Here is the material as it appeared in the student's final draft. With the added topic sentence, sentences explaining the relevance of each example, and a summarizing sentence to connect this material to the thesis, the original paragraph has become two.

Sample Final Draft

If teaching is to be regarded as the important job that it is, pride must first be generated within the profession itself. One way to do this would be to have a more rigorous and effective set of criteria that applicants must meet before they are allowed entrance into the profession. Marleen C. Pugach of the University of Illinois has recommended a set of criteria that would function together to provide "entry-level hurdles to encourage self selection, to serve as initial points in the process of continuous judgment of student progress, and to assist faculty members in making discriminations between applicants based on multifaceted data" (161). Pugach recommends these selection criteria: 1) basic skills testing, consisting of entry-level tests in reading, mathematics, and written and oral communication; 2) a minimum grade point average; and 3) a structured interview to assess the applicant's personal qualities (161-63).

Another criterion used in universities such as Oregon State and Northern Kentucky is also helpful in selecting suitable candidates. Students must successfully complete a two- to five-day full-responsibility teaching experience prior to being accepted into a teacher training program. The number of drop-outs increased from approximately 5% to 25% (Edgar 96). Clearly, such intensive selection policies would be a strong force in attracting applicants who seriously wish to pursue teaching. At the same time, these policies would deter students who now casually drift into teacher education, such as those I overhear in the undergraduate lounge. The sense of personal achievement that would come from gaining entrance to a faculty with such high entrance standards would contribute to a feeling of professionalism among candidates.

—Carol Murray

14d Documenting Sources

Plagiarism and Inadequate Documentation

When you use facts and opinions from outside sources, you must document where you found them. Failure to do so constitutes **plagiarism**. Plagiarism is a form of stealing: stealing someone else's words or stealing someone else's facts and ideas. And, like other forms of stealing, it is illegal.

Occasionally students, in a panic over deadlines or low marks, may be tempted to pass off as their own work a paper they have copied in whole or in part from another student or, more often, from a published source. Instructors can usually spot this kind of plagiarism easily, either because they are familiar with the original or because the writing is noticeably different from the student's other work.

Plagiarism includes more than the deliberate theft of someone else's words, however. Using facts or ideas without identifying their source is also plagiarism. Plagiarism of this sort usually arises from sloppy note-taking: the writer has failed to record the necessary information for references. Appending a list of works cited is not an adequate indication of the source of specific facts and ideas.

The consequences of both kinds of plagiarism can be severe. The student who plagiarizes may be required to rewrite the paper, may be given a failing grade on the paper or the course, or may be expelled.

You can prevent the panic that leads to deliberate and unintentional plagiarism by allowing three weeks to gather material, draft, and revise your research paper. Make sure you provide appropriate documentation of your sources at each stage of the process.

Documenting Paraphrased Material

To show how you can paraphrase research material and identify its source appropriately, we will use source material from the sample literary research paper *"Tom Sawyer* and *Anne of Green Gables:* Two Models of Heroism"* (14f). If you are not familiar with these novels by Mark Twain and L.M. Montgomery, you may want to read the sample essay first. You will also find a summary of *Anne of Green Gables* in Summaries (12c).

Imagine that you were doing research on these novels and came across the following paragraph in James L. Johnson's book *Mark Twain and the Limits of Power* (Knoxville: U. of Tennessee, 1982). In this paragraph, Johnson argues that because Tom's village is not portrayed realistically, Tom is not changed by his seemingly serious experiences:

> Simply put, St. Petersburg is not a world in which children are easily turned into adults, for such a change requires that the child meet a real world and adjust himself, painfully but with more or less success, to its undesirable circumstances. Much of the idyllic quality of St. Petersburg is attributable to the fact that Twain has excluded from the novel a world in which experience produces consequent changes in character. Tom's world is one in which "adventure" replaces "experience"; his encounters with the alcoholic Muff Potter, the grave-robbing Dr. Robinson, the vengeful Injun Joe—encounters which should ordinarily produce some difference in his perception of the world—leave his character essentially untouched. (51)

You might decide that this paragraph would strongly support a point you had made in your rough draft, and so you might paraphrase Johnson's passage in your notes:

157

Tom is not turned into an adult by the world of St. Petersburg because he is not shown trying to adjust himself, with more or less success, to a real world. As St. Petersburg is presented as idyllic, Tom has adventures, but not experiences that would change his character. His encounters with Muff Potter, Dr. Robinson, and Injun Joe do not change him, although encounters such as these would ordinarily affect how a person sees the world.

If you were to use this paragraph in your paper without acknowledging that the ideas were Johnson's, you would be guilty of plagiarism. Adding a citation to identify the source will protect you from a charge of plagiarism, but it may not clearly distinguish your own thinking from the work of others. If we were to add a page reference at the end of the paraphrase from Johnson, for example, a reader would not be sure whether all the ideas in the paragraph were Johnson's, or merely the last point. Using his name at the beginning of the paragraph, with the page reference at the end, would make clear that all the points come from Johnson's book:

> As James L. Johnson points out, Tom is not turned into an adult by the world of St. Petersburg . . . although encounters such as these would ordinarily affect how a person sees the world (51).

In most cases, you would not rely so heavily on a single critic; you would at least use your own examples to illustrate the point. Even so, this paragraph is an improvement because the reader knows whose ideas are being presented. If you are careful to identify others' facts and opinions, your reader has more confidence that what remains is your own.

14e Integrating Research Material

To see how to integrate research, we will look first at a draft paragraph on *The Adventures of Tom Sawyer* written before consulting the critics. Then we will discuss two revisions that show ways of incorporating other interpretations.

Sample Draft Paragraph: Student's Analysis

In *The Adventures of Tom Sawyer,* the adults are not presented as models of behaviour. In fact, they are often shown to be acting like children. When Tom tricks Aunt Polly at the beginning of the book, for instance, Aunt Polly has been attempting to trick him. Similarly, Tom shows off at Sunday School when Judge Thatcher visits, but the superintendent and the teachers are also described as "showing off." Even serious events in the adult world seem to parallel Tom's actions. The fight that ends with Injun Joe murdering Dr. Robinson has many of the same elements as Tom's fight with the new boy in town. It is no wonder then that even after his harrowing escape from the cave and his recovery of the treasure, Tom returns to playing at robbers. The adult world is not portrayed as different from the world of childhood, and so there is no reason for Tom to grow up.

Sample Draft Paragraph: Adding Support from Research Material

In this revised paragraph, the material from Johnson that we noted earlier is added to summarize and expand the point that the writer made in the topic sentence.

The adults in *The Adventures of Tom Sawyer* are not presented as models of behaviour, but simply as older versions of Tom himself . . . [continue with examples from the original draft]. It is no wonder then that even after his harrowing escape from the cave and his recovery of the treasure, Tom returns to the boyhood world of playing at robbers, for the adult world offers no incentives for growing up. James L. Johnson argues that Tom's adventures "leave his character essentially untouched" because "such a change requires that the child meet a real world and adjust himself, painfully but with more or less success, to its undesirable circumstances" (51). But St. Petersburg, as Johnson points out, is an idyllic world, not a real world that would bring about change.

Sample Draft Paragraph: Synthesis of Student's Analysis and Research

In outstanding research papers, the writer does more than cite authorities to support points: he or she synthesizes material from various sources by showing basic similarities and differences. This synthesis then provides a context for the writer's own interpretation.

In the following paragraph, the writer of the sample research paper demonstrates her grasp of the debate about Tom Sawyer's relationship to the adult world by synthesizing opposing critical views and stating her own position.

What, then, is the relation between Tom and his world? Robert Regan supports the view, originally put forward by Walter Blair, that the narrative strands of the novel "trace Tom's progress from childishness to maturity" (Regan 116). Several critics disagree. They argue that because the adults of St. Petersburg are essentially childish, there is no impetus for Tom to change (Fetterley 300; Johnson 51; Miller 73; Whitley 60).

Numerous incidents in the book support this contention . . . [continue with examples from the original draft].

Crediting your sources, integrating research material, and synthesizing different points of view are never easy tasks. We have used a literary topic to demonstrate these techniques because essays on literature are the first type of research paper that many students have to write. As you continue in college or university, however, you will find that these skills are increasingly important in all your courses.

14f Sample Literary Research Paper

Tom Sawyer and Anne of Green Gables:

Two Models of Heroism

by Lanette Thornton

When we think of heroic quests, we usually envision a pattern very much like that of Mark Twain's The Adventures of Tom Sawyer: the hero engages in a series of adventures through which he proves his worth and is rewarded with riches and the love of a beautiful maiden. In this version of the heroic quest, as is obvious from the way I've described it, the hero is male. L.M. Montgomery's Anne of Green Gables, I will argue, presents a female version of the making of the hero. In the mythic pattern of separation, initiation, and reintegration into the society, Tom's tests of courage and his rewards are largely external, and neither he nor his world is transformed by them. Anne's tests, on the other hand, are largely internal, and her rewards depend upon her ability to transform both herself and her world.

Tom's separation from his community lies in his flouting of convention. Although one critic has argued that finally "Tom sacrifices freedom to gain community" (Towers 520), the first episode of the book seems to bear out John Whitley's contention that Tom "is never in any danger of expulsion from the community" (64). In this episode, which sets up our expectations for the rest of the novel, Tom escapes punishment for sneaking jam by outwitting his Aunt Polly. Her response—"a gentle laugh" (8)— immediately establishes her as an indulgent parental figure who likes Tom's mischievousness:

> He 'pears to know just how long he can torment me before I get my dander up, and he knows if he can make out to put me off for a minute, or make me laugh, it's all down again, and I can't hit him a lick. I ain't doing my duty by that boy, and that's the Lord's truth, goodness knows . . . . Every time I let him off my conscience does hurt me so; and every time I hit him my old heart 'most breaks. (8)

Furthermore, the "model boy" of the village—Tom's half brother Sid—is presented as dull and self-righteous, always willing to get Tom into trouble by tattling. Whenever we as readers, like Aunt Polly, are ready to condemn Tom's lying, his thoughtlessness, his prankish behaviour, Twain reminds us, usually through Aunt Polly, that Tom is good at heart. And we, like his aunt and the community gathered for his mock funeral (Miller 71-72), forgive him.

Although Leslie Willis dismisses *Anne of Green Gables* as sentimental because Anne "suffers no real hardships" except over her initial reception and Matthew's death at the end of the novel (250), Anne does not have the security in her world that Tom has in his. Tom is at home in St. Petersburg, under the care of a doting, if at times punitive, aunt. But the orphaned Anne has already lost a series of homes. When she reaches Green Gables, she learns that Matthew and Marilla had wanted a boy to help with the farm, not a girl at all. Furthermore, although Marilla soon discovers that Anne is "smart and obedient, willing to work and quick to learn" (57), the girl is also a talkative, imaginative, hot-tempered redhead. Anne, like Tom, is presented as essentially good. But unlike Tom, if Anne is to have the home she so desperately wants, she must learn to control her behaviour.

This control, moreover, must come from her desire to please others rather than from a fear of punishment. When Anne's temper flares up over Mrs. Rachel Lynde's disparaging comments about her looks, for example, Marilla admits that her neighbour "is too outspoken. But," she adds, "that is no excuse for such behaviour on your part. She was a stranger and an elderly person and my visitor—all three very good reasons why you should have been respectful to her" (72). Although at first Anne refuses to apologize to Mrs. Lynde—the punishment Marilla lights upon—Anne eventually does so to please Matthew. As Matthew had immediately recognized, Anne is "one of the sort you can do anything with if you only get her to love you" (52). The threat of expulsion is always present, however, for as Muriel Whitaker points out, Marilla's favourite punishment when Anne has misbehaved is isolation, banishment, ostracism (53).

To secure a place in the community, Ann must learn "the importance of keeping fantasy and reality segregated," as Julie Fenwick points out (61). Tom, on the other hand, learns to translate his imaginary heroism into real heroism. If Tom were a "model boy" like his half brother Sid, he would not fight, play truant from school, sneak out at night, "hook" provisions, and so on. But without these boyish pranks, he would not have the courage and resourcefulness he needs to become a hero. Thus the ingenuity, self-sufficiency, and leadership Tom demonstrates when he, Joe, and Huck run away to Jackson's Island to become pirates are the same qualities he needs to find a way out when he and Becky become lost in the cave. Similarly, Tom's desire to act on his book-knowledge of buried treasure and the ways of robbers leads him and Huck to discover the whereabouts of

Injun Joe and his treasure. As a result of these exploits, Tom becomes rich, by his standards, and wins the approval of Becky's father, the imposing Judge Thatcher. As Lyall Powers puts it, "the heroic game becomes impressively the Heroic reality" (321).

Anne's quest, on the other hand, leads her to heroic sacrifice: she gives up her hard-won scholarship to university to stay on the farm and care for Marilla. She is able to make this loving choice because she has learned to consider the rights and welfare of others without sacrificing her own individuality. As she tells Marilla on several occasions, Anne never does "the same naughty thing twice" (102). When her scrapes are her own fault—as in losing her temper with Mrs. Lynde, meddling with Marilla's brooch, and hitting Gilbert Blythe with her slate—Anne takes her punishment and mends her ways. But when her scrapes are not entirely her own fault—as when Diana gets drunk on mulberry wine or Anne puts liniment in the cake instead of vanilla— Anne also learns valuable lessons, for the willingness of Marilla and other adults to admit their own failings makes possible the sense of love and security that turn this initially hostile world into the home Anne so intensely desires. When her romantic views are "sabotaged by 'life' in incident after incident," Anne learns to distinguish romance from reality (Ross 46-48).

In the process of learning from her experiences, Anne is both transformed and transforms others (Whitaker 55). She overcomes Matthew's fear of females; awakens Marilla's undeveloped sense of humour; humbles the judgmental Mrs. Barry; sweetens the temper of Diana's crochety Aunt Josephine. By the end of the novel, even Mrs. Rachel Lynde, who is initially presented as the norm of the village, has become less rigid (Rubio 29). Anne is thus presented as a child who can exert some control over her environment by furnishing the "psychological, emotional, and imaginative dimensions which are lacking" in the adults' own lives (Rubio 35). In the process, as Whitaker points out, Anne has come to conform

"pretty closely to the adult view of propriety"
(52). By the time she reaches seventeen, Anne has
become what Marilla wanted: "All I want is that you
should behave like other little girls and not make
yourself ridiculous" (89). But she has done so
because this is what she too wants. Her essential
nature, like her imagination, has been tempered by
her trials, but not destroyed. This match between
desire and fulfillment is possible because the world
of Green Gables, like Anne herself, is essentially
good. Integration into the community is thus itself
the goal of Anne's heroic quest and her reward,
earned through experience.

In contrast, neither Tom nor his world is transformed by his adventures. Although Robert Regan supports the view, originally put forward by Walter
Blair, that the novel "trace(s) Tom's progress from
childishness to maturity" (Regan 116), several critics disagree. They argue that because the adults of
St. Petersburg are essentially childish, there is no
impetus for Tom to change (Fetterley 300; Johnson
51; Miller 73; Whitley 60). Numerous incidents in
the book support this contention. Thus Tom's trick-
ery is echoed by Aunt Polly's attempt to catch him
out, and Tom's showing off when Judge Thatcher visits the Sunday School by the antics of the staff:

> Mr. Walters [the Sunday School superintendent] fell
> to *showing off* with all sorts of official bustlings
> and activities . . . . The librarian *showed off*,
> running hither and thither with his arms full of
> books. . . . The young lady teachers *showed off—*
> bending sweetly over pupils that were lately being
> boxed. . . . The young gentleman teachers *showed
> off* with small scoldings and other little displays
> of authority . . . . (33) [emphasis mine].

Similarly, the fight that ends in the murder of
Dr. Robinson is an adult version of Tom's fight, at
the beginning of the book, with the new boy in town.

It is no wonder then that even after his harrowing escape from the cave and his recovery of the
treasure, Tom returns to playing at robbers. The

adult world is not portrayed as different from the world of childhood, and so there is no reason for Tom to grow up. Indeed, as Harold Aspiz remarks, "The town exists largely as a setting for Tom's adventures . . ." (147) In this respect, the worlds of Tom Sawyer and Anne of Green Gables are not similar, as Mary Rubio suggests (30), but radically different. If, as one critic suggests, Tom is not required "to sacrifice his boy's freedom in return for his success" (Regan 121), the reason may be that Twain "protects Tom from any experience that might seriously impair his 'unrestricted domination': boredom, humiliation, the serious threat of death, lasting or serious disappointment, growing up . . ." (Johnson 59). Tom's initiation thus consists of a series of adventures, not experiences that would lead to maturity (Johnson 51), and his rewards are correspondingly external.

I suggested earlier that these novels can be seen as presenting male and female models of heroism, Twain's novel celebrating individual exploits that lead to external rewards and Montgomery's celebrating a reciprocal process of internal change that leads to transformation of self and society. Robert Keith Miller points out that Twain saw himself as rebelling against the stereotype of the Model Boy portrayed in nineteenth-century children's books and creating instead a portrait of (in Walter Blair's words) "what a normal boy should be" (67). Montgomery's goal seems somewhat different. As we have seen, Anne's first task is to convince Matthew and Marilla that she is worth keeping even though she is not a boy. Anne's rivalry with Gilbert throughout the novel establishes their equality, in keeping with Montgomery's view of there being little difference between men and women (Burns 44-45). If we are tempted to read Anne's story as stereotypically that of the female who triumphs through self-sacrifice, we must remember that Gilbert is also forced to relinquish his chance for a university education because of his responsibility for his family.

This observation leads us to the possibility that the difference between the models of heroism portrayed in the two novels is not merely one of gender but also one of nationality. Tom's story, Lyall Powers argues, reflects the American dream and the American paradox: "The ideal hero is the stout individualist, the non-conforming natural man, American Rousseau, who yet lives snugly in suburbia as a regular fellow" (323). Does Anne then reflect the Canadian dream of social harmony with the recognition of the price we pay in individual sacrifice?

Works Cited

Aspiz, Harold. "Tom Sawyer's Games of Death." *Studies in the Novel* 27.2 (1995): 141, 13p. Online. AcademicSearch. 04 June 1999.

Burns, Jane. "Anne and Emily: L. M. Montgomery's Children." *Room of One's Own* 3.3: 37-47.

Fenwick, Julie. "The Silence of the Mermaid: *Lady Oracle* and *Anne of Green Gables*." *Essays on Canadian Writing* 47 (1992): 51, 14p. Online. MasterFILE. 07 June 1999.

Fetterley, Judith. "The Sanctioned Rebel." *Studies in the Novel* 3.3 (1971): 293-304.

Johnson, James L. *Mark Twain and the Limits of Power: Emerson's God in Ruins*. Knoxville: U of Tennessee P, 1982.

Miller, Robert Keith. *Mark Twain*. New York: Ungar, 1983.

Montgomery, L. M. *Anne of Green Gables*. Toronto: McGraw, 1968.

Powers, Lyall. "The Sweet Success of Twain's Tom." *Dalhousie Review* 53.2 (1973): 310-24.

Regan, Robert. *Unpromising Heroes: Mark Twain and His Characters*. Berkeley: U of California P, 1966.

Ross, Catherine S. "Calling Back the Ghost of the
Old-Time Heroine: Duncan, Montgomery, Atwood,
Laurence, and Munro." *Studies in Canadian Literature*
4.1 (1979): 43-58.

Rubio, Mary. "Satire, Realism, and Imagination in
Anne of Green Gables." *L. M. Montgomery: An
Assessment*. Ed. John R. Sorfleet. Guelph:
Canadian Children's P, 1976. 27-36.

Towers, Tom H. "I Never Thought We Might Want to Come
Back: Strategies of Transcendence in *Tom Sawyer.*"
Modern Fiction Studies 21.4 (1975-76): 509-20.

Twain, Mark. *The Adventures of Tom Sawyer*. London:
Penguin, 1986.

Whitaker, Muriel, "'Queer Children': L. M.
Montgomery's Heroines." *L. M. Montgomery: An
Assessment*. Ed. John R. Sorfleet. Guelph:
Canadian Children's P, 1976. 50-59.

Whitley, John S. "Kids' Stuff: Mark Twain's Boys."
Mark Twain: A Sumptuous Variety. Ed. Robert
Giddings. London: Vision, 1985. 57-76.

Willis, Leslie. "The Bogus Ugly Duckling: Anne
Shirley Unmasked." *Dalhousie Review* 56.2 (1976):
247-51.

14g Sample Non-Literary Research Paper

When you write on a non-literary topic, your research includes finding facts as well as opinions about your subject. You must clearly indicate the source of these facts as well as the source of opinions from experts in the field, whether you use direct quotations or put the information into your own words. The following research paper shows how to give in-text citations and bibliographical references using the American Psychological Association (APA) format. For guidelines on APA format, see Appendix B, Documentation.

What Is Psychology?

Tatiana LoVerso

14g

Sample Non-Literary Research Paper

If I did a research project on the public perception of psychology, I predict that I would collect many different answers to the question "What is psychology?" Almost all of these definitions would be correct because psychology is a discipline with an array of theories, topics, and even subjects, a discipline which continues to change its focus and to branch off in various directions. Although the word *psychology* comes from Greek roots meaning "the study of the soul," it is sometimes difficult to see how the different branches of psychology contribute to our understanding of the human mind, soul, or experience. This difficulty stems in part from a basic disagreement among psychologists over a key question: How should the human mind, soul, or experience be studied? Beyond this disagreement over methodology lies a more basic question: What does it mean to be human?

According to the dominant school of academic psychologists, human behaviour can best be studied using the scientific method, with its emphasis on description, prediction, and control. The aspiration to be a natural science has led the discipline to favour a predominantly quantitative and experimental methodology.

Psychology as an academic discipline has emphasized this orientation from its beginnings around 1879, when Wilhelm Wundt began studying human unconscious processes through systematic introspection in controlled conditions. In this early work, Wundt viewed psychology as a natural science, a study of the nervous system as a means to learn about human consciousness (Leahey, 1997, p. 197).

The intellectual climate in North America was very focused on the scientific method as the path to all knowledge. Thus the theories that monopolized academic psychology were those based on Darwinian evolutionary explanations and assumptions (Leahey, 1997). Through the influence of several prominent psychologists, this antimentalistic trend slowly eliminated consciousness from the topic of study.

As a result, North American academic psychology was fertile ground for the introduction of John B. Watson's behaviourism. Watson and later B.F. Skinner managed to develop a psychology that ignored the human mind. They completely rejected the notion that psychology was the study of the soul or the mind. Instead, they viewed psychology as an indisputably natural science that studies behaviour. Watson held that psychology should not be concerned with consciousness at all because it is not causal or influential in behaviour. What is influential is our environment; thus psychology should be the study of environmental conditions that cause us to behave in particular ways. The environment provides a stimulus: we emit behaviour in response. He also held that animal behaviour and human behaviour had the same causal source, the environment; thus there was no difference in studying the two. Following in Watson's footsteps, Skinner concluded that our environment controls our behaviour by providing either rewards or punishments. According to this view, we are merely a product of this system of environmental rewards and punishments.

This view of human nature ignores free will, creativity, imagination, and purpose. It is these aspects of being human, among others, that a different strand in psychology has focused on. The father of academic psychology, Wilhelm Wundt, who came to see his experimental psychology as the "sin of [his] youthful days" (Leahey, 1997, p. 197), developed a more philosophical approach after he went to work at the philosophically focused University of Leipzig. Here he abandoned physiology as the link to mental processes in favour of the theory that one can study the higher functions of the mind by studying the products of our culture throughout history.

It was not until Sigmund Freud, however, that psychology began to deal with truly unique elements of the human mind such as the unconscious. Like

Wundt, Freud too began his inquiries into the human mind through physiology. A profound self-analysis convinced Freud that mental and emotional factors are causal in our behaviour. His goal was to understand the human mind in order to help men and women live psychologically healthy and rational lives, a goal that led him to found the important tradition of psychotherapy. Freud's theories, which were formed through his work with his patients, reintroduced the mind and emotions to the study of psychology. Psychologists in the Freudian tradition hold that the best way to study the human mind, soul, and experience is what Lawrence LeShan calls La Science de la Humanité: the study of human beings with the goal of gaining a "deeper understanding, for the ability to feel more and more empathy with individuals . . . [in this method] we are concerned rather with our own consciousness being able to 'feel the feelings and think the thoughts' of another person, to so expand our own inner life that it is true that 'nothing human is alien to me'" (LeShan, 1990, p. 145).

Which of these two methods, the method of experimental research or the psychotherapeutic method, tells us more about what it means to be human?

While experimental research has increased our understanding of human physiology and related areas, the very conditions under which most experimental research is done limits its relevance. Much of present day psychology is taken up with research using animals. Indeed, a study by Charles Kutsher "showed that the rat, representing less than 0.0001 percent of all living creatures, was used in 58 percent of reported studies" (as cited in LeShan, 1990, p. 75). Rats are popular as laboratory animals because researchers can eliminate all other factors and study the particular thing in which they are interested in a controlled fashion. As LeShan argues, "It has been that rat who has become the Pied Piper, leading the psychologists away from their homes, away from their concern with meaningful aspects of human life" (1990, p. 75).

Yet rats, like other organisms, have been shown to act differently in the wild than they do in the lab. If nothing in real life is isolated like it is in the lab, studying something in this way will give us a very limited understanding of that which we are studying. This is especially true of the study of humans; we are complex organisms who live and act in complex environments. Karl Popper illustrates this issue very elegantly: "Robinson Crusoe can never be a useful model for any economy whose problems arise precisely from the interaction of individuals and groups" (Popper, 1964, p. 18).

What of the psychotherapeutic method? Even today, Freud's methods are criticized for being unscientific, and yet no other psychologist has made discoveries or proposed theories that tell us as much about what it means to be human. His major discoveries, such as the concept of the unconscious and the Oedipus complex, were obviously not made through experimental methods, and undoubtedly experimental research would never have been able to reveal them. Freud's methods to some extent reproduced those of an artist. He would talk to the subjects of his research, and he would use both his reason and his intuition to formulate his theories. Moreover, his research was conducted while helping people, and with the goal of increasing professionals' capacity to help.

Most people would agree with Freud that one of the goals of psychology is, or should be, to help people have healthy mental lives. In therapy the practitioner cannot help a person without understanding his or her problem and life circumstances. This deep understanding cannot be, and is never thought to be, found through empirical tests such as questionnaires. It is the method of long-term interaction one-on-one, where open-ended questions lead therapists to a deeper understanding of each particular person's point of view. It is that element of "living with" someone who is depressive,

Sample Non-Literary Research Paper

schizophrenic, or psychopathic that gives a true understanding. This is true in great art as well. Art allows us to subjectively experience the inner world of others, anyone from a murderer to a saint. As Kurt Lewin explains:

> The most complete and concrete descriptions of situations are those which writers such as Dostoevsky have given us. These descriptions have attained what the statistical descriptions have most notably lacked, namely a picture that shows in a definite way how the different facts in an individual's environment are related to each other and to the individual himself. The whole situation is presented with its specific structure (1939, p. 13).

I became most acutely aware of the importance of seeking a deep understanding a couple of months ago when both my mother and I were doing research on breast cancer patients. She was doing this research because the main character in her latest novel has breast cancer, and my mother has to understand the experience before she tries to write about it. I was doing this research because I was possibly going to use breast cancer patients in my honors research project, and I too needed to understand the experience before I planned my research.

But our methods of research were very different. My mother read memoirs, novels, and poetry that dealt with breast cancer. She came to understand the emotional experience of breast cancer patients through works such as Alice J. Davis' poem "After Surgery' (1988):

> I am lopsided
> flatter than a boy.
> S-shaped stitches
> frame washboard ribs.
> Why should I remember
> after seven years
> the way a hand
> curved my breast?
> Old griefs sift through
> this excavation. (Lifshitz, p. 42)

My mother also interviewed friends and acquaintances who had breast cancer. She vicariously lived through the experience with imagination and empathy as her facilitators.

In contrast, I went on to PsycINFO and found everything that I could find on breast cancer and Post Traumatic Stress Disorder as well as other psychological reactions to this illness. The language of this research was quite different. One study of traumatic distress symptoms among women recently diagnosed with breast cancer reached this conclusion:

> . . . nearly half of the patients reported a high level of intrusive thoughts during the days immediately following diagnosis. Intrusion as measured with IEA has been found to correlate strongly with anxiety and acute symptoms of post-traumatic stress as defined in the DSM-III-R and DSM-IV. . . . The strong correlation between intrusive thoughts and overall distress suggests emotional pain and suffering in a high proportion of the patients. (Tjemsland, Soreide, & Malt, 1996, p. 6)

At the end of our research, my mother had a far better understanding of the experience of this disease than I did. She knew the breast cancer experience; I could cite studies on how likely these women were to develop a mental disorder like PTSD.

Traditionally, people have turned to art rather than to academic psychology to understand themselves. Through their experience of the work of art, readers or viewers have access to the artist's deep comprehension of human life. In his essay "What Psychology Is About," D.O. Hebb, an eminent researcher in the field of memory, emphasizes this function of art:

> It is to the literary world, not to psychological science, that you go to learn how to live with people, how to make love, how not to make enemies; to find out what grief does to people, or the stoicism that is possible in the endurance of pain, or how if you're lucky you

may die with dignity; to see how power corrupts
or does not corrupt. For such knowledge and such
understanding of the human species, don't look
in my *Textbook of Psychology* . . . try *Lear*, and
Othello, and *Hamlet*. (Cited in LeShan, 1990,
p. 12)

These then are the methods most useful for the
study of the human mind, soul, and experience: self-
analysis like that practised by Freud; "living with"
the experience of others to develop empathy; and the
analysis of human expression in works of art. By
employing these methods, psychology will become more
useful to therapeutic practice. This understanding
and the knowledge that accompanies it will not be
obsolete in a year's time, as has been true with
many of the theories and so-called truths in
psychology. The wisdom gained from this method is
the same kind that is revealed in Shakespeare and
Dostoevsky, knowledge that is relevant across time
and space. If I use this method to ask myself what
psychology is, or should be, I find that it is a
discipline that works towards the comprehension of
the human soul for the eventual betterment of
individual human life.

References

Davis, Alice J. (1988). After surgery. In
L. Lifshitz (Ed.), *Women's poetry on breast
cancer: Her soul beneath the bone* (p. 42).
Chicago, IL: University of Illinois Press.

Leahey, T.H. (1997). *A history of psychology: Main
currents in psychological thought.* New Jersey:
Prentice Hall.

LeShan, L. (1990). *The dilemma of psychology.* New
York: Dutton.

Lewin, K. (1939). Principles of topological
psychology. (F. Heider & G.M. Heider, Trans.).
New York: McGraw-Hill.

Popper, K. (1957). *The poverty of historicism.* New
York: Harper Torchbooks.

Tjemsland, L., Soreide, J.A., & Malt, U.F. (1996).
Traumatic distress symptoms in early breast
cancer I: Acute response to diagnosis.
Psycho-oncology, 5, 1-8.

- Ryerson Polytechnic University—The Writing Centre Guide #3: Writing a University Essay

  gopher.ryerson.ca:70/0/.services/.write/.essay

- The Purdue Online Writing Laboratory research paper guidelines

  owl.english.purdue.edu/writers/introduction.html

- Directory of Academic Internet Resources—listings of best Internet sites for each subject.

  www.academicinfo.net/

Part 4

BUSINESS WRITING

CHECKLIST

Business Writing

	OK	NEEDS WORK
1. Is your purpose clear?	☐	☐
2. Does the content meet your readers' needs? (Is there too much or too little information?)	☐	☐
3. Is the organization effective?	☐	☐
4. Is the tone effective?	☐	☐
5. Is the information accurate and complete?	☐	☐
6. Are the explanations and details adequate?	☐	☐
7. Is the sentence structure appropriate?	☐	☐
8. Is the word choice effective? Have you avoided outdated expressions?	☐	☐
9. Are the transitions between statements clear?	☐	☐
10. Is the format of the document correct? (See Appendix C.)	☐	☐

Chapter 15

Writing Letters, Reports, and Brochures

All good business writers focus on plain, clear language that leaves no doubt about the intended message. They also try to gain readers' goodwill, both by the tone and style of writing and by keeping in mind the readers' needs and point of view.

15a Business Writing

Audience and Purpose

Both business letters and reports often involve writing to someone you do not know personally. For this reason, you will need to make educated guesses about what your reader—a prospective employer, a grant committee, a student loans officer—needs to know. It's worthwhile to ask yourself these questions before you begin:

- What is my position in relation to this reader—taxpayer? employee? client? supplier?

- What tone, style, and format are appropriate for this relationship?

- How much background information does this reader need?

- What do I want my reader to do in response to this letter or report?

Although the purpose of some business writing is solely to convey facts, in many cases you will need to analyze and explain information. You may also want to persuade your reader to take action. If you were writing a report on an accident in which a restaurant employee burned herself, for example, you would include all the facts of the case. To explain why the accident occurred, you might point out that food preparation staff are

179

inexperienced and that the deep fat fryer is in an awkward location. You would also propose changes to prevent future accidents. Thus your report, like most business writing, would have both an explanatory and a persuasive purpose.

Guidelines

Your readers will appreciate business writing that is complete, accurate, and easy to follow.

- *Check your letter or report for completeness.* Include all the background information (*who, what, when, where, why, how*) your reader needs to understand the context of your subject and all the factual information and analysis required to support your conclusions and recommendations.

- *Be sure that your information is accurate and precise.* Telling your insurance agent that *The car skidded twenty metres* is more precise than saying *The car skidded a short distance,* but neither statement is accurate if the car actually skidded forty metres.

- *Make your writing clear, businesslike, and friendly.* You can use contractions (*can't, we'll*) in most business writing except formal reports, but avoid slang. Also avoid outdated expressions, such as *with regard to your inquiry,* and contemporary bureaucratese, such as *prioritize our objectives* (set our goals) and *implement procedures* (take action).

- *Keep your sentences and paragraphs fairly short.* Put main points in short sentences. Use longer sentences to fill in details. Varying the length of your sentences will give your writing a more conversational tone. Avoid stringing together a series of very short sentences (which can sound monotonous or aggressive) or a series of one-sentence paragraphs (which can make it difficult for a reader to see connections among your ideas).

In this chapter we will illustrate three kinds of business writing you are likely to do: letters, reports, and brochures. For more complete information, see Mary Ellen Guffey and Brendan Nagle, *Essentials of Business Communication* (Scarborough: ITP Nelson, 1997).

15b Business Letters

Requesting information, sending special messages (such as thank-yous, sympathy, and congratulations), and making complaints are common reasons for writing letters. These days, people are more likely to use faxes and the 1-800 number service, rather than writing a letter, to request information and order products. It's interesting to note, however, that e-mail and faxes have renewed people's enthusiasm for letter-writing. Most businesses place a high value on "special message" correspondence because of the goodwill it brings.

Here we will focus on letters of complaint. In Chapter 16 you will find a sample job application letter (16g) and letter of request (16i). For the format of business letters and memos, see Appendix C.

15c Letters of Complaint

Complaint letters are designed not only to voice your concerns, but often to request a positive resolution. If you believe you have a legitimate issue, assume that the company receiving your complaint will honor it and make it right. That mind-set will enable you to maintain a courteous and friendly tone throughout. (If you're really angry about the situation, write a rough draft that allows you to vent all those hostile feelings—then tear it up and start over!)

The letter of complaint typically has three parts:

1. The opening paragraph describes clearly what you want.

2. The main body explains the nature of the problem, complete with details, and gives reasons why the claim is justified.

3. The closing expresses appreciation for the help you hope to receive and, if appropriate, provides a deadline for response by the reader.

See the sample letter of complaint below.

15d Sample Letter of Complaint

CEDARS LANDING
182 Creek Road
Victoria, B.C. V5N 1X2

May 18, 1999

Marcella VanDamme
Bulbs Galore! Wholesale
135 Burwell Drive
Mississauga, Ontario N0J 1T0

Dear Ms. VanDamme:

Please honour your lifetime guarantee for the 200
Dutch bulbs we ordered and planted last September. We
would like a full refund for $129.99 (including GST)
as outlined on the enclosed invoice.

Cedars Landing is a seniors' complex that was
built four years ago. Your catalogue arrived at the
perfect moment, as the garden committee had chosen
tulips for this year's project and were wondering
where to buy them. Your bulbs arived on time and appeared to be in good condition. All planting and wa-
tering instructions were followed carefully.

Once spring arrived, everyone watched eagerly for
new growth. Imagine our disappointment when only 12
of the 200 bulbs grew and flowered. We have not been
able to discover the source of the problem. If you
would like a sample of the defective product, please
let us know. Your guarantee states 100% satisfaction,
with a choice of refund or replacement. At this time,
we would prefer a refund in order to purchase annuals
to fill in the bed.

Thank you for looking after our problem. We look
forward to receiving a refund by the middle of June.

Your truly,

Michael Ainsley

Michael Ainsley
Garden Committee Chair
encl.

15e Reports

The term **report** can refer to many kinds of communication, from an informal discussion over the telephone to a lengthy, formal document with a title page, table of contents, and bibliography. In most work situations, you will be given detailed guidelines for the content and the form of the reports you are expected to write. You can then adapt the more general information in this text to your particular task.

Audience and Purpose

15f

Analytical Problem-Solving Reports

All reports are based on factual information, which is collected, analyzed, and then presented in an organized form. The two general categories of reports are **informational** and **analytical**.

The information report provides details and data, such as weekly sales reports or progress reports on specific projects. It does not analyze any of the information presented. Most companies create standard forms to handle routine material.

In contrast, analytical reports evaluate information in order to make recommendations, provide options, or attempt to solve problems. When crafting an analysis report, you may choose either to present your problem and fact-finding at the beginning and end with recommendations, or to begin your report with the recommendations, followed by the background, facts, and description of the problem.

If your audience has little knowledge about your topic, start with the background. For busy executives familiar with the subject, provide the recommendations first.

The more objective and credible your information is, the more useful it will be to your reader. Don't let your interests and biases (such as personal involvement with any of the participants) slant your presentation of the facts. Opinions have their place, but not if they're disguised as facts.

15f Analytical Problem-Solving Reports

As its name suggests, a **problem-solving report** is appropriate when you want to analyze a problem and suggest ways to solve it. A dance student, for example, might write a report on the reasons for injuries to first-year students. A restaurant manager might write a report on the effects of staff reductions on the quality of service.

The more specifically you define the problem you want to solve, the more useful your report is likely to be. Try to narrow a general subject, such as security problems, to something more precise, such as *a 30-percent increase in locker room thefts in the last six months.*

A problem-solving report usually has three sections:

1. *Background*

Fill in enough information to give your reader a good sense of the context and the importance of the problem. How often does the problem occur? When and where does it occur? How many people are affected? What are the costs in money, efficiency, safety, prestige, morale?

2. *Analysis*

You should develop this section of your report through causal analysis. Make a list of all the factors contributing to the problem. Be sure to include both immediate causes (inadequate supervision contributes to theft by employees) and more remote causes (employees are dissatisfied with their wages and benefits and therefore some feel entitled to steal).

You can organize this analysis as a list of independent causes or as a chain of interdependent causes (low wages cause employee dissatisfaction; this dissatisfaction causes resentment against the employer; this resentment causes employees to steal). Depending on the complexity of the problem you are analyzing, you may want to combine both methods of developing a causal analysis. (For more information, see Explaining Causes and Effects, 6d.) Connect your analysis directly with the information in the background section so that your reader can see how your analysis explains the causes of the problem.

3. *Recommendations and implementation*

Suggest solutions to the problem you have analyzed. Your recommendations should follow logically from the analysis section. If you are suggesting a number of possible solutions, indicate which one is best and explain why. If appropriate, describe how the recommendations could be implemented.

Case Study

ABC Pharmacy has been operating in Trenton for six years and is part of a Canada-wide chain. When the manager retired, Henry Wong, a senior pharmacist at the Saskatoon location, took over. He promoted Jenna Janovich from head cashier to merchandise manager. She has worked at the Trenton store since it opened. In addition to Henry and Jenna, there are four other full-time staff and nine part-time.

When Henry first started a month ago, the division manager, Martha Cohen, showed him two letters of complaint from customers concerned about poor service and indifferent staff. She was also concerned about dropping sales and reduced profits from the store. The division manager requested a report that tracked the causes of these concerns and his plans for improvement. The first step Henry took was to place an employee suggestion box in the staff room to collect feedback about customer service challenges and ideas for fixing them. He instructed Jenna to clear the box after two weeks and pass along all comments.

The comments in the box had more to do with staff morale than customer relations:

- Staff morale is lousy.

- I never know what's going on.

- I get all the worst shifts.

- It's no fun working here.

- The lineups at the checkout are too long.

Henry was not surprised at some of the comments. This new store had a very different atmosphere from his old one, where all the staff and even the customers were treated like family. He met with Jenna to learn the store history and get her perceptions about current problems. Jenna sensed that no one was clear about roles and responsibilities for each position, and some staff seemed resentful of her recent promotion. A staff meeting was called to discover specific concerns. Jenna was asked to run this meeting so Henry could listen and observe. Together, they carefully planned the meeting in order first to uncover the root causes of both customer and staff complaints, and then to look for possible solutions to those problems.

The meeting was very productive. Most of the participants gave specific feedback and examples, and the brainstorming session generated good ideas for overcoming the existing problems. With this new information, Henry and Jenna wrote the report for the division manager. They chose a memo format and used key headings to organize their information. Recommendations were positioned toward the end of the report.

15g Sample Problem-Solving Report

TO: Martha Cohen, Division Manager
Toronto office

FROM: Henry Wong, Store Manager and
Jenna Janovich, Merchandise Manager,
Trenton store

DATE: March 29, 1999

SUBJECT:CUSTOMER COMPLAINTS-PROBLEMS AND
RECOMMENDATIONS

INTRODUCTION

In February, two customer complaint letters regarding treatment at the Trenton store initiated a request from the division for a report regarding the issues and any recommendations for solving them. The information and suggestions in the following paragraphs were compiled from feedback sessions with the staff.

PROBLEM

Our suggestion box that was meant to get feedback about fixing customer problems generated instead the most concern about staff morale. We believe that these two matters are closely connected. On March 15, a staff meeting was held to explore the contributing causes of poor customer treatment and employee concerns. The following causes seem to be the major ones:

1. The staff rotation for weekend hours is not fairly handled, resulting in a few staff working more than their share of weekends, and causing resentment amongst co-workers.

2. Part-time staff are not kept informed of policy and price changes. Mistakes are made and profit is lost.

3. Due to the current method of scheduling shifts, day and evening staff rarely have a chance to talk to one another. Not only does this cause the problems listed in #2, but there is also no opportunity to build staff loyalty and a sense of belonging.

4. Day staff often find unfinished pricing left by the evening shift and have an extra load to face. Sometimes customers are ignored in order for employees to catch up with the work.

5. Even the most senior staff are unsure of their specific roles and duties. No one is sure who to take orders from and what their responsibilities are, so day-to-day activities are not as productive and customers get shuffled from one person to another.

RECOMMENDATIONS

Most of the ideas below can easily be implemented at the store level. Some of the recommendations will require the support of the division office.

Scheduling:
1. Find a better scheduling system for handling weekend hours.
2. Schedule an extra half hour for one part-time person per evening to collect work instructions from the merchandise manager.

Communications:
1. Create job descriptions that clearly outline roles and duties.
2. Provide customer service training and updates for all staff.
3. Schedule monthly staff meetings.
4. Plan quarterly social functions for all employees.
5. Choose a staff rep. to gather feedback and voice concerns.

CONCLUSION

We believe that by implementing the above plan, our level of customer service will climb dramatically and our staff will be happier and more productive. As mentioned, Martha, we will need your help with items #1 and #2. Work will begin immediately on the other items. We look forward to your comments and support.

On the surface, it seemed as if ABC Pharmacy was only having customer service problems. If Henry and Jenna had considered just the service problem, they might not have uncovered the root issues that caused it. Whenever you write any kind of problem-solving report, it's important to be diligent in sorting out symptoms and causes, then looking for solutions that will deal with the causes.

15h Brochures and Flyers

Despite the invasion of television advertising, most organizations still rely on written communication to promote their products and services. Newspaper and magazine ads, promotional letters, brochures, and flyers are the most common types of persuasive pieces.

A company with a large budget can hire professionals to create a marketing portfolio that will bring in plenty of business. However, even with no budget and just eager volunteers, you can produce a simple, yet effective brochure that will get your business off the ground.

Creating a Brochure or Flyer

Complete these three stages in order to produce an effective brochure or flyer: create a framework, write the contents, and design the format.

Creating a Framework

Before you begin to write, answer the following questions to provide your framework.

1. What do you want the brochure to do for you (inform existing customers, find new customers, give information about new products or services, advertise a sale)?

2. Who is your target audience (households, other businesses, specific income levels or age groups)?

3. What needs does your product or service fill?

4. How will you use this piece (mail-out, drop-off, handout, leave-behind)?

5. What format will be most effective (full-page text, 6-panel–2 folds, half-page fold-over)?

Once you've answered the who, what, how, where, and why, you will know whether a brochure or a flyer is more appropriate, and you will be ready for the next stage.

188

Note: A flyer is either a full- or half-size, unfolded sheet (8-1/2 X 11) with all the text on one side of the page. A brochure has one or two folds in the paper and the text is printed in columns on both sides of the page (8-1/2 X 11 or 8-1/2 X 14 are the typical sizes).

Writing the Contents

Marcia Yudkin, in her book *Persuading on Paper* (New York: Penguin, 1996, 65–73), outlines five steps to creating your piece.

1. ***Brainstorm ideas.*** For at least a week, jot down all ideas and thoughts. A thesaurus is a great tool for generating even more ideas. Allow enough extra time for these ideas to take shape.

2. ***Craft an attention-getting opener.*** This important first line helps you capture your readers' attention. These grabbers can be in the form of questions, news headlines, promises, or results (testimonials).

   Ever Wondered How to Get More for Your Money?

   Wake Up and Smell Our Coffee!

3. ***Spell out the offer or the action you want readers to take.*** Keep it simple and direct.

   This is a limited offer. Book your appointment by calling . . .
   Take advantage of our gift with purchase.

4. ***Select and arrange supporting facts and ideas gathered in Step 1 above.*** Provide details about your product or service that explain why people should buy from you. This is your chance to persuade your readers.

5. ***When your rough draft is done, get an unbiased second opinion.*** Make changes and then proofread carefully.

Designing the Format

Gather samples of other brochures and ads, and decide what you like and don't like. Visit your local copy shop and ask to see samples of paper. Pick out suitable paper in the weight and color you think will get your message across.

The format needs to align closely with the tone and intent of the brochure. Choose the fonts, graphics, and layout that most closely match the content. It's a bit like choosing the right frame for a beautiful picture—isn't your content worthy of a great frame?

Because there are so many choices in a typical graphics package, remember to keep it simple. A clean, uncluttered look will have a more positive impact than too much text or too many graphics on the page.

The example below provides some insights about the brochure-writing process and the resulting sample flyer.

Case Study

Four university friends—Harry, Ahmed, June, and Shandy—all needed to make some money over the summer. Summer jobs were scarce in their town, so they had to be creative. When they assessed their combined talents, skills, and interests, they discovered that a variety of duties, preferably outdoors, would suit them best. And if they could all work together, that was even better.

"But what should we do?" asked Shandy.

"Well my mom will pay me to water and weed her garden when she's away," said Ahmed.

"And my dad has a pile of fence boards to be replaced and painted," said Harry.

"Maybe we should start some sort of home and garden service," suggested June.

The more they talked, the more this idea grew. Harry's dad, a salesman, told them that selling their idea was critical to their success and that a good brochure or flyer could really help them. Ahmed's desktop publishing software and laser printer would help them produce their advertising piece for very little money.

The company name they chose was Handy Hammers Home & Garden Care. Their goal was to offer holiday house sitting, indoor and outdoor plant care, fence-building and small household repair jobs. Customers could hire them either for one project or for ongoing work over the summer.

They started by creating a framework:

1. **Purpose of the brochure**—attract customers and create an awareness of their services

2. **Target audience**—homes in their neighbourhoods

3. **Needs of customers**—help with household chores, more free time

4. **Delivery method**—hand deliver to people's homes and talk to potential customers at the door

5. **Format**—an 8-1/2 X 11, unfolded, full-text flyer

After much discussion and re-writing, the team created the draft shown next. Harry's father declared it a winner. Once it was printed, all they had to do was knock on those doors and get the business!

15i Sample Flyer

TOO MANY CHORES & TOO LITTLE TIME FOR FUN?

Give yourself a summer break—
Let Handy Hammers do those jobs for you!

Plagued by weeds?
Worried about your plants during vacation time?
Frustrated with a falling-down fence?
Tired of spring cleaning?
Bored with tending your garden?
Concerned about leaky eavestroughs?

GIVE US A CALL

At your service, Shandy, Harry, June, and Ahmed are all eager to fix pesky problems and reduce those tiresome tasks so you'll have time for sun, surf, and relaxation. Our dedicated staff has a combined total of over 12 years' experience in household and yard maintenance. We guarantee our work—if you're not satisfied, we'll make it right!

FREE CONSULTATION & ESTIMATE
SPECIAL PRICES FOR SENIORS
REASONABLE RATES

CALL 555-6677 NOW & GET YOUR JUNE DISCOUNT

Handy Hammers Home & Garden Care
123 Elm Street, Parkerville, ON M3C 1X1
Phone: 555-6677; Fax: 555-5544

Chapter 16

Getting a Job

Getting a job these days requires a great deal of effort. You are more likely to be successful if you are organized and thorough in your approach and present yourself, on paper and in person, in a professional, businesslike manner. In order to be well-prepared for the job search, you will need to create the following documents:

- Résumé

- Cover letter

- List of references

This section will guide you through each of these, step by step, and give you examples to follow.

16a Résumés

A résumé is a one- or two-page summary of your work experience and educational background. It's important to tailor the contents of your résumé to fit the requirements of each prospective employer. The wider the variety of jobs you have had, the more you'll need to do this. Computers make this much easier with the "cut and paste" features they provide. Simply type in a standard résumé, save it on disk, and modify as needed.

A word here about professionally prepared résumés. While they do look very impressive, they are costly. Another drawback is that these documents sometimes inflate the applicant's abilities. In an interview, employers look for a match between the person they have seen on paper and the one facing them. Any discrepancy will raise questions about suitability. There is nothing wrong with getting some help to create the best portfolio you can; just be sure the words and descriptions fit with your personality and experiences. In other words, make it your own.

Contents of a Résumé

1. *Personal information*

At the top of the page, type your name, address, telephone and fax numbers, and an e-mail address. If any of these numbers are temporary, provide any permanent ones where you can also be reached.

2. *Objective*

If it's a part-time or summer job you're applying for, this statement is optional. However, if you are searching for a job that will provide experience to reinforce your career path, then include this information. Briefly describe your career goal and state the skills and abilities you would like to use.

> To broaden my administrative responsibilities in the health care field where my nursing background and effectiveness in dealing with people would be assets.

3. *Work experience and educational background*

These are the most important parts of the résumé. The way you present this information depends on the kind of résumé you are writing (see below), but your main purpose is to demonstrate that you can do the job you are applying for. Emphasize your achievements and the range of your responsibilities rather than merely giving your job title. Include the names of the institution(s) you have attended and the degrees or certificates you have received. If you haven't gone beyond high school, include the name of the school you attended and the type of diploma you received. You might also indicate that you have met the entrance requirements for college or university. If you are a college or university student, you can omit information about your high school education. List any work-related workshops, training sessions, and non-credit courses you have completed, because they indicate enthusiasm for your field.

4. *Interests, activities, recognition, and awards*

This personal information is optional in a résumé. You can include sports, hobbies, and awards to indicate that you have diverse skills and interests (some of which might be relevant to the job) and qualities, such as courage or perseverance, that an employer would value. This information should be current, so don't include everything you have ever been interested in.

5. *References*

List three names, addresses, and phone numbers of people willing to provide references. Include their job titles and their relationship to you. Be sure to ask referees' permission before you include their names.

To choose your references, pick the people who can provide the best information about you for the type of job you're applying for—former employers, supervisors, and teachers. When you have an interview scheduled, it's a good idea to alert those on your list and remind them of skills and abilities you may want them to comment on, such as reliability, performance, teamwork. You will find a sample letter requesting a reference below.

A frequently asked question about references is whether to include them on your résumé or just provide them when asked. Though there's no right or wrong answer, we have noticed that if names and references aren't on the résumé, potential employers will often choose someone else whose references are right there.

Three Types of Résumés

There are three types of résumés: the *chronological*, the *functional*, and the *combination* résumé. Each has advantages and disadvantages.

The Chronological Résumé

Also known as the traditional résumé, this style presents your work experience and educational background in a chronological sequence from most recent to least recent. It is easy to read and prepare. Use this format if you have a consistent work record and steady employment. However, if you are new to the job market, haven't worked for some time, or have gaps in your work history, this type may not be the best because it quickly reveals these potential weaknesses.

The Functional Résumé

Headings for the functional résumé focus primarily on specific skills and accomplishments related to the prospective job, rather than the chronological listing of education and work experience.

If you've been away from the job market for a while, have an erratic work history, or have gained most of your experience from volunteer activities, then this format may be the best to emphasize your strengths. The major disadvantage of the functional résumé is that some employers distrust it, mainly because it's different. Even in a functional résumé, it's a good idea to include a brief employment history.

The Combination Résumé

As its name suggests, this résumé combines the features of the chronological résumé and the functional résumé. As in the functional résumé, you use skills and accomplishments as the major headings, but within these headings, you list the relevant information in a chronological sequence. The major advantage of a combination résumé is that you can present a more complete picture of yourself. The major disadvantage is that it is harder to organize. It may also be difficult to restrict to the maximum two pages.

Case Study

Marcel Bruneau has just finished his first year of Computer Sciences at the University of Lethbridge and needs a full-time summer job that could convert to part-time hours for the rest of the year. In the local paper, there were two very different opportunities that closely matched his skills and interests.

> Qualified lifeguards and instructors for summer. Drop resume @ Queen Elizabeth Pool, 912 Garner Street.

> Franco's on Victoria Trail now hiring servers & bartenders, f/t & p/t. Apply: 140 Victoria Trail.

Because Marcel had learned the importance of targeting a résumé toward the type of job offered, he knew he would have to submit a different version for each position. His work and volunteer history for the past four summers was consistent, so he chose the chronological format for both submissions.

16b Sample Chronological Résumé I

MARCEL BRUNEAU
#302, 1021 Legion Ave.
Lethbridge, AB T2X 1Y2
Ph: (555) 325-1191   Fax: (555) 325-6686

Objective: Challenging summer employment as a
              lifeguard with an opportunity to use
              my teamwork and pool-side skills, and
              potential for ongoing part-time work
              in the fall

Employment   Sr. Lifeguard, Borden Park Pool,
             Medicine Hat

Experience: June–August, 1998

   Responsibilities
   • Performed lifeguard duties, pool side and on
     spray deck
   • Maintained pumps and gauges for pool
   • Assigned shifts to other lifeguard staff

   Accomplishments
   • Created and implemented a Summer Fun program
     for 7- to 10-year-olds
   • Received Employee of the Summer award from
     pool management

   Jr. Lifeguard, Camp Winatoo, Waterton Lakes
   July and August, 1997

   Responsibilities
   • Supervised campers during free swim time
   • Taught swimming and water sports
   • Recorded inventory nightly of all life jackets
     and swim accessories

   Accomplishments
   • Learned teamwork skills
   • Placed second in the Most Helpful Staff
     contest

Volunteer Swimming Assistant, Camp Winatoo,
Waterton Lakes
July and August, 1995 and 1996

Responsibilities
* Assisted lifeguard staff with all water
  activities
* Supervised one cabin at night
* Conducted indoor games during rainy weather

Accomplishments
* Discovered a talent for working with children
* Helped plan and present a talent show for
  Parents' Day

Education: Completed first year of Computer
            Sciences at University of Lethbridge
            Achieved certification in National
            Lifeguard Service, AEC First Aid and
            CPR Basic Rescuer

References: Mr. Anthony Chai, Supervisor
            Borden Park Pool
            293 - 52 Street
            Medicine Hat, AB   T1Y 0K2
            (555) 896-2731

            Mrs. Mary Bradshaw, Director
            Camp Winatoo
            Box 42
            Waterton Lakes, AB   T6J 1X3
            (555) 765-3456

            Mr. Frank Holbright, Professor
            Computer Sciences Department
            University of Lethbridge
            10 University Avenue
            Lethbridge, AB   T3Z 5J4
            (555) 229-3314

*Sample
Chronological
Résumé*

16c Sample Chronological Resume II

MARCEL BRUNEAU
#302, 1021 Legion Ave.
Lethbridge, AB T2X 1Y2
Ph: (555) 325-1191   Fax: (555) 325-6686

Objective: Challenging full-time summer
             employment as a waiter in the food
             industry with an opportunity to use my
             hospitality and teamwork skills, and
             potential for ongoing part-time work
             in the fall.

Employment   Waiter, Earl's Restaurant, Lethbridge

Experience: October 1998-March 1999

Responsibilities
- Managed a 10-table section, took customer orders, served food and cleared tables
- Relieved host/hostess for breaks
- Completed cash and credit card transactions

Accomplishments
- Suggested and designed a Winter Food Fair menu insert
- Received Employee of the Month award for December

Volunteer Swimming Assistant, Camp Winatoo, Waterton Lakes
July and August, 1995 and 1996

Responsibilities
- Assisted kitchen staff with meal set-up and service when water activities finished
- Kept juice containers and snack trays filled

Accomplishments
- Learned proper sanitation procedures
- Helped plan the menu for Parents' Day
- Learned teamwork skills
- Placed second in the Most Helpful Staff contest

```
Education:    Completed first year of Computer
              Sciences at University of Lethbridge
              Achieved certification in AEC First
              Aid and CPR Basic Rescuer


References:   Ms. Belva Drucker, Manager
              Earl's Restaurant
              653 Plains Road
              Lethbridge, AB T2X 1K3
              (555) 635-1121

              Mrs. Mary Bradshaw, Director
              Camp Winatoo
              Box 42
              Waterton Lakes, AB T6J 1X3
              (555) 765-3456

              Mr. Frank Holbright, Professor
              Computer Sciences Department
              University of Lethbridge
              10 University Avenue
              Lethbridge, AB T3Z 5J4
              (555) 229-3314
```

16d Sample Functional Résumé

A social worker changing jobs might prepare a résumé like this
one.

```
WILLIAM FORREST
1235 Elm Street
Halifax, NS    B3M 3J6

Ph: (555) 663-7854  Fax: (555) 663-7725
email: wforrest@iconn.com

Objective:    Personnel manager in a major retail
              firm where problem-solving,
              communication, and administrative
              skills would be assets.
```

Communication
Skills:
- Set up and provided editorial assistance for an information newsletter for people on welfare
  Results: Achieved a readership of over 10,000 in Halifax area

- Delivered talks and lectures on family problems, organizational dynamics, and liaisons with government agencies
  Results: Regarded as an interesting and informative speaker

- Wrote proposals for special projects requiring provincial government funding
  Results: Succeeded in securing an annual grant of $30,000 for special services to runaway teens

Administrative
Skills:
- Set up and directed a special project to assist runaway teenagers
  Results: Provided assistance to over 100 young people and their families

- Hired, supervised and assisted recent social work graduates in their first year of employment
  Results: Improved the efficiency and effectiveness of all employees

Employment
Highlights: Worked with a caseload of 150 families for five years. Counselled and provided practical assistance to parents and children. Had the reputation of offering skilled assistance to families in economic and emotional crisis.

Education: Bachelor of Social Work (University of Calgary, 1990)

Bachelor of Arts (major in sociology and English, Mount St. Vincent, 1986)

Certificates from workshops in group dynamics, crisis intervention, and effective management skills

```
Activities:     President, Toastmasters Club, 1990,
                92-94; member 1988-present

                Treasurer, Mount Pleasant Community
                Assoc., 1986-87

Recognition
and Awards:     Volunteer Service Award, Westside
                United Church, 1991


References:     Dion Harris, Director
                Youth Emergency Shelter
                1310 Glengarry Avenue
                Halifax, NS    B5J 2P4
                (555) 685-4221

                Jean-Paul Sartre, Editor
                No Exit
                Box 1341, Postal Station B
                Halifax, NS    B2N 1J7
                (555) 673-0000

                Alastair MacLeod, Supervisor
                Families in Transition
                123 Boat Harbour Drive
                Halifax, NS    B2R 3P6
                (555) 633-2957
```

16e Sample Combined Résumé

This résumé was prepared by a person returning to the work force.

```
MURIEL LE BLANC
445 - 25 Street
Winnipeg, MN    R3T 2N2

Ph: (555) 335-6529  Fax: (555) 335-7331

OBJECTIVE:    To use my knowledge of the community
              and my communication skills to assume
              administrative responsibilities in the
              Portage and Main Recreation Centre for
              Senior Citizens.
```

SKILLS:
- Able to communicate effectively to build consensus amongst a diverse group of people.
- Can think creatively, build on others' ideas, and follow a plan through from inception to completion.
- Work productively with others to emphasize team strengths and minimize weaknesses.

ACHIEVEMENTS: Initiated and helped to manage a community-based relief day care centre, now in its tenth year of operation.

Voted President of the River Flats Community League, 1992-94
- Coordinated new building project
- Negotiated financing
- Oversaw construction activities

Results: Community League is debt-free with yearly profits and now serves over 500 families per year with a variety of fitness and recreational activities

Participated actively with parents' music support group for Central Junior High, coordinated volunteers for band camps and chaperoned fifty students performing in London, England

Assigned as a returning officer in municipal, provincial and federal elections, 1988-present.

EDUCATION: Awarded Bachelor of Arts degree (major in Fine Arts), University of Manitoba, 1978
Completed university extension courses on retirement planning, alcoholism and the elderly, and recreation for seniors.

```
PERSONAL:        Skilled at budgeting, purchasing, and
                 household management.
                 Experienced in recreational and
                 holiday planning.
                 Interested in opportunities for the
                 retired person.
                 Enjoy hiking, bowling, and playing
                 bridge.

REFERENCES:      Harriet Johnsen, President
                 River Flats Community League
                 105 Fernwood Drive
                 Winnipeg, MN   R4S 3N1
                 Phone: (555) 337-2424

                 Renee Bischof, Coordinator
                 Helping Hands Daycare
                 Sherwood Community Centre
                 Winnipeg, MN   R5J 2E2
                 Phone: (555) 335-1121
```

16f Cover Letters

The cover letter accompanies your résumé when you apply for
a job. Your aim in both pieces of writing is to create enough
interest to secure an interview.

In your letter, you create interest principally by showing how
your qualifications meet the requirements for the position. To
achieve this purpose, you need a clear sense both of what your
qualifications are and of what the job demands. Before you write
your cover letter, then, you need to do two things: prepare your
résumé (see Chapter 14) and find out as much as you can about
the position. Examine the job ad carefully and note any particular
skills and abilities the job demands, such as a driver's licence or
experience with a particular computer program. Talk with anyone
you know who has had a similar job or worked for the same
employer. Then make a matching list of job requirements and
your qualifications so that you can anticipate questions and
provide answers.

You also create interest by the way you present yourself. Your
letter should convey those aspects of your personality that are
most appropriate for the job—your enthusiasm, initiative,
personal warmth, experience in the field. But don't get carried

away; this is a business letter. Choose your words carefully so that you don't sound too gushy, too pushy, or overly casual.

Warning: Proofread carefully. Mistake-ridden letters end up in the trash!

Contents of the Cover Letter

Job application letters usually have three parts:

1. An **introductory paragraph** stating the position you are applying for and indicating where you found out about the job. If possible, establish a connection with the employer by naming the person who suggested you apply. Express enthusiasm for the aims of the organization you want to join.

2. A **summary of your skills**, knowledge, and personal characteristics that are most relevant to the specific requirements for this position. This may take more than one paragraph. (See the sample cover letter, 16g.)

3. A **closing paragraph** referring to your résumé and indicating that you are available for an interview at the employer's convenience.

16g Sample Cover Letter

The sample letter was written in response to an advertisement for summer lifeguards. (See 16b for the applicant's résumé.)

```
#302, 1021 Legion Ave.
Lethbridge, AB    T2X 1Y2
Ph: (555) 325-1191  Fax: (555) 325-6686


May 10, 1999


Ms. Jane Terrachuk
Queen Elizabeth Pool
912 Garner Street
Lethbridge, AB   T2X 7J6


Dear Ms. Terrachuk:


Please accept this letter of application for the
position of summer lifeguard which was advertised
```

in the *Lethbridge Times* on May 9, 1999. As you will
see by my attached résumé, I have both experience
and the necessary certification for a lifeguard
position. I swim at your pool regularly, and it
appears to be a great place to work.

For the past four summers, I have worked either
at the lake or the pool in a variety of positions,
with a steady progression from volunteer swimming
assistant to senior lifeguard. The Borden Park Pool
in Medicine Hat, one of the busiest in Alberta,
proved to be a great challenge last summer. Not
only was I in charge of staff scheduling and
rotation, but in addition to my lifeguard duties I
had to learn more about pool chemicals, maintenance
and sanitation.

Working as a lifeguard has been very rewarding
over the years. I particularly enjoy teaching the
kids water safety and water sports.

If you are looking for a conscientious and
enthusiastic person to work with your swimmers,
then I look forward to an opportunity to discuss
this position further. I can be available for an
interview at your convenience. Please call or fax
me at one of the above numbers.

Yours truly,

Marcel Bruneau

Marcel Bruneau
Enc.

16h Letters of Recommendation

In addition to your résumé and cover letter, it's a good idea to
include one or two letters of recommendation. If you make a
habit of collecting them when you leave a job or complete a
course, they will be readily available as attachments.

Most supervisors, employers, and teachers will need to know
what type of letter you want—a basic character reference, for
example, or highlights of abilities and successes. Be clear about
this before you ask them. If appropriate, remind them of your
past contributions and any positive results. Most of the time
you'll be able to call the people you want letters from, especially

those who are local. For long-distance communication, it's better to write a letter of request.

16i Sample Letter of Request

The following sample demonstrates the basic format for this kind of request.

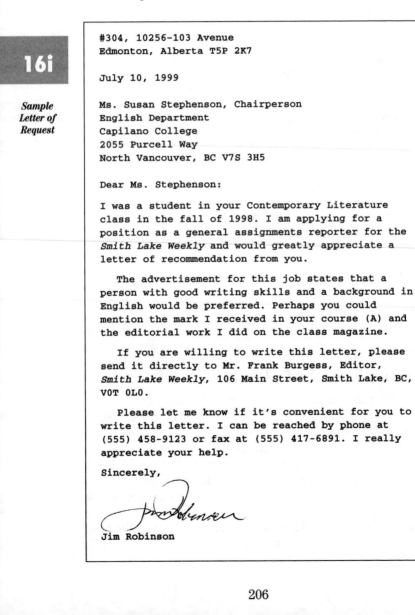

```
#304, 10256-103 Avenue
Edmonton, Alberta T5P 2K7

July 10, 1999

Ms. Susan Stephenson, Chairperson
English Department
Capilano College
2055 Purcell Way
North Vancouver, BC V7S 3H5

Dear Ms. Stephenson:

I was a student in your Contemporary Literature
class in the fall of 1998. I am applying for a
position as a general assignments reporter for the
Smith Lake Weekly and would greatly appreciate a
letter of recommendation from you.

    The advertisement for this job states that a
person with good writing skills and a background in
English would be preferred. Perhaps you could
mention the mark I received in your course (A) and
the editorial work I did on the class magazine.

    If you are willing to write this letter, please
send it directly to Mr. Frank Burgess, Editor,
Smith Lake Weekly, 106 Main Street, Smith Lake, BC,
V0T 0L0.

    Please let me know if it's convenient for you to
write this letter. I can be reached by phone at
(555) 458-9123 or fax at (555) 417-6891. I really
appreciate your help.

Sincerely,


Jim Robinson
```

- Punctuation Guide—from NASA's *A Handbook for Technical Writers and Editors*

  sti.larc.nasa.gov/html/Chapt3/Chapt3-TOC.html

- Capitalization Guide—from NASA's *A Handbook for Technical Writers and Editors*

  sti.larc.nasa.gov/html/Chapt3/Chapt3-TOC.html

- Online Careers Resources—a collection of sources of information about résumé writing, interview skills, success in the workplace, rights in the workplace, and Canadian career and job search centres

  www.cln.org

- The Rensselaer Writing Centre offers a variety of online handouts including information on résumés and cover letters.

  www.rpi.edu/dept/llc/writecenter/web/handouts.html

- Business and Technical Writing Links from the Purdue OWL

  owl.english.purdue.edu/writers/introduction.html

- The Riley Guide: Employment Opportunities and Job Resources on the Internet

  www.rileyguide.com

Part 5

WRITING WITH STYLE

CHECKLIST

Improving Your Style and Proofreading

	OK	NEEDS WORK
1. Is your **word choice** appropriate and effective for your purpose and audience?	☐	☐
2. Have you used **quotations and other devices** to enliven your writing?	☐	☐
3. Have you varied **sentence patterns and sentence length** effectively?	☐	☐
4. Have you used **transitional devices** to provide continuity?	☐	☐
5. Is your writing **concise**?	☐	☐
6. Have you corrected errors in a. **sentence structure**? (Chapter 15) b. the use of **modifiers**? (Chapter 19) c. the use of **verbs**? (Chapter 20) d. the use of **pronouns**? (Chapter 21)	☐	☐
7. Have you corrected errors in a. **punctuation**? (Chapter 22a–h) b. **spelling** and related matters? (Chapter 22i–k) c. **word usage**? (Chapter 22l)	☐	☐

Chapter 17

Improving Your Style

Style is the result of all the conscious and unconscious choices you make as you write, including choices about the words you use, the kinds of sentences you construct, the length and structure of your paragraphs. So you already have a style—in fact, you likely have many styles you shift among as you write for different purposes and audiences.

But perhaps you would like your writing to be more vivid or more concise, or to flow more smoothly. If so, you will find numerous suggestions below.

17a Improving Your Word Choice

Some writers use informal language in writing that requires more formal diction. Others adopt a formal vocabulary so completely that their writing becomes stilted. Still others coast along, using words that are safe but dull. Paying attention to the words you use will help you remedy these problems.

Understanding **levels of language** will help you choose words appropriate for your purpose and audience. Consider these words meaning *poor*:

Formal	Standard	Informal

impecunious, destitute, poverty-stricken, poor, hard up, broke, busted.

These words illustrate what we mean by levels of language, with "big words" such as *impecunious* and *destitute* at the formal end of the scale; colloquial and slang terms such as *hard up* and *busted* at the informal end; and the standard vocabulary of public writing and speaking in the middle (*poverty-stricken, poor*). Most of the words you use in writing for college or university should come from a standard vocabulary. You will find suggestions below about when and how to use formal and informal language.

17b Choosing Appropriate Language: Formal Writing

When you are writing academic essays, reports, and business letters, keep these suggestions about word choice in mind.

1. *Aim for a serious, knowledgeable, and businesslike tone, but avoid sounding stuffy or pompous.*
In general, choose standard words rather than more formal terms (*need* rather than *necessity*, *uses* rather than *utilizes*). Emphasize key points by selecting words from the slightly formal range (*poverty-stricken* or *destitute*, but not *impecunious*).

2. *Use specialized terms only when necessary.*
Part of what you learn when you study psychology, sociology, and other academic disciplines is the language that specialists in the field use in talking and writing to other specialists. In an essay discussing Freud's theory of the unconscious, for example, you would use Freud's terms *id*, *ego*, and *superego*. There are no other words that would precisely convey the meaning of these concepts.

But when a specialized vocabulary is used inappropriately, it is called *jargon*. Jargon obscures meaning rather than making meaning more precise. When jargon combines with an unnecessarily formal vocabulary, writing can become almost unintelligible, as in the examples below.

NOT   As the precepts of individual psychology are ultimately reflected in social psychology, the psychic impairment experienced by the student as part of the educational process will be augmented within the context of the social environment.

BUT   Since students carry their perceptions of themselves into the larger social world, any damage to their self-esteem will become more severe when they leave school.

NOT   Management will access the input of all interested parties, prioritize their responses, and introduce modifications to the terms of the proposal accordingly.

The manager will ask all interested parties for their reactions to the proposal, review their responses, and make changes accordingly.

3. *Avoid slang and colloquial expressions.*

many rather than *a lot of*
an acquaintance rather than *a guy I know*

4. *Avoid clichés.*

Clichés serve a useful purpose in spoken language, but in formal writing they may suggest that the writer is treating the subject superficially, as in this example:

> Undoubtedly, there is pressure for change from within Iraq. The number may be small but every little bit helps.

5. *Use contractions sparingly.*

Some readers object to contractions in formal writing; others don't. If you use an occasional contraction to keep from sounding too stiff, make sure you use the apostrophe correctly (see Apostrophes, 22h).

6. *Use **I** and **you** sparingly.*

Don't distract your readers from your subject by constant references to yourself: *I think, I feel, I believe, it seems to me that.* When it is appropriate to use *I,* use it rather than substituting *one* or *this writer.*

NOT

It seems to me that this anthology is unsuitable for the high school curriculum.

NOT

In the opinion of this writer, this anthology is unsuitable for the high school curriculum.

BUT

This anthology is unsuitable for the high school curriculum.

OR

Although other reviewers consider this anthology suitable for the high school curriculum, I disagree.

Similarly, avoid using *you* in formal writing to mean *people in general.*

17b

Choosing Appropriate Language: Formal Writing

NOT	The university's marking system can be frustrating when all of your professors have their own scale within the scale.
BUT	The university's marking system can be frustrating when professors have their own scale within the scale.

Exercise 17.1

Comment briefly on the effect of jargon and big words in the following paragraph, taken from a research paper on the back-to-basics movement in education. Then rewrite the paragraph in simpler, more concrete language.

> The teacher I interviewed perceived her role as a socializing agent with a humanistic approach. She added that although students lacked skills to handle grade five curriculum, her priority was to allow student-directed activities in a safe environment free of negative labelling. Correcting exams and clerical tasks presented a strain on her role. She felt psychology was the most beneficial course she had taken at university: she taught many children experiencing stress from broken families or families who did not share time.

Exercise 17.2

Underline inappropriate word choices in the following paragraph, adapted from a research paper on impaired driving. Then rewrite the paragraph so that the diction is more appropriate for the subject and audience.

> Kathy Stechert's research on drunk driving (1984) has suggested some prevention techniques that you should consider when entertaining guests in your home: serve lots of food; provide non-alcoholic beverages; don't pressure guests to drink; water down drinks when guys are consuming too much alcohol. Don't let guests leave the house if they're tanked; ask them to wait until they've sobered up or to stay overnight. If they make a fuss and insist on leaving, drive them home. It is really amazing that many people don't think about what could happen after guests leave the party. It doesn't take a genius to see that these measures would help reduce drunk driving.

17b

*Choose
Appropriate
Language:
Formal
Writing*

17c Choosing Appropriate Language: Informal Writing

For personal and persuasive writing intended for a general audience, follow these guidelines.

1. ***Try for the friendly, engaged tone of one person talking to another.***
That means choosing most of your words from the standard to slightly informal range (*poor, hard up*). Choose short, common words over longer synonyms.

possess=own, have	automobile=car
retain=keep	residence=house
purchase=buy	difficulties=troubles

2. ***Use more formal words to create suggestive images, humour or satire, and subtle shades of meaning.***

the undulations of the wheat
the writer was lionized in London, lampooned in L.A.
serpentine streets

3. ***Choose concrete nouns over abstract nouns and specific nouns over general nouns.***

Abstract nouns name qualities (*friendship, heroism*) or concepts (*the state, conservatism*). **Concrete nouns** name things we can perceive through our senses (*your friend, the brain*). **General nouns** apply to a class of things (*adolescents, buildings*) rather than to a single, specific thing (*the teenager who works at The Bay, the CN Tower*). Abstract and general nouns keep your reader at a distance.

4. ***Use first- and second-person pronouns (I, you), where appropriate, to establish a personal relationship with your reader.***

5. ***Use occasional contractions, colloquial expressions, or slang terms, if appropriate to your subject and audience.***

6. *Choose* active verbs *over* state-of-being verbs *and* verbs in the passive voice.

By changing **state-of-being**, or **linking** verbs (*is, seems, exists, has, contains, feels*) to active verbs, you can often make a vague general statement into a precise, vivid image.

NOT	She *has* short brown hair. Her face is round.
BUT	Her short brown hair *cups* her round face.
NOT	I *felt* angry.
BUT	I *throbbed* with anger.
OR	I *stalked* out of the room.

Verbs in the **passive voice** may take the energy out of your writing:

NOT	The winning goal was scored by me.
BUT	I scored the winning goal.

To see how changing the diction can improve a piece of writing, compare the following versions of a paragraph on the perils of sailing. In the first, the formal language makes the danger seem remote.

Sample Draft Paragraph

Of course there are those who endure the elements as necessitated to earn a living. Traditionally they are the men of the sea. Sailors maintain many fears in terms of the elements. For instance, atmospheric electricity playing around the mast might cause a fire. To the sailor's peril, ice can cover the rigging, leaving the ship top-heavy and in danger of "turtling." Thrashing waves and Titanic swells can consume both craft and crew.

In the revised paragraph, the simpler language, active verbs, and concrete nouns create a vivid image of a ship in danger.

Sample Revised Paragraph

Sailors have traditionally earned their living by enduring the dangers of the elements. Sailors fear the blue haze of St. Elmo's fire encircling the mast, and its acrid smell of burning. They fear the surge that rises twelve metres above the mizzen and the waves that slam the hull from every direction. The wind, as it sings through the stays, charts a new course without aid of a compass, without earthly reason. But at no time is a sailor's job so perilous as when the wind chill plunges the mercury to minus thirty-five and droplets of mist condense on the supercooled rigging. Then layer upon layer of ice forms. When an ice-laden ship gets top-heavy, no amount of praying will keep it afloat. The captain's call goes out: "The gyros are toppling."

—*Chris Paterson*

Exercise 17.3

Underline word choices in the following paragraph that you find ineffective for a personal essay. Then rewrite the paragraph using more vivid language.

Adding Interest

Chuck is, simply put, a mean person. One would not say that he is a sadist, exactly. He is not of the character to pull the wings off flies, albeit he does on occasion step on ant hills. He merely loves practical jokes—mean-spirited practical jokes. One time a small, plastic-wrapped packet of cloves was left by Chuck on the desk of a fellow student named Ramona. Attached to the packet with tape was a note that read, "Cloves make an effective breath freshener." Ramona was, with justification, mortified and offended. On other occasions sample bottles of deodorant and acne medication have been left on classmates' desks. One could say that these tactics work to undermine a person's self-confidence. Chuck also has an inconsiderate mouth. In the recent past, on the day we were being photographed for the yearbook, Jerry Johnson wore a new suit. Hiding behind his most sincere smile, Chuck told Jerry, "Jer, my man, that suit really suits you, ha, ha. I donated one just like it to the Sally Ann last week." I used to laugh at Chuck's peccadilloes, until this morning. As we were walking out of math class, the teacher directly behind us, that insensitive Chuck enunciated clearly, "Ken, I wish you would not say those things about Mr. Mueller. I think he is a fine teacher." I am planning how to asphyxiate Chuck in his sleep. The deed will definitely be done with malice aforethought.

17d Adding Interest

Enliven your writing by using quotations and other kinds of allusions, dialogue, and figurative language.

Quotations

Use familiar quotations—proverbs, lines from songs, advertising slogans, sayings of famous people, well-known bits of poetry and prose—to make an emotional appeal and to create a sense of shared experience. You don't need to give complete bibliographical information for quotations used in passing, but do put them in quotation marks and identify the source.

> When you are backpacking through Europe, your money will start to dwindle and you will feel moments of fear and desperation. As *The Hitchhiker's Guide to the Galaxy* so wisely advises, "Don't panic."
>
> —*Lori Yanish*

Allusions

An allusion is a casual reference to a figure, event, or document from history, literature, mythology, popular culture, or religion. Allusions help to establish your authority as a writer by indicating the breadth of your knowledge or experience. They may also have a strong emotional impact because they evoke shared experiences.

> Like Caesar, he came, he saw, he restored order where confusion reigned. —*Chris Carleton*
>
> Her hopes, like Miss Havisham's wedding cake, had been eaten away. —*Chris Carleton*
>
> I suspected life at Stephanie's house might be just like life at Dick and Jane's. —*Suzanne Cook*

Dialogue

Use dialogue for dramatic effect. Direct speech allows you to show what happened rather than merely to tell the story. It also gives variety to your writing by introducing other voices.

> My parents were glued to a small black and white television in room #107. I wandered into the room and tugged on my mother's skirt until she lifted me into her lap. "Look, it's Neil Armstrong," she said as she directed my gaze at the small screen. "He's about to walk on the moon."
>
> —*Mario Trono*

Figurative Language

Figures of speech create vivid mental images for your readers. Use them to sharpen your descriptions and to convey your attitude toward your subject. Try your hand at the five types illustrated below: simile, metaphor, personification, hyperbole, and irony. Avoid clichés (*dead as a doornail*) and mixed metaphors (*flooded with an iron resolve*).

> A clock, hanging like a sign of doom over my head, showed the lateness of the hour [simile]. —*Terri Dana*

> We are nothing but a jar full of flour beetles, continually eating and reproducing [metaphor]. —*Cheryl Lewis*

> The unruly maple holds fast to her golden gown [personification]. —*Lillian Darling*

> Those demonic savages, those cruel, sadistic, verminous beings, those bus drivers, have persisted in their heinous acts [hyperbole]. —*Amanda Thompson*

> Mr. Simpson would pretend to drive into Miss Merril's little BMW just to terrify her in a neighbourly way [irony]. —*Alex Cheung*

Exercise 17.4

Rewrite a paragraph from one of your personal essays so that it includes two or more of the devices discussed in this section.

17e Improving Your Sentence Structure

Keep your sentence structure consistent with your purpose and audience. To create a conversational tone in personal essays and other informal types of writing, use occasional sentence fragments (see Fragments, 18c) and avoid sentence patterns that require formal punctuation such as semicolons and colons. For more formal writing, avoid using sentence fragments and informal punctuation such as dashes and exclamation marks.

Reading your work out loud, to yourself or to a classmate, will help you determine whether your writing "flows." If in places the rhythm of your sentences seems jerky, monotonous, or at odds with the effect you want to create, try these suggestions.

- Vary your sentence patterns.
- Vary your sentence length.

Sentence Patterns

Most of your sentences are likely to follow the first pattern below, Subject + Verb + Modifier. But if all your sentences fall into this pattern, your writing is likely to become monotonous. You can use the other five sentence patterns to create emphasis, to mimic the process of thinking, or to engage your readers more directly.

The Loose Sentence: Subject + Verb + Modifier

Karen never won, no matter how hard she tried.

This sentence illustrates the most common sentence pattern in English, and the one most easily understood by readers: subject + verb + modifier. Since the most emphatic position in the sentence is normally at the end, this sentence would lead naturally into a discussion of how hard Karen tried.

The Periodic Sentence: Modifier + Subject + Verb

No matter how hard she tried, Karen never won.

Because we have to wait for the subject and verb, this sentence pattern creates interest and suspense. It also throws heavy emphasis upon Karen's inability to win, and thus would prepare readers for a discussion of the reasons for her lack of success or for examples of her failures.

The Embedded Sentence: Subject + Modifier + Verb

Karen, no matter how hard she tried, never won.

Here subject and verb are separated by a lengthy modifier. Because this sentence pattern slows the reader down, it effectively imitates the process of thinking through a problem or situation. The modifier also shifts the emphasis to the beginning of the sentence. As readers, we might therefore expect to explore less obvious aspects of Karen's personality or background that would account for her lack of success.

Sentences Employing Parallelism

There are two ways to use parallelism in sentences.

- Join two or more closely related clauses with a coordinate conjunction or semicolon. (This pattern is also called a **balanced construction.**)

You can allow your anxieties to rob you of sleep and satisfaction, or you can plan your time wisely and then enjoy your free time thoroughly.

—Wendy Amy

- Arrange a series of words, phrases, or clauses in order of increasing importance.

Friends listen to you babble, tell you honest opinions when you prefer lies but need the truth, tell you *I told you so* at annoying times, defend your reputation from others, and generally mother, father, grandparent, and sibling (brother or sister) you.

—Amanda Thompson

Rhetorical Questions

How many times have you waited in the rain or snow for a bus that is ten minutes late? How many times has a surly bus driver snapped an answer to your innocent question? How many times have you stood for half an hour in a bus crammed with people?

—Cheryl Lewis

Uncommon Constructions

- Use paired conjunctions (*both/and, neither/nor, not only/ but also*) to link ideas.

Neither fear of failure nor desire for glory drove her to practise that trumpet hour after hour.

- Use a noun clause as the subject.

That he would win the election was certain.

Sentence Length

To create rhythm and emphasize important points, use a combination of short sentences (ten words or fewer), long sentences (thirty words or more), and medium-length sentences.

Short sentences are effective for rendering abrupt actions, giving directions, stating main points, and creating emphasis.

ABRUPT ACTIONS	She stopped.
DIRECTIONS	First stop the bleeding.
MAIN POINTS	One cause of high unemployment is government policy. [Essay topic sentence]

	Safety violations have increased 10 percent over last year. [Report topic sentence]
EMPHASIS	He loved no one.
	The war was over.

Long sentences are effective for expressing continuous action, giving a series of details or examples, and creating a sense of closure.

CONTINUOUS ACTION	After discovering Jack's country address, Algernon assumes his friend's secret identity and poses as wicked Ernest Worthing for his meeting with Cecily, Jack's sheltered young ward; but when they meet for the first time, the worldly, cynical Algernon is momentarily confounded by the sophisticated wit of "little" Cecily.
DETAILS	According to the criteria for student loans, students are considered to be financially independent only if they have no parent, guardian, or sponsor; are married or a single parent; have been out of secondary school for four years; or have been in the labour force for twenty-four months.
CLOSURE	In the final analysis, the losers are not merely those who have been jailed for insider trading, nor the firms whose reputations have been sullied, nor the stockholders who have lost money; the losers are all those who have lost confidence in the integrity of the stock market.

Exercise 17.5

The following paragraph on how actors learn a scene has been reduced to a series of short sentences. Rewrite the paragraph using a variety of sentence lengths and sentence patterns to make it more interesting.

Preparing a scene of a play is time-consuming. It may not appear time-consuming. First the actor reads the scene. The actor becomes familiar with it. Then he or she reads the entire play. The play gives the actor an idea of the events that lead up to the scene. It also gives the actor insights into the characters. The actor then asks questions about the character. The actor asks what the character looks like. The actor asks questions about the character's family. The actor asks what happened in the past. The actor asks these questions until he or she can picture the character. Then the actor goes back to the script. The actor reads each line. The actor is looking for hidden meanings. The actor figures out what is not being said. The actor thinks about what the character wants. The actor thinks about what the character does. The two things may be in conflict. Next the actor plays the scene. He or she does what the script indicates. He or she thinks about what the character really wants. For example, the character may look happy. Inside the character may want to cry. Finally the actor knows the character inside out. Then the actor can memorize the scene.

Exercise 17.6

The following paragraph sounds choppy because it is written almost entirely in short, simple sentences. Rewrite the paragraph to improve the rhythm, using several of the techniques discussed above.

Being your own boss has its down side. I learned the hard way. One summer I decided to go into business for myself. I was tired of my usual part-time jobs. I was tired of the long hours and low pay at the fast-food restaurants and laundries I'd worked at in the past. I decided to strike out on my own. I started up the Domestic Bliss Home and Pet Care Service. It was a house-sitting service for clients away on vacation. I contracted to water plants, take in mail and newspapers, and feed pets. This last responsibility soon proved the most challenging. One of my charges was Baby. Baby was lonely. She was affectionate. She was untrained. She was a twenty-five kilogram Golden Retriever who leapt into my arms with joy every time I stepped into her house. Another of my charges was the Queen of Sheba. She was an overstuffed Persian cat with surgical steel claws capable of slicing through even the thickest denim. Another of my charges was Jabberwocky, the parrot, who had apparently committed to memory *A Complete Dictionary of the Vulgar Tongue*. I spent a month cleaning up accidents and cleaning up litter boxes. I longed to be back in uniform behind a counter serving up chicken and fries. I completed the contracts with my current customers. I said farewell to all my furry and feathered friends. I closed the door on Domestic Bliss.

17f Providing Continuity

As you move from sentence to sentence and paragraph to paragraph, you constantly present your readers with a mixture of known information (terms and ideas you have already introduced) and new information. You can emphasize the continuity between known and new information by using these stylistic devices.

1. ***Repeat key words or phrases.***
Repeating a key word lets your readers know you are still talking about the same subject. If you introduce synonyms, readers may think you are offering new information. For example, in this short paragraph, the many synonyms for *bear* and *hunting partner* distract attention from the main subject, the father.

> Dad was fearless. Once when he and a hunting partner were tracking deer in the foothills, they surprised a wounded bear in a thicket. When the maimed animal knocked his friend down, Dad struck the brute with an empty rifle, distracting the angry monster long enough for his companion to get up and shoot the beast.

The paragraph reads much more smoothly when fewer terms are introduced:

> Dad was fearless. Once when he and a hunting partner were tracking deer in the foothills, they surprised a wounded bear in a thicket. When the bear knocked George down, Dad struck it with an empty rifle, distracting it long enough for George to get up and shoot it.

2. ***Use personal pronouns to refer to subjects you have previously named.***
Pronouns (*he, she, it, they*), like repeated terms, signal known information; in the example above, the pronoun *it* refers to the bear.

3. ***Put the idea you plan to discuss next at the end of the sentence.***
Link sentences by repeating the last word(s) of one sentence at the beginning of the next or by using a synonym and a demonstrative pronoun (*this, that, these, those*).

> British suffragettes challenged the existing system first through marches on Parliament, then through civil disobedience. When civil disobedience failed, they turned to property damage.

British suffragettes challenged the existing system first through marches on Parliament, then through civil disobedience. When these measures failed, they turned to property damage.

4. *Use sentence structure to indicate logical relationships.*
To show that two or more sentences contain equivalent points (as when you are giving a list of reasons, examples, or actions), use **parallel sentence structure** (see 18d).

FIRST SENTENCE	Slander may involve . . .
SECOND SENTENCE	It can also be . . .
THIRD SENTENCE	It is quite often . . .

When you move from a general point to a specific detail, or vice versa, signal the shift by changing your sentence structure.

GENERAL POINT	To be blunt, slander is an ugly, malicious lie about someone. [The sentence begins with an introductory modifier.]
SPECIFIC EXAMPLE	It may involve . . . [The sentence begins with a subject and verb—change in sentence structure.]

5. *Use transitional words and phrases.*
The transitions in the list below can help your readers to understand how you have organized your material, making it easier for them to move from one point to the next in your writing. (The terms listed before each semicolon are less formal; those listed after the semicolon are more formal.) For examples showing the importance of transitions within paragraphs, see Transitions, 4e.

NARRATION	first, next, then, last, as soon as, early the following morning, later that day; in the beginning, in the end
DESCRIPTION	nearer, farther, on the right, on the left, at the top, at the bottom, to the east, beside, between, above; adjacent to
CLASSIFICATION	one group, another kind, a third type; one subcategory, moreover, furthermore
EXAMPLE	for example, for instance; to illustrate, a case in point

PROCESS ANALYSIS	first step, second step, next stage, final stage
SYSTEMS ANALYSIS	one component, another part, the most important element
CAUSAL ANALYSIS	one reason, a final reason, the most important effect, although, because, despite, however; therefore, nevertheless, consequently, as a result, thus, if/then, provided that
DEFINITION	one meaning, another meaning, the most relevant meaning; primary meaning, secondary meaning
COMPARISON	and/also, but/too; in comparison, in contrast, similarly; just as/so too, not only/but also, neither/nor
EVALUATION	a practical advantage, a logical inconsistency, another legal aspect, from a moral perspective, an aesthetic weakness

If you compare the following paragraphs, you will see how these devices for achieving continuity can dramatically increase the flow of your writing. The material is from a personal essay on the writer's experiences with judo.

Sample Draft Paragraph

Bullies always have their little rituals. They go through a talking phase with a new kid who might be tough. If they aren't sure, they leave subtle threats and go away. After this little talk they hammer an opponent who reveals a weakness. They try to make friends with the "mark" who appears too formidable. I was skinny and scared, and so bullies always beat me up.

Sample Revised Paragraph

When bullies encounter a "mark" who might be tough, they go through little rituals. First they talk to him. If this talk reveals a weakness in their opponent, they hammer him. If they still aren't sure, they leave subtle threats and go away. If he appears too formidable, they make friendship gestures. But when the new kid is skinny and scared, like me, there is no ritual. It's all fists.

—*Dan Martin*

Exercise 17.7

Write a paragraph describing one of the items below. Be sure to use transitional devices that allow your reader to visualize spatial relationships between the things you describe.

- a room where you live or work
- the view from your window
- a painting
- a favourite place

Exercise 17.8

Improve the following paragraph by adding transitions and revising sentences to show how the events are related in time.

> For fifteen years Boots, our barn cat, and Alice, our spaniel, lived together outside, inseparable friends. Alice died. Boots was inconsolable. We moved Boots inside the house. We rarely saw her. She slept all day and sneaked to her food dish at night. My husband was making his lunch. He accidentally dropped a piece of cheese. Boots was nearby. Boots dove in and devoured it. The next morning my husband had the cheese in his hand. Boots started talking cat language. The morning ritual continued. Boots was trained to wait for her cheese until my husband was sipping his morning coffee. She followed him everywhere, including the bathroom. Boots began to make friends with the rest of the family. She is over her depression.—
> *Adapted from an essay by Darcy Colwell.*

17f

*Providing
Continuity*

Exercise 17.9

Improve the following analysis paragraph by adding transitions and revising sentences to show the cause-and-effect relationship between ideas.

> There are a number of reasons for the rise in customer complaints against our department store. We have not been living up to our promises. We have a sale. Usually several items advertised in our flyers remain on back order. Often the selection of available items is very poor. Customers complain that the store is poorly laid out. Aisles are blocked by overflowing display tables and unpacked boxes. Trying to get from one department to another becomes an exercise in frustration. Finding particular merchandise is difficult. Customers have to wrestle with clothes jammed onto racks or struggle with linens stuffed into shelves. The store is chronically understaffed. Service is slow and at times nonexistent. Customers are annoyed at having to wait too long for assistance and at standing in crowded lines at sales counters. We must solve these problems as quickly as possible.

17g Being Concise

In good writing, every word counts. Pruning the deadwood—words, phrases, and sentences that are not essential to your purpose—clarifies your meaning and makes your writing easier to read.

To make sure that every word counts, many writers set a goal of cutting their writing by 10 percent. If you tend to be wordy, you may want to set your goal higher. Here are four practical suggestions.

1. *Eliminate unnecessary repetition of words and ideas.*

Often whole sentences merely repeat a previous point.

REPETITIOUS PHRASE	Formerly women's clothes were much more restrictive in the past.
REVISED	Women's clothes were much more restrictive in the past.
REPETITIOUS SENTENCES	Macbeth seems shaken by the witches' announcement that he will become king. He is uneasy when they tell him he is destined to gain the throne.
REVISED	Macbeth seems shaken by the witches' announcement that he will become king.

2. *Reduce phrases, clauses, and sentences.*

Reduce phrases to single words (*in a short time* = *shortly; a lot of* = *many* or *much; at this point in time* = *now*).

Reduce clauses beginning with *that, which,* or *who* to words or phrases.

NOT	the person who owns the store
BUT	the store owner
NOT	at the position that I was assigned
BUT	at my position
NOT	*School Violence,* which is another study of this problem
BUT	*School Violence,* another study of this problem

228

NOT	The magazine is designed for women who are from 25 to 50 years of age.
BUT	The magazine is designed for women aged 25 to 50.

3. *Rewrite wordy constructions.*

NOT	It is a fact that the car has been stolen.
BUT	The car has been stolen.
NOT	What this means is that profits are down.
BUT	This means that profits are down.

4. *Eliminate unnecessary modifiers.*

WORDY	The small, sporty-looking red car just left us in the dust.
BETTER	The red sportscar left us in the dust.

17g

Being Concise

To see how being concise can make your meaning clearer, consider these two versions of a paragraph from an essay on the importance of options in the school curriculum.

Sample Draft Paragraph

There are a lot of other courses that are very important to children growing up today. Courses such as home economics, industrial education, accounting, and computer courses help children function better in the outside world—whether in the job market or in the home. These courses enable the children to be able to learn about a wide variety of things. Students today learn about health and nutrition, they learn about first aid, how to look after a home (boys as well as girls), they learn how to look after a vehicle, and even how to budget themselves and to do their own taxes. [106 words]

Sample Revised Paragraph

Many other courses are also important to today's adolescents. Courses such as home economics, industrial education, accounting, and computer science help them function better in the home as well as in the job market. These courses enable students to learn about health and nutrition, first aid, and home maintenance. Students also learn how to look after a vehicle, how to budget, and how to do their own taxes. [69 words]

Exercise 17.10

Underline unnecessary words, phrases, and sentences. Then rewrite the paragraph in 200 words or fewer. Do not leave out any ideas.

At the base of the argument for an education based on facts lies a dangerous assumption: that a person with a good grasp of general knowledge has the will and the means to examine information critically to determine whether it is true and valid. Realistically, most people who get through school by memorizing information lack either the ability to think critically or the desire to think critically. A simple science fair project conducted by a junior high school student exposes people's failure to think critically and make reasoned judgments. At the Greater Idaho Falls Science Fair in April 1997, the student presented a presentation about the dangers of dihydrogen monoxide. The student asked people to sign a petition to have the chemical banned because of its harmful effects. The harmful effects included the statements that "accidental inhalation can cause death" and that dihydrogen monoxide "is a major component of acid rain." Of fifty people asked, forty-three supported elimination of the chemical, six people were undecided, and one person recognized that dihydrogen monoxide is the chemical term for H_2O. That is, dihydrogen monoxide is water. Clearly, these people did not analyze the situation effectively. The mental habits that enable people to make sound judgments are not inherent. Educators cannot expect that an individual will use his mind to reason, analyze, and make sound judgments simply because that person has a solid base of facts and knowledge. [235 words]

Exercise 17.11

Using the Checklist for Improving Your Style (p. 210) and the specific suggestions in this chapter as a guide, evaluate the stylistic strengths and weaknesses of the following paragraph.

As I returned home I could not stop thinking about Jane. She had done nothing unusual during the interview. In fact, if I had not read her chart she would have appeared like the babysitter next door, except smarter. I felt that, for my own peace of mind and the safety of society, Jane should be wearing a tattoo on her forehead that said "psychopath." Inside I felt entirely unclean. The only emotion that came through clearly was fear. She was not someone who made me feel afraid for my personal safety, but she made me feel afraid for the world. She challenged the way I had categorized the world up until then. Jane was a woman with no mental illness, no deficits of intelligence or social skills, and apparently no conscience. She tortured and killed toddlers. She terrified me.

Exercise 17.12

Evaluate the stylistic strengths and weaknesses of two paragraphs of your own writing: one from an academic essay and one from a less formal piece. Then revise the paragraphs.

Being
Concise

Chapter 18

Proofreading: Sentence Structure

18a Proofreading Strategies

Proofreading involves looking for errors in sentence structure, grammar, spelling, and punctuation. Don't skip this last step, even if you are pressed for time or simply tired of a piece of writing. Awkward, wordy sentences and slips in grammar or spelling can bring an A paper down to a B, or a D paper down to an F. Spelling errors in a résumé or cover letter can mean that you are not asked for an interview. Wordy writing in a report might mean that your carefully thought-out recommendations are ignored. You will assure your reader of your credibility and competence if you take the time to give your writing a final polish.

To locate the rough spots in your writing, try these strategies:

- Leave your paper for at least a day. You will then be able to see what you actually wrote more clearly.

- Read your paper aloud either to yourself or to a friend. Revise awkward or unclear sentences.

- Read your paper backwards, sentence by sentence. This strategy is especially good for highlighting sentence fragments and spelling errors.

- Recheck the format of your letter, report, or essay using the guidelines in Appendix C.

18b Comma Splice

When you're proofreading for errors in sentence structure, be especially careful to watch for **comma splices**. This error, sometimes called a *comma fault*, occurs when two main clauses are joined by only a comma.

The wind whipped up dead leaves in the yard, violent drops of rain beat against the ground.

Recognizing Comma Splices

1. *Figure out whether your sentence contains two or more clauses.*

You can do this if you understand the difference between a clause and a phrase. A **clause** is a group of words with a subject and a verb.

she waved at the helicopter
when *she waved* at the helicopter

A **phrase** is a group of words without a subject and a verb.

after waving at the helicopter
to wave at the helicopter
in the sky overhead

Exercise 18.1

Underline the clause(s) in each of the following sentences:

1. To prove yourhypothesis, you must not falsify data or ignore contradictory evidence.

2. Clarence cut the questioning short with a caustic remark and a withering glance.

3. Furrowing her brow in concentration, Kathryn wound up for the pitch.

4. At the end of the project, Govind admired his handiwork: a two-storey birdhouse with a railed porch and cedar roof.

5. After pulling the pen from his pocket, Hans noticed a large blue stain on his shirt front.

2. *Figure out whether the clauses are main clauses or subordinate clauses.*

A **main clause** can stand alone as an independent sentence.

Marta stared in disbelief.

A **subordinate clause** cannot stand alone.

While Marta stared in disbelief

18b

Comma Splice

Adverbial subordinate clauses begin with subordinate conjunctions (*after, during, while, when, if, unless, until, because, although*).

Exercise 18.2

Underline the main clause(s) in each of the following sentences.

1. When I worked as a cashier in a local supermarket, I dreaded the monthly special on quarter chicken legs.

2. The packages, each containing three legs oozing raw chicken juices and blood, were poorly sealed.

3. As a result, the juices leaked all over the conveyor belt and all over my hands as I scanned and packed the chicken.

4. Rightly concerned about contamination, I sanitized the belt and my hands with antibacterial cleanser after each order.

5. Despite my best efforts to rid myself of the smell of chicken, when I returned home after my shift, my dog would practically knock me to the ground in his efforts to "kiss" me hello.

3. *If the sentence contains two main clauses, are they joined by only a comma?*

If so, the sentence contains a comma splice.

Be especially careful to avoid comma splices when a main clause is followed by a subordinate clause and another main clause.

COMMA SPLICE	Tim completed a four-year degree in nursing, when he graduated, however, there were no jobs.
REVISED	Tim completed a four-year degree in nursing; when he graduated, however, there were no jobs.

Correcting Comma Splices

There are six ways to correct a comma splice.

1. *Use a period to separate the two clauses.*

COMMA SPLICE	An enormous wave hit the boat, all those on deck were swept overboard.

REVISED	An enormous wave hit the boat. All those on deck were swept overboard.

2. *Use a semicolon to join the two clauses if they contain closely related ideas.*

COMMA SPLICE	Fish stocks have declined in the last ten years, fishing licences are now difficult to obtain.
REVISED	Fish stocks have declined in the last ten years; fishing licences are now difficult to obtain.

3. *Use a colon to join the two clauses if the second clause explains, expands, or emphasizes the first.*

COMMA SPLICE	After six months of treatment, Louisa was feeling much better, she now eagerly anticipated returning to school.
REVISED	After six months of treatment, Louisa was feeling much better: she now eagerly anticipated returning to school.

4. *Use a semicolon and a conjunctive adverb, such as* moreover, however, therefore, thus, *or then to join the two clauses.*

COMMA SPLICE	Sean drifted out of high school without a diploma, he now has the job of his dreams.
REVISED	Sean drifted out of high school without a diploma; however, he now has the job of his dreams.

5. *Use a comma and coordinate conjunction (and, but, or, nor, yet, so, for) to join the two clauses.*

COMMA SPLICE	Peering through the darkness, they could see the lights of the settlement, they struggled onward.
REVISED	Peering through the darkness, they could see the lights of the settlement, so they struggled onward.

6. ***Change one of the main clauses into a subordinate clause.*** Put a comma after the subordinate clause if it comes first in the sentence.

COMMA SPLICE   You need more rest, you will get sick.

REVISED   If you don't get more rest, you will get sick.

Exercise 18.3

Revise the following sentences to eliminate all comma splices. Try a number of revision methods.

1. A loud crackling sound alerted Gerta to the fact that she had left the foil cover on the dish, both the meal and the microwave oven were ruined.

2. Alicia offered to replace my shift, when I called to confirm the arrangement, however, she had changed her mind.

Comma Splice

3. As we waited in line, we heard Jason's unmistakable braying laugh, we hoped he wouldn't see us before we could disappear into the darkened theatre.

4. Tina groaned in dismay at the error message, she pulled out the massive user guide and started her search for help.

5. Neither team chose Maria, she took her ball and went home.

Exercise 18.4

The following passage is from an essay comparing two science fiction horror movies, *Dr. Jekyll and Mr. Hyde*, made in the 1930s, and *The Fly*, made in the 1980s. Revise it to eliminate all comma faults.

> Technology is presented as much less powerful in *Dr. Jekyll and Mr. Hyde* than in *The Fly*. Dr. Jekyll remains recognizably human as Mr. Hyde, Seth Brundle becomes completely non-human by the end of *The Fly*. Of course, Dr. Jekyll remains human-looking partly because special effects were more limited in the 1930s. Thus there are only minor changes in his appearance when he becomes Mr. Hyde, his hair is longer, his eyes are brighter and darker, and his jaw is larger to accommodate his bigger teeth. The focus in this movie is less on

the power of science than on the evil part of Dr. Jekyll's nature when it is acted out by Mr. Hyde. Science is much more threatening in *The Fly*, it has the power to change not only a man's appearance but his species as well. In fact, the focus in *The Fly* is almost entirely on the horrifying changes taking place in Seth Brundle's appearance. By the end of the film, he is spitting teeth into a sink and accidentally tearing off parts of his face, his inner organs are now mostly outside his skeleton. This, the film is telling us, is what happens to scientists who do not know how to control the technology they have created. They can turn the machine on, they cannot predict what it will do or stop it once it has started.

18c Fused Sentences

A **fused sentence**, sometimes called a *run-on sentence*, occurs when two main clauses are written as one with no punctuation between them. The length of the sentence will not tell you whether or not it is fused. A sentence can be quite long without being run-on.

CORRECT   Wendy stopped and glared angrily at the mischievous children as another snowball flew by her head.

On the other hand, some fused sentences are quite short.

FUSED   Open the window I need some fresh air.

You can correct this error by using one of the following techniques:

1. *Separate the two clauses with a period.*

   Open the window. I need some fresh air.

2. *Use a semicolon to join the two clauses.*

   Open the window; I need some fresh air.

3. *Use a comma and a coordinate conjunction to join the two clauses.*

   Open the window, for I need some fresh air.

4. *Change one of the main clauses into a subordinate clause.*

   Open the window because I need some fresh air.

Exercise 18.5

Revise the following to eliminate all fused sentences.

1. Marvinder shifted slowly and repeatedly between forward and reverse she was therefore able to gain traction and move the car out of the mud.

2. Beatrice checked e-mail three times a day she didn't want to miss any messages.

3. Watch where you're going you'll walk into the wall.

4. Without thinking, Delmar opened the side door and was startled by a shrieking siren he had forgotten to deactivate the alarm.

5. Washing four loads of shirts this morning was a chore even more daunting is the prospect of all that ironing.

Fragments

Exercise 18.6

The following paragraph is the conclusion to an essay comparing two science fiction horror movies, *Dr. Jekyll and Mr. Hyde*, made in the 1930s, and *The Fly*, made in the 1980s. Revise it to eliminate all fused sentences.

> The contrasting endings of the two films reveal very clearly the difference fifty years have made in people's attitudes towards scientific technology. In the earlier film, Mr. Hyde becomes Dr. Jekyll again as soon as the potion wears off in the later film Seth Brundle can do nothing to stop his transformation into a fly once the computer has locked him into its program. In *Dr. Jekyll and Mr. Hyde*, the focus is more on the character and intentions of the scientist than on the technology he employs the implication in this film is that we have nothing to fear from science as long as it is in the hands of the right people. In *The Fly*, on the other hand, the technology is so powerful that the character and intentions of the people who use it are much less important. In this film, scientists create machines with minds of their own these machines are indifferent to the wishes and best interests of their creators. In the 1930s scientists could control their creations they were responsible for them. In the 1980s no one could be sure what would happen when high-tech machinery was set into motion.

18d Fragments

A **fragment** is an incomplete sentence. In some contexts, such as informal personal letters, press releases, and advertising, a fragment is a good way to catch your reader's attention.

A wonderful occasion for all of us.

The best buy ever!

The end of the line for him.

A small step, but an important one.

If the rest of your sentences are grammatically complete, a fragment will stand out effectively for emphasis. On the other hand, if you mix unintentional fragments with intentional fragments, you'll confuse your reader and lose your intended emphasis.

Remember, too, that fragments will make your writing seem less formal. Unless you wish your work to appear somewhat casual, avoid fragments in reports, business letters, and essays. When you are proofreading for sentence fragments, watch for the following errors.

Recognizing Sentence Fragments

• *Phrases or subordinate clauses punctuated as complete sentences*

Sometimes the fragment belongs with the complete sentence that comes before or after it in the passage.

Fragments

FRAGMENT	Bill could balance a glass of water on his head. Without spilling a drop. [The second construction is a prepositional phrase and, like all phrases, lacks a subject and a verb.]
COMPLETE SENTENCE	Bill could balance a glass of water on his head without spilling a drop. [The phrase has been joined to the sentence before it.]
FRAGMENT	Because there had been two major rent increases in the last two years. Maureen decided to look for a new apartment. [The first construction is a subordinate clause, not a complete sentence.]
COMPLETE SENTENCE	Because there had been two major rent increases in the last two years, Maureen decided to look for a new apartment. [The subordinate clause

239

has been joined to the following sentence. There is a comma between the clauses because the subordinate clause is first.]

• *Sentences with missing verbs*

If you remember that every verb ending with *ing* must have an auxiliary in order to be a complete verb, you'll be less likely to write this kind of fragment.

| FRAGMENT | The child frantically searching for her mother. |
| **COMPLETE SENTENCE** | The child was frantically searching for her mother. |

Be especially careful with *being*, which is a participle, not a verb. Avoid the phrase *the reason being*. Use *because* instead.

| FRAGMENT | The reason for her sore back being that she had fallen. |
| **COMPLETE SENTENCE** | Her back was sore because she had fallen. |

Exercise 18.7

Revise the following constructions to make them complete sentences.

1. Wendell driving around in circles, unable to find his date's house in the maze-like neighbourhood.

2. According to *The Hitchhiker's Guide to the Galaxy*, forty-two being the answer to the meaning of life, the universe, and everything.

3. After getting up to change channels himself because the remote control battery was dead. Brad sank back exhausted onto the couch.

4. Lydia, the last person I expected to quit school.

5. Angry at the parking attendant for writing up a ticket because the metre had expired.

Exercise 18.8

Revise the following constructions to make them complete sentences. If the sentence is correct, write **C**.

1. Always quick to judge others, but he bridled at even the mildest criticism.
2. Open your booklets and begin the exam.
3. The fans cheering wildly as the defenceman raced down the ice.
4. Turning his head for an instant to look at his program, Brendan missed the winning goal.
5. A woman with fierce pride and a determined spirit.
6. The reason for the fire being a pot of hot oil left burning on the stove.
7. Last year Donald was the grand prize winner in the Bulwer-Lytton bad writing contest.
8. Tearing open the envelope and nervously removing the transcript of her final grades.
9. Although I could detect movement inside, no one answering my knock.
10. Because he didn't phone in or show up for work.

Exercise 18.9

Restore the following paragraph to its original form by eliminating all inappropriate **sentence fragments**.

Marsha slammed the car into the parking spot, jumped out, and raced across the lot. Prayed she wasn't too late. The usual crises that morning having delayed her escape from the house. Darren's little tirade—he would *not* eat peanut butter sandwiches for lunch two days in a row—had taken a good five minutes. Krista's venting—why did Marsha keep buying her such stupid clothes for school?—lasting another ten. The clock read 8:30 as Marsha shoved in her card for imprinting. Official; she was on time. Marsha couldn't afford to keep losing a quarter-hour's pay as penalty for punching in late. She opened the supervisor's memo and looked over the day's orders. "(1) Dust all the shelves from top to bottom. Don't miss any shelves," the list began. "(2) Put the new price labels on the shelves. Be sure to use the correct prices." *Yes, the correct prices*, Marsha thought. Well, maybe she could do something right today. Marsha picked up the feather duster. And set to work.

18e Faulty Parallelism

The principle of **parallelism** is that similar ideas should be
expressed in grammatically similar ways.

> Her New Year's resolutions were to **quit smoking, lose weight,**
> and **exercise regularly.**

Faulty parallelism occurs when ideas of equal value are not
expressed in the same grammatical form.

Avoiding Faulty Parallelism

- *Use the same part of speech for each item in a series
  of words.*

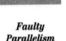

NOT	The family has wealth, reputation, and **is powerful.**
BUT	The family has wealth, reputation, and **power.**

*Faulty
Parallelism*

- *Use the same construction for each phrase or clause in
  a series.*

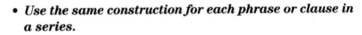

Do not mix phrases and clauses, or even different kinds of
phrases.

NOT	Maurice decided to complete his second year at college, look for a job, and **then he and Eva would get married.**
BUT	Maurice decided to complete his second year at college, look for a job, and **then marry Eva.**

- *Include both elements in a comparison.*

NOT	My paper is as long as **Bill.**
BUT	My paper is as long as **Bill's.**
NOT	The more I work on this assignment, **I don't seem to accomplish much.**
BUT	The more I work on this assignment, **the less I seem to accomplish.**

242

- *Make sure correlative conjunctions join grammatically similar sentence elements.*

The correlative conjunctions are *either/or, neither/nor, not only/but also, whether/or, both/and.*

NOT	Not only did the horse lose, **but the right leg of the jockey was broken**.
BUT	Not only did the horse lose, but also **the jockey broke her right leg**.

Exercise 18.10

Make elements in the following sentences parallel. Put *C* beside a correct sentence.

1. Robert can either work and save money for college, or he can take out a student loan.

2. The more I try to convince him otherwise, he is more determined to dye his hair green.

3. The Bennetts' house is smaller than their neighbour.

4. My car needs new paint, new tires, and the transmission is shot.

5. Not only did Marvin borrow my book without asking, but he also bent the cover and wrote in the margins.

6. The store went out of business because of inferior merchandise, their prices were high, and poor customer service.

7. I haven't decided whether to study or whether I should go skiing during reading week.

8. Gina is both a skilled pianist and she is a talented baseball player.

9. Before becoming actors, some famous stars worked in other fields. For example, Harrison Ford was a master carpenter, and there is Michelle Pfeiffer, who was a cashier.

10. Some people keep repeating their mistakes; others keep making new ones.

Faulty Parallelism

Exercise 18.11

The errors in parallel sentence structure introduced into this passage make it wordy and confusing. Revise where necessary to make sentence elements parallel.

The flu symptoms started with a minor sore throat that slowly evolved into searing pain with every swallow. Tiredness progressed to exhaustion, a burning fever and drenching perspiration were the transmutations of a slight flush, and general discomfort metamorphosed into the fact that I felt totally miserable. All my major joints and most of my major muscles ached profoundly. To make matters worse, the pain of past injuries returned to torment me. The scar on my left thumb, the result of stitches needed to close a gash caused by the slip of a paring knife, hurt as intensely as a fresh wound. There was a merciless throbbing in my right hamstring, which I'd pulled years ago in a skiing accident. Several knuckles, mashed last summer when I misjudged my distance to the end of the swimming pool, stiffened in agony. With this flu virus I was double cursed. All I could do was gulp down aspirins, lie in bed, and pray for an end to the pains, both present and those that I'd suffered in the past.

18f

Faulty
Subordination

18f Faulty Subordination

Faulty subordination occurs when you fail to differentiate less important ideas from more important ideas.

Avoiding Faulty Subordination

- ***Check that you have attached the subordinate conjunction to the appropriate clause.***

Some common subordinate conjunctions are *before, after, since, while, when, if, unless, until, because, although.* You can signal the connections among your ideas more accurately by putting the less important idea in the subordinate clause and by beginning the subordinate clause with the appropriate conjunction.

NOT	He wanted to make a good impression, **because** he dressed carefully for the interview.
BUT	**Because** he wanted to make a good impression, he dressed carefully for the interview.

- *Use the most precise subordinate conjunction.*

Pay particular attention to your use of *since* and *as*. *Since* can mean *because*, but it can also mean *from the time that*. In some sentences, *since* is confusing. In such cases, it is best to rephrase the sentence.

CONFUSING   Since Sandy broke her leg, she hasn't been playing basketball.

CLEAR   Sandy hasn't played basketball since she broke her leg.

CLEAR   Because Sandy broke her leg, she hasn't been playing basketball.

As is another troublesome conjunction. Sometimes *as* means *because*, but it's clearer to use *as* to mean *during the time that*.

CLEAR   **As** the rain poured down, we made our way to the deserted cabin.

CONFUSING   **As** she cycles to work, she never gets stuck in traffic.

CLEAR   **Because** she cycles to work, she never gets stuck in traffic.

*Faulty
Subordination*

Note: Don't be afraid to begin a sentence with *because*. Just make sure to include a main clause in the sentence.

- *Limit the number of subordinate clauses in a single sentence.*

By piling subordinate clauses on top of each other you can make it difficult for the reader to judge how your ideas are related. Revise sentences with too many subordinate clauses by rephrasing the sentence or by reducing some of the clauses to phrases or single words.

NOT   **Because the committee could not reach a decision**, the project was stalled **because no one knew what to do next**.

BUT   The **committee's failure to reach a decision** stalled the project because no one knew what to do next.

NOT	The party **that wins the election, which will be held on November 10**, will set economic policies **that will affect the country** for the next ten years.
BUT	The party **that wins the November 10 election** will set the **country's** economic policies for the next ten years.

Exercise 18.12

Revise the following sentences to correct faulty or excessive subordination.

1. Since their home was badly damaged by fire, the Wongs have been living in a rented house.

2. Although Gina used the proper amount of bromine, the pool sides were still covered with algae although she also shocked the pool regularly with chlorine.

3. The fireplace that is in the basement has a pilot light that frequently goes out when snow blocks the outside vent.

4. Todd forgot to include his charitable receipts in his income tax return because his refund was delayed.

5. If you want to buy a computer, the person whom you should call is Roman, who is an expert on what are the best buys.

6. Craig isn't doing well in physics although he doesn't seem particularly concerned.

7. When I entered the building, I knew I was late for class when I heard the final bell.

8. Marina hates the taste of ketchup even though she likes ketchup-flavoured potato chips.

9. As I couldn't hear what he was saying, I asked him to speak up.

10. Since the air conditioner broke down, everyone has been complaining about the heat.

Mixed Constructions

18g Mixed Constructions

Mixed constructions get their name because they mix incompatible grammatical units and thus produce sentences that will seem awkward to your reader. Mixed constructions result from the writer thinking of two similar sentences and then using parts of each in a single sentence. For example, let's say you have these two perfectly reasonable sentences in mind:

Because June has three small children, she is exhausted.

June's three small children are the reason she is exhausted.

If you are not paying attention, you might change your mind as you are writing and produce a mixed construction:

MIXED   June has three small children is the reason she is exhausted.

You can recognize awkward constructions like this by reading your work aloud to yourself or to a classmate. Here are some tips to help you avoid three common types of mixed constructions.

1. *Avoid* **is when** *and* **is because** *constructions.*

MIXED   **An example** of her snobbery **is when** she criticizes her neighbours for their ungrammatical speech.

REVISED   An example of her snobbery is **her criticism** [noun] of her neighbours' ungrammatical speech.

REVISED   She **reveals** her snobbery when she criticizes her neighbours' ungrammatical speech. [linking verb replaced]

MIXED   **The reason** the brakes failed **is because** the brake fluid was accidentally removed.

REVISED   The reason the brakes failed is **that the brake fluid was accidentally removed**. [noun clause]

REVISED   The brakes **failed** because the brake fluid was accidentally removed. [linking verb replaced]

Occasionally the subordinate clause appears before the verb.

MIXED   **Because he was always late** [subordinate clause] **was** [verb] **the reason** he was fired.

18g

Mixed Constructions

REVISED	**His lateness** [noun] was the reason he was fired.
REVISED	Because he was always late, he **was fired**. [linking verb replaced]

2. *Make sure you have a subject in the main clause.*

Remember that a prepositional phrase is never the subject of a sentence.

MIXED	In the article "Anorexia and the Adolescent" [prepositional phrase] explains Lilian Donaldson's views on the connection between self-starvation and the adolescent's need for control.
REVISED	In the article "Anorexia and the Adolescent," Lilian Donaldson [subject] explains the connection between self-starvation and the adolescent's need for control.
REVISED	The article "Anorexia and the Adolescent" [subject] explains Lilian Donaldson's view on the connection between self-starvation and the adolescent's need for control.

3. *Don't confuse questions with statements.*

MIXED	She wondered how long will it be until I see him again?
REVISED	She wondered how long it would be until she saw him again.
REVISED	She wondered, "How long will it be until I see him again?"

Exercise 18.13

Revise the following sentences to eliminate mixed constructions.

1. Geraldine asked her brother Ben how much longer will he be in the shower?
2. Because my dog ate my computer disk is the reason my paper is late.

3. Portaging is when you carry a boat overland between navigable lakes or rivers.

4. In Darrin's letter explained why he resigned his position.

5. The reason we cut our vacation short is because it rained for a solid week.

6. Without more donations means that the shelter will have to close.

7. Looking at his bank statement, Domenic wondered how did he spend so much money in only a month?

8. An example of Mary's thoughtfulness is when she cuts the lawn for her elderly neighbours.

9. In the threatre program lists all the actors in the play.

10. The next day is when Frank finally thought of a snappy comeback to Vincent's insulting remark.

18g

Mixed Constructions

Chapter 19

Proofreading: Modifiers

19a Key Terms to Know

Adjectives modify nouns and pronouns.

> The quick brown fox jumped over the lazy dog. [*Quick* and *brown* modify *fox*; *lazy* modifies *dog*.]

Adverbs modify verbs, adjectives, and other adverbs.

> The cat stretched lazily in the sun. [*Lazily* modifies the verb *stretched*.]

> Dr. Lucas' lecture on the shortage of clean water in Ghana was extremely interesting. [*Extremely* modifies the adjective *interesting*.]

> The car went by too quickly for me to see who was in it. [*Too* modifies the adverb *quickly*.]

19b Comparative Forms of Adjectives and Adverbs

Adjectives and adverbs have degrees of comparison (*pretty, prettier, prettiest; interesting, more interesting, most interesting*). If you are not sure of the comparative form of a particular adjective or adverb (should it be *clearer* or *more clear*?), consult your dictionary.

Avoid using double comparisons, such as *more happier* or *most fastest*. Some adjectives (such as *unique, perfect, empty*) express absolute concepts. One piece of pottery cannot be *more unique* than the rest, one math test cannot be the *most perfect* in the class, one glass cannot be *more empty* than another.

19c   Troublesome Adjectives and Adverbs

- *Well* is usually an adverb.

NOT   Declan **ran good** in the last race.

BUT   Declan **ran well** in the last race.

- *Well* in reference to health is an adjective.

  Jane hasn't been **well** since her bout of mononucleosis.

- *Good* is an adjective.

  I haven't seen a **good** movie for ages.

  His health is **good** now because he has his allergies under control.

- *Bad* and *real* are adjectives.

  This is a **bad** photograph of me.

  The huge boulder looks **real**, but it is actually made of papier-mâché.

- *Badly* and *really* are adverbs.

NOT   The roof was damaged **bad** in the hailstorm.

BUT   The roof was **badly** damaged in the hailstorm.

NOT   Ben is **real** eager to begin his new job on Monday.

BUT   Ben is **really** eager to begin his new job on Monday.

- *Less* and *fewer* are used differently. *Less* (the comparative of *little*) is an adjective used with items that cannot be considered as separate objects: *less* food, *less* kindness, *less* snow. *Fewer* (the comparative of *few*) is an adjective used with things that can be counted individually: *fewer* students, *fewer* courses, *fewer* responsibilities.

NOT   I have **less** errands to run tomorrow than I had anticipated.

BUT   I have **fewer** errands to run tomorrow than I had anticipated.

Exercise 19.1

Revise the following sentences so that adjectives and adverbs are used correctly.

1. He looked at me serious and began to speak.
2. The engine still runs good, but the body is badly rusted.
3. Less players have registered for hockey camp this summer.
4. The supervisor is real interested in your opinion of the proposal.
5. Clarence gets good grades in physical education, but he doesn't do so good in chemistry.

Exercise 19.2

Revise the following sentences so that adjectives and adverbs are used correctly. If the sentence is correct, write **C**.

1. Lynette is the most liveliest member of my aerobics class.
2. You will feel considerable better after you have taken this medication.
3. The play went good in rehearsal, but opening night was a disaster.
4. Since landing a full-time job, Satpal has been able to afford more dressy clothes, but she has less social occasions on which to wear them.
5. The milk bottle in the refrigerator is completely empty.
6. Of the two reports, which is the more informative?
7. Eric answered all of the questions as honest as he could.
8. Although the hikers were real tired, they decided to press on.
9. The door opened more easily after Jack adjusted the hinges.
10. Max is less happier living on his own than he was living at home.

19d Misplaced Modifiers

A **misplaced modifier**, as its name suggests, is in the wrong place. The resulting sentence is confusing and sometimes unintentionally amusing.

> Mr. Kowalski saw a horse by the side of the road on his way home from work.

Since Mr. Kowalski is more likely to be on his way home from work than the horse is, the prepositional phrase *on his way home from work* should be placed closer to *Mr. Kowalski* in the sentence.

> On his way home from work, Mr. Kowalski saw a horse by the side of the road.

Words such as *only, hardly, barely, nearly,* and *almost* are especially troublesome because they can easily be misplaced.

NOT	After a few lessons, James could **almost swim** the entire length of the pool.
BUT	After a few lessons, James could swim **almost the entire length** of the pool.
NOT	**I only want** a minute of your time.
BUT	I want **only a minute** of your time.

Note: Do not use *hardly* and *barely* with *not.*

NOT	**I can't hardly** hear you.
BUT	**I can hardly** hear you.
NOT	**She couldn't barely** hear the faint sound coming from the basket on the front steps.
BUT	She **could barely** hear the faint sound coming from the basket on the front steps.

19e Split Infinitives

An **infinitive** is *to* + a verb: *to think, to walk, to breathe.* A **split infinitive** occurs when a modifier (usually an adverb) is misplaced between *to* and the verb (*to quickly run*). It is best to avoid splitting an infinitive, especially when the resulting construction is awkward. You can correct a split infinitive by rephrasing the sentence.

SPLIT INFINITIVE	Marjorie needed time to **mentally prepare** for the exam.
REVISED	Marjorie needed time to **prepare mentally** for the exam.

Sometimes, however, a split infinitive sounds less awkward than when the modifier is relocated in the sentence.

> The diners asked the man at the next table **to please stop** smoking his cigar. [Putting *please* anywhere else in the sentence would be clumsy.]

Exercise 19.3

Revise the following sentences to avoid split infinitives and to place modifiers as close as possible to what they modify.

1. Soak the shirt in cold water with the spaghetti sauce stain.

2. Sonia could almost run ten full circuits around the field.

3. Preserved in formaldehyde, the students examined the jar of tapeworms.

4. I promise not to unfairly judge you.

5. I had difficulty hearing the conversation standing by the band.

Split
Infinitives

Exercise 19.4

Revise the following sentences to avoid split infinitives and to place modifiers as close as possible to what they modify. If the sentence is correct, write **C**.

1. The singer's fans couldn't hardly wait for the concert tickets to go on sale.

2. Properly cooked, you can eat hamburger without fear of food poisoning.

3. I want to thoroughly consider all my options before making a decision.

4. Greg has only enough money to cover this month's rent.

5. Seeing the accident ahead, the car pulled to the side of the road, and Tran got out to investigate.

6. We enjoyed the beautiful lawn and gardens eating our lunch on the patio.

7. You must be ill; you only ate half the pizza.

8. Jim heard the phone ring with his mouth full of toothpaste.

9. There is a family picture of our trip to Nassau on the hall table.

10. I asked him one final time to please stop pestering me.

19f Dangling Modifiers

An introductory phrase normally modifies the closest noun in the sentence. When it does not, it is called a **dangling modifier**.

DANGLING   **Driving down the mountain**, three bears were seen.

Recognizing Dangling Modifiers

1. *Does the sentence begin with a participial phrase or an infinitive?*

Participial phrases are formed with the present or past participle of a verb.

hanging on the wall
stricken with AIDS

Infinitive phrases are formed with an infinitive (*to* + verb).

to drive defensively
to bake the perfect cake
to listen carefully

2. *Does this participial or infinitive phrase logically modify the closest noun or pronoun in the sentence?*

NOT   Sitting on the beach under the boiling sun, **a swim** was inviting.

BUT   Sitting on the beach under the boiling sun, **we** looked forward to a swim.

NOT   To swim a mile, **endurance** must be built up gradually.

BUT   To swim a mile, **you** must build up your endurance gradually.

3. *Is the verb in the main clause in the passive voice?*

Verbs have two voices: active and passive. When the verb is in the active voice, the subject of the sentence performs the action: *Amin signed the documents.* When the verb is in the passive voice, the subject of the sentence is acted on by the verb: *The documents were signed by Amin.*

Be careful with passive constructions. Introductory phrases are more likely to dangle when the verb in the main clause is in the passive voice.

NOT	After hours of frustrating discussion, an agreement on the verdict was finally reached by the jury.
BUT	After hours of frustrating discussion, the jury finally agreed on a verdict.

Exercise 19.5

Identify the verbs in the following sentences as **A** (active) or **P** (passive).

1. The newsletter was distributed to every home in the neighbourhood.

2. Rajiv was listening to the conversation on the extension phone.

3. The basement was flooded when a water pipe burst.

4. After a two-hour delay, our flight was cancelled.

5. The robins have built a nest in the hanging planter.

Correcting Dangling Modifiers

When an introductory phrase dangles, you can revise the sentence in one of two ways. You can either expand the phrase to a subordinate clause or revise the main clause so that the introductory phrase logically modifies its subject.

NOT	Intending to finish the report by the end of the day, my plan was to work through lunch and coffee breaks.
BUT	Because I intended to finish the report by the end of the day, my plan was to work through lunch and coffee breaks.

OR

Intending to finish the report by the end of the day, I planned to work through lunch and coffee breaks.

You could correct the dangling modifier in the next sentence by changing the prepositional phrase to a clause, with the subject clearly stated.

NOT

After being honoured by sports writers and fellow athletes, the retired hockey star's name was inscribed in the Hall of Fame.

BUT

After the retired hockey star was honoured by sports writers and fellow athletes, his name was inscribed in the Hall of Fame.

Sometimes it is necessary to revise a sentence extensively to eliminate the dangling modifier.

NOT

Upon learning about the budget cutbacks, it was difficult for Ruth to hide her concern that her position would be abolished.

19f

BUT

When Ruth learned about the budget cutbacks, she found it difficult to hide her concern that her position would be abolished.

Dangling Modifiers

Exercise 19.6

Correct each dangling modifier.

1. Walking into the room, a strange sight caught my eye.

2. While in high school, George's father was promoted and the family moved to Vancouver.

3. Exhausted by a heavy work schedule, a complete rest was recommended by the doctor.

4. To make a perfect omelette, the freshest ingredients are required.

5. After pleading earnestly, the curfew was extended to midnight.

Exercise 19.7

Correct each dangling modifier. If the sentence is correct, write **C**.

1. To have a chance at winning the lottery, a ticket must first be bought.

2. Hoping to catch the final inning of the baseball game on television, Michael left the office early.

3. Driven by arrogance and greed, Joe's friends were soon alienated from him.

4. After working so hard on the committee, our gratitude is definitely deserved.

5. To extend your cable service, you may call any time during office hours.

6. While reading Stephen King's *Cujo*, my dog began barking in the backyard.

7. Concerned by the noise, I went outside to investigate.

8. Driving on the highway, Hank's care engine suddenly seized.

9. Staring intently at the small print, spots began to swim before my eyes.

10. To build a better mousetrap, the proper tools are essential.

Exercise 19.8

The following paragraphs contain errors in the use of modifiers. Revise the passage to correct these errors.

When the morning radio announcer reported that snow was moving in rapid from the country and had already reached the city limits, Karen went to the window in anticipation. Soon the first flakes filtered down and clung to bare tree branches, bushes, and the few hardy annuals that had survived the last frost in the front flower bed. The snow that reached the lawn, driveway, and road melted immediately. *Oh, I hope some of it stays*, thought Karen. *The first snow makes everything look so much more cleaner and fresher.*

The snow had only been falling for a few hours, but already the world was transformed. Merging into one smooth, pristine expanse, Karen looked out at the road and yard. "Exquisite," she sighed. She pushed away thoughts of tomorrow and work; she wanted to merely enjoy the beauty of the snow, the warmth of the fireplace, and the cozy security of her family room. She went back to her novel wishing there were more days like this.

As she stood again at the window in late afternoon, Karen couldn't barely see through the dense whiteness. Turning on the radio, there were reports of numerous cars in ditches and two injury accidents downtown. City crews were struggling to clear major arteries, while most side streets remained impassable. Motorists were advised to avoid area highways because of white-out conditions. "Well, folks," the announcer continued, "with no end to the snow in sight, it looks as though we're going to have a few more days like this."

19f

*Dangling
Modifiers*

Chapter 20

Proofreading: Verbs

Because the English verb system is quite complex, it's easy to make errors involving both verb tenses and verb forms.

20a The Principal Parts of Verbs

Each verb has four principal parts, from which all its other forms can be derived.

- The **infinitive** form (*to* + a verb) names the verb: *to walk, to run, to think*.
- The **past tense**: *Yesterday I **walked** to school*.
- The **present participle**: I **am walking** *to school right now*.
- The **past participle**: I **have walked** *to school every day this week*.

Regular verbs form the past tense and the past participle by adding *ed* to the infinitive: *walked, have walked; visited, have visited*.

Irregular verbs form the past tense and the past participle in a variety of ways: *drank, have drunk; brought, have brought*. If you are not sure of the principal parts of an irregular verb, check your dictionary.

20b Auxiliary Verbs

A number of verb tenses are formed by combining a participle with one or more **auxiliary verbs**:

am, is, was, were	*can, could, may, might*
be, being, been	*shall, will, should, would*
have, has, had	*ought to, have to, used to*
do, does, did	*supposed to*

20c Common Errors with Verbs

- *Using the past participle instead of the past tense*

NOT   I **seen** [past participle] him yesterday.

BUT   I **saw** [past tense] him yesterday.

- *Using an auxiliary verb with the past tense*

NOT   Ahmed **had went** to visit his parents in Manitoba.

BUT   Ahmed **went** to visit his parents in Manitoba.

OR   Ahmed **had gone** to visit his parents in Manitoba.

- *Using* being *as a main verb instead of* is *or* was

NOT   The reason **being** that I was already late.

BUT   The reason **is** that I was already late.

- *Using* of *to mean* have

NOT   He should **of** known better.

BUT   He should **have** known better.

- *Using too many* coulds *or* woulds *in* if/then *statements*

NOT   If you **would have asked** me, I would have helped.

BUT   If you **had asked** me, I would have helped.

20c

Common Errors with Verbs

Exercise 20.1

Revise the following sentences so that auxiliaries and principal parts are used correctly. If the sentence is correct, write **C**.

1. You should of did the dishes instead of playing computer games.

2. How could you have wore a hole in your new running shoes already?

3. Whenever Martin gets the urge to work, he lays down until he feels better.

4. If I would have known you were in town, I would have invited you to the party.

5. The reason being that they couldn't find a baby-sitter.

6. Yvette rung the doorbell and waited to be admitted.

7. Susan has not wrote to her parents in over two months.

8. If Tom had submitted the essay on time, he would not have lost marks.

9. I am positive that I seen Jocelyn at the concert, but she insists that she wasn't there.

10. Rosa has swum in that lake every summer since she was a child.

20d   Keeping Verb Tenses Consistent

Once you have decided on the tense—present, past, or future—of a particular piece of writing, be consistent. You may have to shift tenses to clarify time relationships, but don't do so unnecessarily. Use the present tense when you are writing about literature.

Keeping Your Verb Tenses Consistent

Note the use of the present tense in the following paragraph analyzing Stacey MacAindra, who is the central character in Margaret Laurence's novel *The Fire Dwellers.*

> Stacey's inability to communicate with her husband and children is a manifestation of the "tomb silences" of her own parents. Again we see Laurence's concern with the past as a source of isolation, for Stacey's background does not give her the means to be fully open with others. Moreover, she is a victim not only of her own past but also of the past influences that shape her husband, Mac, who inherits his reticence and his tendency to misinterpret Stacey's remarks from a father who is himself often restrained and imperceptive. Because of their childhoods, both Stacey and Mac believe that "nice" people do not talk about fear or pain. Stacey understands the limitations of this belief, but her inability to free herself from its influence leads her to remark that everyone in her family is one-dimensional. This image conveys Stacey's feelings of dissociation from her husband and children.

Exercise 20.2

Revise the following paragraph to eliminate unnecessary tense shifts. Use the present tense. The paragraph deals with Margaret Laurence's collection of short stories *A Bird in the House*.

> As a child, Vanessa expresses her imaginative concerns in the stories of "spectacular heroism" that she composes in her head to counteract the boredom of Sunday School lessons. Essentially, she rejected any ties between her fictional world and the reality she experiences growing up in a little prairie town. Although she acknowledges Manawaka in her tale of the infant swept away in its christening robe by the flooding Wachakwa River, she transformed this muddy little river into an agent of the grotesque. Beyond this, Manawaka seems hardly worthy of literary note. For Vanessa, the "ordinary considerations" of life were completely divorced from the dramatic considerations of art. Thus she abandons her heroic epic, "The Pillars of the Nation," when she learned that Grandfather Connor, with his boring stories of the past, is himself one of those pillars.

20e Active and Passive Voice

English verbs have two voices: the **active** and the **passive**. In an active construction, the subject performs the action of the verb. In a passive construction, the subject is acted upon.

> Edward made the announcement. [active]
>
> The announcement was made by Edward. [passive]

In most writing situations, it's best to use the active voice. Occasionally, however, the passive voice can be useful.

When to Use the Active Voice

In most writing situations, don't rely heavily on passive constructions, especially if you are using them merely to sound more formal. Active constructions are usually clearer, more concise, and more forceful.

PASSIVE	The home owners were informed by the city that the weeds would have to be cleared from their lots immediately.
ACTIVE	The city informed the home owners that they would have to clear the weeds from their lots immediately.

263

When to Use the Passive Voice

Sometimes the passive voice is necessary. There are two main occasions.

- Use it when you don't know who or what performed the action.

  The house was constructed of limestone from the local quarries.

- Use the passive voice when you want to emphasize what was done rather than who did it.

  The solution was heated in a beaker.

Note: Passive constructions have always been common, and often preferred, in scientific writing because they place the emphasis on what was done rather than on who did it. The use of the passive voice suggests that anyone performing the experiment would get the same results. Recently, however, passive constructions in scientific writing have become less popular as more importance has been given to the role of the researcher. Because scientific writing styles vary, check to see which voice your instructor prefers.

Being Consistent

20e

Active and Passive Voice

Avoid mixing active and passive constructions in the same sentence.

NOT	A letter was written by the home owners saying the weeds would be cleared when they (the home owners) were good and ready.
BUT	The home owners wrote a letter saying they would clear the weeds when they were good and ready.

Exercise 20.3

Change passive constructions to active constructions where appropriate. If the passive voice is preferable, write **C**. Be prepared to defend your choices.

1. The light changed to amber before the intersection was reached by Oliver.

2. The municipal swimming pool was opened for the summer last week.

3. My directions were completely misunderstood by Burt.

4. After much lengthy debate, the meeting was finally adjourned.

5. The milk was spilled, but Marietta made no effort to wipe it up.

6. The building site has been shut down until all safety hazards have been eliminated.

7. Marcia was hurt by Sarah's careless remark.

8. After the lawn was trimmed and raked, we weeded the front flower bed.

9. Before setting out to write my exam, I searched for my good luck pen, but it couldn't be found anywhere.

10. The newspaper was delivered late again this morning.

20f Making Subjects and Verbs Agree

The principle of **subject–verb agreement** is that singular subjects take singular verbs and plural subjects take plural verbs.

> This **ornament goes** on the top of the tree. [singular]
>
> The **lights go** on first. [plural]

Here are the most common causes of errors in subject–verb agreement.

• *A prepositional phrase separating subject and verb*

The subject and verb may be separated by a prepositional phrase (*of the workers, between the houses, across the field, including all team members, along with all his supporters*). The subject of the sentence is never located in the prepositional phrase.

> **One** of the workers **has filed** a complaint with the grievance committee.
>
> **Neither** of the women **wants** to press charges.
>
> **Mrs. Murphy** along with her five noisy children **attends** mass regularly.

- ***Sentences beginning with* there *or* here**

There or *here* may be the first word of the sentence, but neither will be the subject of the sentence. Look for the real subject after the verb.

> There **are** only five **bananas**, not enough for everyone.

> Here **come** the **Jackson twins**, just in time for dinner.

- ***Subjects linked by paired conjunctions:* either/or, neither/nor, not only/but also**

In sentences with paired conjunctions, the subject closer to the verb makes the verb singular or plural.

> Neither Reuben nor **his cousins were prepared** to kiss the bride.

> Not only the students but also the **teacher was delighted** by the unexpected holiday.

- ***Subjects that may be singular or plural***

Collective nouns, such as *team, group, committee,* are considered singular when they refer to people or things acting as a unit.

> Our **team is** on a five-day road trip.

> The **herd has settled down** for the night.

Collective nouns are considered plural when they refer to people or things acting individually.

> The **team do** not **agree** about the need for a new manager.

> The **herd have scattered** in every direction.

Making Subjects and Verbs Agree

Collective nouns of quantity (*number, majority, percentage*) are singular when preceded by *the,* plural when preceded by *a.*

> **The number** of unemployed people **is increasing**.

> **A number** of unemployed people **are** still **looking** for jobs.

The pronouns *all, none,* and *some* can be either singular or plural, depending on the noun to which they refer.

> **None** of the cake **is** left.

> **None** of the cookies **are** left.

Words joined by *and* are considered singular when they refer to a single unit or to the same person.

Bread and butter makes a fine basis for a sandwich.

My **neighbour and best friend has moved** to another city.

Exercise 20.4

Make subjects and verbs agree in the following sentences. If the sentence is correct, write **C**.

1. Neither Stephanie nor her sisters is available to help at the bazaar on Saturday.

2. The team have won the championship fours years in a row.

3. Neither of the applicants are willing to relocate to a branch office.

4. There goes the Pied Piper, along with all the children of Hamelin.

5. Fear of falling and of loud noises are instinctive.

6. Either the love birds or the gold fish make a suitable pet for an apartment resident.

7. The number of hamburgers sold has increased significantly this quarter.

8. The jury have been sequestered for three days.

9. Each of the committee members have made a different selection for Citizen of the Year.

10. Nothing I've seen in the last three clothing stores seem suitable for graduation.

Chapter 21

Proofreading: Pronouns

Pronouns substitute for nouns or other pronouns. The word to which the pronoun refers is called its **antecedent**.

> My **grandmother** goes bowling every Wednesday. Then **she** eats lunch at **her** fitness club. [*Grandmother* is the antecedent of *she* and *her*.]

We will discuss the five most common types of pronoun problems.

1. Pronoun agreement errors
2. Pronoun case errors
3. Errors with possessive pronouns
4. Pronoun reference errors
5. Shifts in pronouns of address

21a Pronoun Agreement

21a

Pronoun Agreement

Errors in pronoun agreement occur when you don't match a singular pronoun with a singular noun or a plural pronoun with a plural noun. Pronoun agreement errors occur most frequently in the following situations.

Agreement with Singular Nouns: Avoiding Gender Stereotypes

Pronoun agreement errors often involve using a plural pronoun to refer to a singular noun. Most often, the noun names a type of person (the alcoholic, the mature student, the typical worker) rather than an individual, as in the following example:

ERROR   The **alcoholic** may blame **their** drinking problem on unsympathetic family members.

There are four ways to avoid this kind of agreement error.

1. *Use a singular pronoun.*

   The alcoholic may blame **his** drinking problem on unsympathetic family members.

   Although this version is grammatically correct, the use of *his* is unappealing because it implies that all alcoholics are men.

2. *Use the phrase* **his or her.**

   The alcoholic may blame **his or her** drinking problem on unsympathetic family members.

   This correction works well in single sentences but becomes cumbersome when repeated frequently. Avoid using *he/she*, *s/he*, or *him/her* in any piece of writing.

3. *Make the noun plural.* Pluralizing is often the simplest and most effective way to ensure pronoun agreement.

   Alcoholics may blame **their** drinking problems on unsympathetic family members.

4. *Alternate masculine and feminine pronouns.* If you were writing about types of people, such as the teacher and his or her students or the doctor and his or her patients, you could alternate masculine and feminine pronouns by referring to the teacher or doctor as *he* in one paragraph and as *she* in the next paragraph. Alternating masculine and feminine pronouns paragraph by paragraph is much less confusing and distracting than alternating them within a single paragraph.

Exercise 21.1

Revise the following sentences to make antecedents and pronouns agree.

1. Every manager has been asked their opinion of the merger.
2. A new immigrant generally suffers from culture shock, no matter how well they have prepared for the move.
3. A day-care worker must ensure that their qualifications in basic first aid are current.
4. It is not unusual for even an experienced actor to suffer from stage fright before they begin a performance.

5. A customer service representative needs to remain calm and polite in their dealings with the public.

Agreement with Collective Nouns

Collective nouns are words such as *jury, team, band, audience, group, family, committee, congregation, herd,* and *flock* that refer to people or things taken together.

When a collective noun refers to people or things acting as a single unit, the collective noun takes singular verbs and singular pronouns.

The **jury was** unanimous in **its** verdict.

The **band was** doomed without **its** leader.

When a collective noun refers to people or things acting as individuals, the collective noun takes plural verbs and plural pronouns.

The **jury were divided** in **their** judgment of the defendant.

The **band were arguing** over **their** next number.

When a collective noun is followed by a prepositional phrase, be careful to match the pronoun with the collective noun and not with the noun inside the prepositional phrase.

A small **group** of hecklers made **its** impact on the meeting.

The stranded **herd** of horses lost **its** way.

Agreement with *Either/Or, Neither/Nor, Or, Nor*

21a

Pronoun Agreement

Singular nouns joined by *either/or, neither/nor, or,* and *nor* are matched with singular pronouns.

Neither Farida nor Barbara has contacted **her** lawyer.

Either Mark or Craig will lend you **his** truck for the move.

Plural nouns joined by these conjunctions take plural pronouns.

Neither the students nor the teachers had time to collect **their** belongings when the fire alarm sounded.

When mixed singular and plural nouns are joined by these conjunctions, put the plural noun last and use a plural pronoun.

Neither the lead singer nor **the dancers** have been fitted for **their** costumes.

Exercise 21.2

Revise the following sentences where necessary to make antecedents and pronouns agree. If the sentence is correct, write **C**.

1. Neither the employees nor the supervisor believed that their position was wrong.

2. Either Sheryl or Jennifer will lend you her bicycle for the outing.

3. The herd of cattle left their grazing area and wended their way home.

4. Next week the safety committee will publish the results of their investigation.

5. If you need help with opening night at your restaurant, either Matt or Richard will offer their services.

6. The municipal government has issued their recommendations on property tax increases.

7. The weary group of tourists finally arrived at their hotel.

8. The class were packing their books in anticipation of the bell.

9. A family of bats has made their home in our attic.

10. I know you are curious, but neither Pierre nor Antoine wants me to tell you their plans for the weekend.

Agreement with Indefinite Pronouns

Singular Indefinite Pronouns

The following indefinite pronouns are always singular. They take singular verbs, and any pronouns referring to them should also be singular.

everyone	*anyone*	*no one, one*	*someone*	*either*
everybody	*anybody*	*nobody*	*somebody*	*neither*
everything	*anything*	*nothing*	*something*	*each*

Here is a typical example of an agreement error with an indefinite pronoun:

Everyone in the office had put in **their** request for time off at Christmas.

271

Here *everyone*, which is singular, and *their*, which is plural, do not agree.

You could correct this error by using the strategies suggested above for singular nouns. Alternatively, you could rephrase the sentence to eliminate the pronoun altogether.

> Everyone in the office had requested time off at Christmas.

Don't be misled by prepositional phrases. If a singular indefinite pronoun is followed by a prepositional phrase ending with a plural noun (*of the children, in the houses, under the benches*) the verb and any pronouns referring to the subject are still singular.

> **Neither** of the drivers has contacted **her** insurance agent.

In this sentence, the antecedent of *her* is *neither*. Because *neither* is singular, the pronoun referring to it must be singular.

Plural Indefinite Pronouns
(Many, Few, Several, Both)

The indefinite pronouns *many, few, several,* and *both* take plural pronouns.

> **Both** of the drivers filed claims with **their** insurance companies.

Singular or Plural Indefinite Pronouns
(All, None, Some)

The indefinite pronouns *all, none,* and *some* are matched with singular pronouns when they are followed by a prepositional phrase that contains a singular noun.

> **None of the furniture** has been moved from **its** original position for years.

These pronouns are matched with plural pronouns when they are followed by a prepositional phrase containing a plural noun.

> **None of the chairs** have been moved from **their** original positions for years.

21a

Pronoun Agreement

Exercise 21.3

Revise the following sentences where necessary to make antecedents and pronouns agree. If the sentence is correct, write **C**.

1. Everyone purchasing these selected products is eligible to submit their name for the grand prize in the draw.

2. None of the witnesses on shore were prepared to risk their own safety to rescue the drowning man.

3. Each of the crafters is selling their best creations at the fall fair.

4. Neither of the men left their names when they called this morning.

5. Anyone interested in joining the canoe trip should send his or her payment to Harriet by the end of the month.

Exercise 21.4 Pronoun Agreement Review

Revise the following sentences to make antecedents and pronouns agree. If the sentence is correct, write **C**.

1. An experienced writer considers their readers' needs.

2. Neither of the suspects has confessed their involvement in the embezzlement.

3. The congregation is unanimous in its support of the new minister.

4. No one in the office has submitted their ideas on the proposal.

5. Some of the passengers stowed their baggage in the overhead bins.

6. After dissecting a frog in biology class, neither Stacey nor Veronica could eat their lunch.

7. A gambling addict may go deeply into debt to finance their habit.

8. All of the stolen money has been returned to its rightful owner.

9. An army marches on their stomach.

10. Everyone is expected to be on their best behaviour.

11. The band began its Canadian tour in Halifax.

12. Either Sandra or Brianne will give their oral presentation on Friday.

13. Neither of the two lost little boys knew their home address.

14. Every winner will have their picture in the newspaper.

15. Mr. Warden is a man who does their work without complaint.

21a

Pronoun
Agreement

Exercise 21.5 Pronoun Agreement Review

Revise the following paragraph to eliminate all errors in pronoun agreement.

Psychologists say that altruism, which the dictionary defines as an "unselfish concern for the welfare of others," is actually a form of selfishness. In essence, altruists are motivated as much by self-interest as by interest in others. For example, an altruist genuinely enjoys helping their neighbour build a fence. An altruist feels needed when they offer advice to family and friends. An altruist gains comfort themselves by comforting others in sorrow or pain. In short, being good makes an altruist feel good. This description is not meant to disparage altruism, of course. Someone for whom virtue truly is a reward is a decent and worthy person, and the world deserves more of their kind.

21b Pronoun Case

The **subject pronouns** (*I, we, you, he, she, it, they*, and *who*) are used as the subject of a sentence or a clause. The **object pronouns** (*me, us, you, him, her, it, them*, and *whom*) are used as the object of a verb or a preposition. The most common error in pronoun case involves a confusion of subject and object pronouns.

NOT	**Her** and **I** are going to a movie tonight.
BUT	**She** and **I** are going to a movie tonight.
NOT	You can reach my wife or **I** at home after six o'clock.
BUT	You can reach my wife or **me** at home after six o'clock.

Subject Pronouns

Use subject pronouns in the subject position in the sentence. Don't be confused when the pronoun is part of a compound subject.

NOT	Frances and **me** went to the Farmers' Market on Saturday to buy vegetables.
BUT	Frances and **I** went to the Farmers' Market on Saturday to buy vegetables.

Don't be confused when the subject pronoun is followed by an explanatory noun (*we home owners, we students, we smokers*). The pronoun is still in the subject position.

NOT

Us residents are presenting a petition to city council.

BUT

We residents are presenting a petition to city council.

Use subject pronouns after comparisons using *than* or *as*.

NOT

Peter is as tall as **me**.

BUT

Peter is as tall as **I**.

NOT

No one was more surprised than **her**.

BUT

No one was more surprised than **she**.

Use a subject pronoun as the subject of an embedded subordinate clause. Be especially careful with *that* clauses.

NOT

Ramesh said that **him** and his wife would be glad to help.

BUT

Ramesh said that **he** and his wife would be glad to help.

Object Pronouns

Use object pronouns as the direct or indirect object of a verb.

NOT

The manager assigned Loretta and **she** to work a double shift.

BUT

The manager assigned Loretta and **her** to work a double shift.

NOT

Please let your mother or **I** know when you will be home.

BUT

Please let your mother or **me** know when you will be home.

Use object pronouns in prepositional phrases.

NOT

Between you and **I**, there is something strange about our new neighbour.

Pronoun Case

BUT	Between you and **me**, there is something strange about our new neighbour.
NOT	The city replied to **we** home owners.
BUT	The city replied to **us** home owners.

Note 1: Don't make the mistake of thinking that *me* is an informal version of *I*. *Me* is a perfectly correct pronoun, provided that you use it in the object position in a sentence.

Note 2: Don't use a **reflexive pronoun** (the pronouns that end in *self/selves*) as a substitute for a subject or object pronoun.

NOT	My family and **myself** will be going to Nova Scotia for a camping holiday.
BUT	My family and **I** will be going to Nova Scotia for a camping holiday.
NOT	Ms. Chang asked that all inquiries be directed to **herself** rather than to Mr. Morgan.
BUT	Ms. Chang asked that all inquiries be directed to **her** rather than to Mr. Morgan.

21b

Pronoun Case

Who and *Whom*

Who is a subject pronoun. Use it to refer to a subject noun or pronoun.

Helen is the candidate. She is sure to win.

Helen is the candidate **who** is sure to win. [*Who* replaces *she*.]

Whom is an object pronoun. Use it after prepositions and to refer to an object noun or pronoun.

To whom do you wish to speak?

He is a lawyer. We can trust him.

He is a lawyer **whom** we can trust. [*Whom* replaces *him*.]

Exercise 21.6

Correct all errors in pronoun case in the following sentences. If the sentence is correct, write **C**.

1. Us workers must stand firm in our demand for safer conditions.
2. Him and me agree on hardly anything.
3. Todd is no more likely to know the answer than her.
4. Can you tell me who to contact about this insurance claim?
5. Please let Mrs. Wallace or I know your vacation plans.
6. James said that you can get additional copies of the newsletter from Serena or he.
7. Adrilla and myself share the same birthday.
8. Michael, Stephen, and him will be working for the same tree planting company this summer.
9. Olga told me that her and her sister haven't seen each other in years.
10. She is the kind of person who isn't afraid to express an unpopular opinion.

21c Possessive Pronouns

Use **possessive pronouns** (*mine, yours, his, hers, its, theirs, whose*) to show ownership or possession. Pay especially close attention to the following points.

- Don't confuse the possessive pronoun *its* with the contraction *it's* (*it is*).

POSSESSIVE   The committee has tabled **its** report.

CONTRACTION   Don't call me unless **it's** an emergency.

- Don't confuse the possessive pronoun *whose* with the contraction *who's* (*who is*).

POSSESSIVE   I didn't hear **whose** name was announced as the winner.

CONTRACTION   I don't know **who's** calling.

- Don't confuse the possessive pronoun *their* with the contraction *they're* (*they are*) or the adverb *there*.

POSSESSIVE	The Séguins are attending **their** family reunion in Regina.
CONTRACTION	**They're** staying with Cousin Denis and his family for two weeks.
ADVERB	They hope to see the whole family **there**.

- Remember to use apostrophes with indefinite pronouns.

  Everyone's assignments have been returned.

  Someone's keys were turned in to the receptionist.

- Do not use apostrophes with *hers, his, ours, yours,* and *theirs.*

  The battered canoe tied to the dock is **theirs**.

  This sweater must be **yours**.

Exercise 21.7

Correct all errors in the use of possessive pronouns in the following sentences.

1. It is anyones guess why Greg didn't show up for the interview.

2. Who's piece of chocolate cake is on the table?

3. I know that the suitcases are identical, but I'm certain this one is your's.

4. There's is the most beautiful garden in the neighbourhood.

5. The dog bared it's teeth and growled menacingly.

Exercise 21.8 Review of Pronoun Case and Possessive Pronouns

Correct all errors in pronoun case and possessive pronouns. If the sentence is correct, write **C**.

1. Please tell Nigel or myself if you need a ride on Saturday.

2. Dale promised that him and his brothers would vacuum the pool before the barbecue.

3. No one is happier than me that you and her have won the scholarships.

4. The Vachons sold most of there furniture and moved into a condominium.

5. Do you know who's limousine is stopped at the light?

6. Justine claims that the idea was entirely her's.

7. Between you and I, she is not giving Ian his share of the credit.

8. Put everything back in its proper place.

9. The earliest that Dave and me can be there is noon.

10. Evangeline hopes that her boyfriend and herself are accepted by the same university.

Exercise 21.9 Review of Pronoun Case and Possessive Pronouns

Correct all errors in pronoun case and the use of possessive pronouns in the following passage.

This past spring my sister Adele and me decided to throw a surprise anniversary party for Aunt Charlotte and Uncle Ted, my mother's brother. Swearing our parents to secrecy, we enlisted there help in making up a guest list. That simple request marked the beginning of a heated debate about whom was and whom was not in the family's good graces. Mother vetoed her sister Gerta because Gerta hadn't stopped by or even phoned to say hello the last time she was in town. In fact, Mother said that her and Gerta hadn't spoken since. Father agreed that Gerta was a pain and that he wanted both she and Mother's sister Lucille off the list. Father had never been able to stomach Lucille's constant yackety-yack about those boring Caribbean cruises her and Uncle Dan took every winter.

"And just who's brother never shuts up about his glorious high school football career, as though anyone cares about what happened thirty years ago?" rejoined Mother.

I remained silent, but my sister, always more forthright than me, jumped in with, "Let's not fight. An anniversary is a time of celebration, of loving and caring and sharing. Why can't we all just get along?"

"Good grief," said Mother as she glared at both my sister and myself, "what greeting card have you been reading? Between you and I, ours is not the most functional of families. A special occasion is a time when we can stick it to annoying relatives by leaving them out." With those parting words, Mother went to make supper, and Father to walk the dog.

"Okay," I said to Adele, "its obviously up to we two to send out the invitations ourselves. It will be a surprise party all right. Everyone will get a big surprise when they see who's there."

"Right," Adele replied. "Now, I know you like Cousin Carol, but I have a few thoughts on that matter."

21d Pronoun Reference

When you are speaking, you can usually make yourself understood even if you use pronouns rather vaguely. When you are writing, however, you need to make the connections between pronouns and nouns clear to your reader. When this connection is unclear, you have made an error in pronoun reference.

Here are some of the most common errors in pronoun reference.

Confusing Pronoun References

This problem is most likely to occur in sentences containing indirect speech.

VAGUE	When Kevin told Ali that he was being laid off, he was very upset.
CLEAR	Kevin was very upset when he told Ali, "I'm [or you're] being laid off."

Vague Use of *They* and *It*

Avoid using *they* if it doesn't refer to a specific noun in your writing.

VAGUE	They say that a number of western democracies are shifting politically to the right.
CLEAR	Respected commentators say that a number of western democracies are shifting politically to the right.

You can see a similar problem with *it* in this sentence.

VAGUE	I spent hours working out a detailed budget, but **it** didn't solve my financial problems.

This sentence leaves your reader wondering what didn't help: the time you spent working on your budget? the budget itself? A revised sentence might read like this.

CLEAR	I spent hours working out a detailed budget, but **this effort** did not solve my financial problems.

OR   I spent hours working out a detailed budget, but **the budget itself** did not solve my financial problems.

Vague Use of *That*, *Which*, and *This*

In some sentences, *that*, *which*, or *this* refers to several different ideas.

VAGUE   The cousins fought on different sides in the war, which tore their family apart.

What tore their family apart—the fact that they fought on different sides? the exploits? the war? A clearer version might read like this.

CLEAR   The family was torn apart by the cousins' decision to fight on different sides in the war.

Vague References to Possessive Pronouns

VAGUE   Unable to brake on the icy roads, Jesse slammed into the car's bumper that was stopped at a red light.

In this sentence, *that* refers to *the car's bumper*, an error suggesting that the car's bumper was stopped at the red light. You could revise this sentences as follows:

CLEAR   Unable to brake on the icy roads, Jesse slammed into the bumper of a car that was stopped at a red light.

*Pronoun
Reference*

Exercise 21.10

Revise the following sentences to clarify vague pronoun references.

1. They say that nightmares are caused by anxiety.
2. Why do you tease your sister and call her names when you know it upsets her?
3. Natalie was disappointed when Nicole told her that she didn't get the job.

4. I rested and drank plenty of fluids, but it didn't make me feel better.

5. Maxine wanted to subscribe to the newspaper, but they said that home delivery was not available in her neighbourhood.

6. The cash register stopped working because a customer's child had turned off the main switch, but at the time Giselle didn't know it.

7. Raul added too much water to the dough and beat it mercilessly, which is why the pie crust is tough.

8. Rex is lazy, immature, and irresponsible, but that doesn't bother his friends.

9. I heard that Raul left his wife and children and ran away to Tahiti to paint. This greatly surprised me.

10. Mr. Carlson applied too much weed killer and overwatered the grass, which ruined the lawn.

Exercise 21.11

Revise the following paragraph to eliminate all vague and ambiguous pronoun references.

Benevolence is certainly a desirable quality, but being like this doesn't give us the right to force our good will on others. In performing our good deed or random act of kindness for the day, we must guard against making assumptions about what they need. The fact that we may be too warm, for instance, doesn't mean that we have to turn up the car air conditioner and adjust the vent to blow directly into his or her face. We may love creamed rutabagas, which shouldn't compel us to urge third helpings on a dinner guest. And the fact that we know how to live our lives doesn't justify our constantly advising them on how to live theirs. There are times to help other people and times to respect their independence and their ability to help themselves.

21e

Pronouns of Address

21e Pronouns of Address

You establish your relationship to your reader by the **pronouns of address** you use (or don't use) in your first paragraph. If you want your readers to focus on you—your ideas, your experiences—use first-person pronouns (*I, me, my, mine*). If you want your readers to consider how your subject relates to them directly (as in sermons, advertisements, directions), use second-person pronouns (*you, your, yours*). If you use only nouns and third-person pronouns (*he, she, it, they*), you will encourage your readers to focus on your subject.

These sentences illustrate the different relationships you might establish with your readers in an article about word processors.

FIRST PERSON   When I first began to use a word processor, I lost several files.

SECOND PERSON   When you first begin to use a word processor, you may lose a few files.

THIRD PERSON   When they first begin to use a word processor, most people lose a few files.

Once you have established the basic pronouns of address for a piece of writing, do not shift abruptly and without reason to another set of pronouns.

NOT   When **you** first begin to use a word processor, **one** may lose a few files. [shift from second person to third person]

NOT   When **most people** begin to use a word processor, **you** may lose a few files. [shift from third person to second person]

Confusing pronoun shifts may occur from sentence to sentence as well as within sentences.

NOT   When **I** began to use a word processor, **I** lost several files. **You** find it hard at first to master the sequence of commands. [shift from first person to second person]

These shifts disrupt your relationship with your reader.

Correcting Pronoun Shifts

In the following example, the perspective shifts from the third person, *Conrad* (*he*), to the second person, *you*.

Conrad has invested **his** money wisely because, as an oil rig worker, **you** always face the possibility of seasonal unemployment.

There are two ways to correct this error.

- Replace *you* with *he*.

    Conrad has invested **his** money wisely because, as an oil rig worker, **he** always faces the possibility of seasonal unemployment.

- Rephrase the sentence to eliminate the use of the pronoun.

    Conrad has invested his money wisely because oil rig workers always face the possibility of seasonal unemployment.

Exercise 21.12

Revise the following sentences to eliminate pronoun shifts. Where there are several possibilities, be prepared to explain your choice. If the sentence is correct, write **C**.

1. I dislike asking Pauline for help because you never know whether she will keep her promise.
2. Even when you are knowledgeable and competent, many sales associates find dealing with a difficult customer to be an unnerving experience.
3. When you see Simon, you will be surprised at the changes in his appearance.
4. The owners claim that you can hear their ancestor's ghost on his nightly tour of the old mansion.
5. Colin has agreed to have a root canal rather than an extraction because you don't want to lose a tooth that can be saved.

Exercise 21.13

Revise the following paragraph to eliminate all pronoun shifts.

For Canadians, working in The Bahamas is not simply a matter of finding a job, packing a swimsuit, and heading south. Anyone seeking employment in The Bahamas must meet a number of requirements before you are considered for a work permit. One important requirement is verification from your prospective employer that the position was first advertised in The Bahamas but that no suitable candidate was found. The employer will usually handle this detail. The applicant arranges for the remaining documentation. For example, you must hold a valid passport. Applying for a passport involves submitting an application form along with two passport-size photographs. One photo and the form must be signed by a professional, such as a medical doctor or school principal, who acts as a guarantor. In addition to the passport, applicants must complete an Immigration Form I. In this form you provide information on passport number and date of expiry, all education and work experience, the job applied for, and expected salary. Applicants must also attach two signed, passport-size photographs to this form and enclose the following: police certificate showing no record of conviction for the past five years, a valid medical certificate issued no earlier than thirty days before completion of the form, references from two previous employers, and copies of any results of public examinations described in the section on education. You must have this form signed and dated by a Notary Public. Applicants will not receive permission to work in The Bahamas until you have submitted the Immigration Form 1 and all of the supporting documentation.

Pronouns of
Address

Chapter 22

Proofreading: Punctuation and Mechanics

22a Commas

When you are proofreading for errors in the use of commas, remember the following two principles:

- **Single commas** are used to separate the items in a series of words, phrases, or clauses and to set off elements at the beginning or end of the sentence.
- **Pairs of commas** are used to enclose parts of a sentence.

Key Terms to Know

A **series** consists of three or more similar grammatical constructions.

> To complete grade 12, Petra needs **English, chemistry**, and **physics**. [a series of nouns]

> Before leaving for the lake, Simon needs to **buy groceries, pack the camper**, and **pick up his children**. [a series of phrases]

> **If you can meet the entrance requirements, if you can find a sponsor**, and **if you can arrange your own transportation**, you can run in this year's marathon. [a series of clauses]

A **phrase** is a group of words without a subject and a verb (*around the corner, looking out the window, to finish the test on time*).

A **clause** is a group of words with a subject and verb.

A **main clause** can stand on its own as a sentence (*Sheila looked out the window*).

A **subordinate clause** cannot stand alone as a sentence (*After Sheila looked out the window*).

22a

Commas

Using Commas to Separate

Separating Items in a Series

Use a comma to separate words, phrases, or clauses in a series. Should you use a comma before the last item? Usage varies. We recommend putting a comma before the *and* or other conjunction that joins the last two items in the series, both to provide emphasis and to prevent misreading:

WITHOUT COMMA   I forgot to buy milk, orange juice, bread, peanut butter and jam. [does peanut butter and jam refer to one item or two?]

WITH COMMA   I forgot to buy milk, orange juice, bread, peanut butter, and jam.

- ***Words in a series***

    I forgot to buy orange juice, milk, bread, peanut butter, and jam. [unless you intended to buy a jar containing both peanut butter and jam]

Note 1: Do **not** put a comma between pairs of items considered a single unit.

    The Prime Minister said that full employment, regional development, and **law and order** are the chief priorities.

Note 2: Do **not** put commas between adjectives that could not be joined with *and*.

    James Cook was a highly skilled eighteenth-century navigator.

- ***Phrases in a series***

    The frightened puppy raced **through the door, down the hall,** and **under the bed.**

    Listening to music, playing cards, and **eating peanuts** are my favourite recreational activities.

- ***Clauses in a series***

    Mohammed handles the budget, Judy handles customer complaints, and **Philip handles the advertising.**

Exercise 22.1

Add all necessary commas to the following sentences.

1. Lorraine packed two suitcases called a cab and headed for the airport.

22a

Commas

2. The secret ingredients in my stew are eye of newt toe of frog wool of bat and tongue of dog.

3. We have agreed to put the armoire in the master bedroom the console in the hall and the pine desk in the study.

4. We'll need bread cheese cold cuts fruit and sodas for the picnic.

5. The diner complained that the meat was underdone the vegetables were soggy and the wine was sour.

Setting Off Main Clauses

Use a comma before the coordinating conjunctions *and, but, or, nor, for, yet*, and *so* when they join main clauses.

> The company sold off its unprofitable subsidiaries, **and** within six months its shares had doubled in value.

> Readers of the play may perceive Hamlet as slow to act, **but** on the stage the prince seems to rush headlong towards his death.

The comma is often omitted before *and* and *or* if the clauses are short or have the same subject.

> You stand in line and I'll find a table.

> They may achieve their goals or they may fail.

To prevent misreading, always use a comma before *for, so, yet* when used as coordinating conjunctions, since these words have other uses.

> The dog limped, **for** it was old. [coordinating conjunction]

> The dog limped **for** the door. [preposition]

22a

Commas

Exercise 22.2

Add all necessary commas to the following sentences.

1. We must go now for our ferry leaves exactly at noon.

2. Freida knocked down the wall and David hauled away the rubble.

3. Liam is a painstaking editor yet a few small errors escaped even his sharp eye.

4. The Richardsons knew that they must replace the worn linoleum and repaint the walls a neutral colour or the house would never sell.

5. When Fiona first began working as a cashier she thought that she would never remember the PLU's for produce but she had soon memorized dozens of codes.

Setting Off Introductory Elements

• *After introductory subordinate clauses*

Use a comma after an introductory subordinate clause. These clauses begin with subordinate conjunctions such as *although, because, after, when, before, since,* and *while.*

> Before anyone could stop the baby, she had grabbed the edge of the tablecloth and pulled the dishes to the floor.
>
> Because there has been so much rain, the mosquitoes have been bad this year.

• *After introductory interjections*

Use a comma after mild interjections (*oh, well, my goodness*), and after *yes* and *no.*

> My, what a beautiful baby.
>
> Yes, the merchandise that you ordered last week has arrived.

• *After introductory transitional words and phrases*

The usual practice is to put a comma after transitional phrases such as *for example, on the other hand, in contrast.* Put a comma after conjunctive adverbs of more than two syllables: after *nevertheless,* but not after *thus.*

> On the other hand, many prairie grain farmers are in desperate straits.
>
> Nevertheless, people were optimistic that the economy would improve.
>
> Thus we need to work out a new system to deal with rural bankruptcies.

Commas

Note: Do **not** use a comma after a subordinate conjunction.

NOT	Although, she was desperate for a cigarette, she was too intimidated to smoke.
BUT	Although she was desperate for a cigarette, she was too intimidated to smoke.

- *After introductory phrases of more than five words*

  Sitting patiently beside my neighbour's woodpile, Brutus stood vigilant guard over escaping field mice.

- *After any introductory element to prevent misreading*

  After the Smiths left, the Joneses turned out the porch light and retired for the evening.

  In the evening, darkness settled over the town.

Exercise 22.3

Add all necessary commas to the following sentences.

1. For example pizza has ingredients from all four food groups but it can also be high in fat.
2. During his years at university in Calgary Louis never took the opportunity to visit Banff or Lake Louise.
3. When Bret dropped the iron skillet on the tile floor he heard a sharp crack.
4. High above the planes flew in precise formation.
5. No I don't remember your lending me ten dollars.

Setting Off Elements at the End of a Sentence

Use a comma to set off a word, phrase, or clause at the end of a sentence that qualifies, contrasts with, or questions what comes before.

22a

Commas

  A puppy is a perfect pet, if you have lots of patience. [qualifying clause]

  I ordered the chicken, not the squid. [contrasting element]

  You'll give me a hand, won't you? [question]

Setting Off Direct Speech and Quotations

Use commas to set off direct speech and quotations from the rest of the sentence.

  Alice remarked, "The lights are on, but no one seems to be home."

  We see Hamlet's growing awareness of the burdens placed upon him when he says, "The time is out of joint. O cursed spite / That ever I was born to set it right!"

Note: Do **not** use a comma before a quotation when the structure of the sentence introducing the quotation does not call for one.

> We see Hamlet's hostility when he says that Claudius is "A little more than kin and less than kind."

Exercise 22.4

Add all necessary commas to the following sentences. If the sentence is correct, write **C**.

1. It's best to feed a cold and starve a fever isn't it?
2. Nathan is constantly telling me that "he who hesitates is lost."
3. However I always counter "Look before you leap."
4. Time and tide wait for no man if you catch my drift.
5. Music has its charms to soothe the savage breast not the savage beast.

Using Pairs of Commas to Enclose

Enclosing Interruptions in the Sentence

Use a pair of commas to enclose words, phrases, or clauses that slightly interrupt the flow of the sentence. Such expressions include parenthetical remarks (*of course, indeed, for example*), transitions (*however, therefore*), interjections (*well, oh*), and nouns of direct address (*Henry, Mother*).

> I will, as I have already told you, investigate the matter fully.
>
> The events described in this story are true. The names, however, have been changed to protect the innocent.
>
> I'd say he weighs about, oh, 80 kg.
>
> This decision, Kevin, is for you to make.

22a

Commas

Enclosing Nonrestrictive Phrases and Clauses

Use a pair of commas to enclose a nonrestrictive modifying phrase or clause. These clauses and phrases function as adjectives, but their presence is not essential to identifying the noun they modify. Instead, they supply additional or supplementary information.

Nonrestrictive clauses and phrases usually modify **proper nouns**—nouns that name a particular person or thing.

NONRESTRICTIVE   Bob Edward, publisher of *The Calgary Eye-Opener*, was an influential and controversial figure until his death in 1922.

NONRESTRICTIVE   Clarence's Uncle David, who is an accomplished seaman, is planning to sail around the world.

Clauses beginning with *which* are more likely to be nonrestrictive than are clauses beginning with *that*.

NONRESTRICTIVE   In the story, which is about a seemingly ordinary village lottery, the horrifying nature of the prize is not revealed until the draw has been made.

RESTRICTIVE   I've lost the book that I intended to lend you.

Note: Do **not** use commas to enclose a restrictive phrase or clause that provides essential information in the sentence.

RESTRICTIVE   Men wearing straw hats are a rare sight today. [Only men wearing straw hats are a rare sight.]

RESTRICTIVE   All customers who install a smoke detector are eligible for a discount on insurance premiums. [Only customers who install a smoke detector are eligible.]

RESTRICTIVE   The one book that I am determined to read this summer is *War and Peace*.

22a

Commas

Exercise 22.5

Add all necessary commas to the following sentences. If the sentence is correct, write **C**.

1. Thank you Mr. Sutherland for booking your vacation trip through our travel agency.

2. The people who live next door are covering their entire backyard in artificial grass.

3. Punch Dickins who won the Distinguished Flying Cross in World War I gained fame as a bush pilot in the 1920s.

4. Monty's python which hasn't eaten in a month has escaped from its cage.

5. Monty promised us however that we had nothing to fear.

Using Commas in Conventional Places

- Use a comma to separate the day of the month from the year.

    Canada celebrated its centennial on July 1, 1967.

Note: The comma is optional when only the month and year are given.

    Canada celebrated its centennial in July, 1967 [July 1967].

- Use a comma to separate the elements in geographic names and addresses.

    Architect Douglas Cardinal designed the Museum of Civilization in Hull, Québec.

    The couple were married at St. Joseph's Basilica, 10044-113 Street, Edmonton, Alberta.

- Use a comma after the salutation in personal or informal letters and after the closing in all letters.

    Dear Aunt Margaret,

    Yours truly,

    Sincerely yours,

Exercise 22.6 Comma Review

Add all necessary commas and delete unnecessary commas in the following sentences. If the sentence is correct, write **C**.

1. Have you stood in a winter storm at the corner of Portage and Main in Winnipeg Manitoba?

2. After Christmas the family ate turkey sandwiches turkey casserole and turkey croquettes for a week.

3. Repairing the defective component after the warranty has expired Mr. Fortino is not our responsibility.

4. When the signal on the microwave sounded Ted poured the wine and called his guests to the table.

5. The Sandersons are the only people who did not contribute money to the Victoria Day fireworks display.

22a

Commas

6. Whenever we go camping Father always says "If you don't fish where the fish are you'll be having hot dogs for supper."

7. Albert opened the window took a deep breath and composed his thoughts.

8. The one novel that I didn't read, was the basis for the essay question on the English exam.

9. Lucy Maud Montgomery the author of *Anne of Green Gables* was born in Clifton Prince Edward Island on November 30 1874.

10. Well you have certainly chosen a deep subject for your research paper.

11. To put the matter into its proper perspective I want you to consider the following factors.

12. Yes we do have that shoe style in your size.

13. I decided that Howard would bring the food Cliff would bring the drinks and you would bring the music.

14. The snow blockaded the door in deep drifts and icicles hung like spears from the roof.

15. Here is my estimate of the cost of paving your driveway. Taxes of course are not included.

16. Even during the day light could not penetrate the canopy of leaves.

17. Mr. Ramondo said "We're a few bricks short of a load but I think we have enough to build the fire pit."

18. Anyone who is caught stealing money will be terminated immediately.

19. On a dark stormy night I like nothing better, than to curl up with a good novel.

20. Cynthia went back to university to study engineering, because she discovered, that her B.A. in linguistics was not highly marketable.

22b Semicolons

Use a semicolon in the following ways.

- By itself to join two closely related main clauses

  The storm struck with a destructive fury; the ship was broken by the violent wind and waves.

Note 1: Never use a semicolon to join a subordinate clause to a main clause.

NOT

Although it had snowed heavily during the night; the roads were clear by noon the next day.

BUT

Although it had snowed heavily during the night, the roads were clear by noon the next day.

Note 2: Avoid using a semicolon as a kind of big comma for emphasis.

NOT

Horrified, Nelson watched the tidal wave approach; knowing that his tiny boat could never withstand its force.

BUT

Horrified, Nelson watched the tidal wave approach, knowing that his tiny boat could never withstand its force.

- With a conjunctive adverb (*nevertheless, however, otherwise, consequently, thus, therefore, then, meanwhile, moreover, furthermore*) or with a transitional phrase (*in addition, as a result, for example*) to join main clauses

    The advertisement states that applicants with a degree in a related area are preferred; **nevertheless**, applicants with a diploma and relevant experience will be considered for the position.

- With a coordinating conjunction (*and, but, or, nor, for, yet, so*) when the main clauses contain internal punctuation

    Already late for work, I dressed hurriedly, ran out of the house, and jumped into the car; but when I turned the key, I heard only the ominous clicking sound of a dying battery.

22b

Semicolons

- However, if you are joining two fairly short main clauses with a coordinate conjunction, a comma is a better choice.

NOT

Yvette longed to escape; yet she remained passive.

BUT

Yvette longed to escape, yet she remained passive.

- Instead of a comma between items in a series when the items themselves have internal punctuation

> The lottery prize includes the dream home, custom-built by a leading home builder; custom-made draperies, professional interior decorating, and exclusive furnishings; and free cleaning for one year.

Semicolons can be useful, but too many will give your writing a ponderous tone. If you're becoming addicted to the semicolon, you're probably relying too heavily on coordination to join your ideas.

> For several years, my computer has been working fine; now I'm having major problems. Perhaps a virus has infected the command system; the computer seems to be erasing files randomly. I'll have to be more careful to duplicate my material on backup disks; I'm losing too much valuable information.

You could improve this passage by introducing more subordination.

> Although my computer has been working fine for several years, now I'm having major problems. Perhaps a virus has infected the command system; the computer seems to be erasing files randomly. I'll have to be more careful to duplicate my material on backup disks because I'm losing too much valuable information.

For more information on joining sentences effectively, see Faulty Subordination (18e).

Exercise 22.7

Add semicolons where necessary to the following sentences.

Semicolons

1. Emilio wanted to be a famous astronaut he ended up operating the ferris wheel at the amusement park.

2. Zack thought that he had enough money in his account to pay for the new jeans however, his direct debit payment was not approved.

3. When the smoke had cleared from the oven, Lucas was afraid to open the door but, fortunately, a quick glance showed that the roast still looked edible.

4. Ashley is going camping with her family Erica has therefore agreed to take over the paper route for a week.

5. There was a heavy frost in the night as a result, farmers are concerned about the peach crop.

Exercise 22.8

Add semicolons where necessary to the following sentences. Replace inappropriate semicolons with the correct punctuation. If the sentence is correct, write **C**.

1. Even though the skater was disappointed with the poor marks for artistic interpretation; he was pleased with the high marks for technical merit.

2. Clean the gardening tools after each use otherwise, they will rust.

3. Betty stood at the bus stop; patiently waiting for the children to come home from school.

4. When John graduated from university, he was fortunate to get a junior management position with an accounting firm; he then began setting aside money to repay his student loan.

5. The variety show will feature Vox Populi, a well-known local band, the Crazy Bones, a hilarious comedy act, and the Tumbling Turners, an acrobatic troupe.

22c Colons and Dashes

The **colon** and the **dash** can both be used to introduce a phrase or clause that explains or illustrates what precedes it.

> After the tenth day without food, the subject began to exhibit psychological debilitation: he had trouble concentrating and slept much of the time.

> I still love listening to the Beatles—they remind me of the Sixties.

The colon is more appropriate for most formal writing situations. Use the dash when you want a more informal tone.

A pair of dashes can also be used to enclose parenthetical comments that slightly disrupt the flow of the sentence. By using dashes rather than commas or parentheses, you can set off these comments more emphatically from the rest of the sentence.

> The relationship between father and son—never very good—worsened as the son began to assert his independence.

Be careful not to overuse either the colon or the dash. Too many sentences containing colons will make your writing too formal and stilted. Too many sentences containing dashes will make your writing too choppy and informal.

22c

Colons and Dashes

Colons

Use a colon in the following situations.

- To introduce a list or series preceded by a complete main clause

  You will need the following equipment: a small tent, a sleeping bag, a camp stove, and several bottles of insect repellent.

- In a sentence introducing a list of items, you can use a colon after a verb when *as follows* or *the following* is strongly implied, as in this example:

  Our report includes:

  1. background information about the problem
  2. an analysis of its causes
  3. recommendations for solutions
  4. a detailed budget

Note: Do **not** use a colon with *such as* or *for example*.

NOT	The Robinsons brought back a number of souvenirs, such as: a red plush cushion with "Visit Niagara Falls" emblazoned on it, a slightly pornographic calendar, and two incredibly ugly beer mugs.
BUT	The Robinsons brought back a number of souvenirs, such as a red plush cushion . . .

- To introduce a concluding explanatory phrase

  She dedicated her research to one goal: finding the link between Einstein's theory of relativity and the theory of quantum mechanics.

Colons and Dashes

- To join main clauses when the second clause restates, explains, summarizes, or emphasizes the first

  The movie was a complete waste of time: the plot dragged, the characters were boring, and the special effects were silly.

- To introduce a formal quotation. Both the sentence introducing the quotation and the quotation itself must be grammatically complete.

  In Alice Munro's short story "Boys and Girls," the narrator gradually becomes aware of the full implications of being a girl: "A girl was not, as I had supposed, simply what I was; it was what I had to become. It was a definition, always touched with emphasis, with reproach and disappointment. Also it was a joke on me."

Note: Do **not** use a colon when the sentence introducing the quotation ends with *that* or is otherwise incomplete.

NOT	Hamlet shows a new acceptance of death when he says that: "There is a special providence in the fall of a sparrow."
BUT	Hamlet shows a new acceptance of death when he says that "There is a special providence in the fall of a sparrow."

- In biblical references (John 3:16)
- In time references (9:45, 12:05)
- Between the title and the subtitle of an article or a book
  A Harvest Yet to Reap: A History of Prairie Women
- After the salutation in a business letter
  Dear Business Manager:
  Dear Editor:
  Dear Ms. Bennett:

Dashes

Use a dash in the following situations.

- To indicate a sudden interruption or change of thought
  I left my briefcase—I remember it distinctly—right here by the front entrance.

  And then she said—but I see you've already heard the story.

- To emphasize parenthetical remarks
  Antonia worked hard—perhaps too hard—in spite of her illness.

- After a series at the beginning of a sentence
  Sports figures, entertainers, politicians—all have been invited to the wedding.

- To set off a series that comes in the middle of a sentence
  It had everything—power, grace, beauty—that Chantal wanted in a car.

- To emphasize an expression that explains or illustrates

    Philip worked tirelessly toward his goal—an A in English.

Exercise 22.9

Add colons and dashes where appropriate to the following sentences. Where either is possible, be prepared to explain your choice.

1. Mae West offers an interesting perspective on making moral choices "When choosing between two evils, I always like to try the one I've never tried before."

2. I have registered in the following courses for the winter term Basic Calculus, Fluid Dynamics, and Introductory Drafting.

3. I am convinced I say this without reservation that Luke and Laura will never get back together.

4. None of the suspects Winken, Blinken, or Nod knew that they were under surveillance for stealing the sleeping pills.

5. My cat Puck is an excellent companion he is intelligent, affectionate and infinitely patient.

Exercise 22.10

Add colons and dashes where appropriate to the following sentences. Where either is possible, be prepared to explain your choice. If the sentence is correct, write **C**.

1. He had no means of escape all of the exits were blocked.

2. When Herb boasted that he was a "self-made man," Vernon replied, "That's the trouble with cheap labour."

3. Mrs. Christie you met her last week at the Doyles' party will host a murder mystery dinner at her country retreat.

4. Pottery, weaving, and willow furniture all will be for sale at the spring craft show.

5. The puppy was in a piteous state he was caked with mud, shivering uncontrollably, and close to starvation.

Colons and
Dashes

22d Parentheses and Brackets

Both **parentheses** and **brackets** serve to set apart certain information in a sentence or a paragraph, but they are used in different circumstances.

Parentheses

Use parentheses in these situations:

- To set off supplementary material that interrupts the flow of the sentence

  The council finally agreed (but only after a heated debate) to the proposed amendments.

Note 1: Parentheses, dashes, and commas can all be used to set off nonessential information. When you enclose something in parentheses, you signal to your reader that it is relatively unimportant. Dashes tend to emphasize its importance, while commas will give it approximately equal weight.

Note 2: Do **not** use parentheses to enclose important information. In the example below, the parentheses are misleading because they suggest that essential information is incidental.

  Although he was only fifteen, Victor was sentenced to nine months in a juvenile detention centre. (This sentence was the result of his fifth conviction for theft over $1000 in two years.)

- To enclose explanatory material, such as bibliographical citations, brief definitions, and pieces of historical information

  The Celsius (centigrade) thermometer was invented by the Swedish astronomer Anders Celsius (1701–1744).

For information on parenthetical citations, see Appendix B, Documentation.

- To enclose letters or numerals in a list of items

  Each oral presentation will be graded on (1) delivery, (2) voice, (3) content, and (4) language.

Parentheses and Brackets

- In general, resist the temptation to use parentheses too often. Information enclosed in parentheses interrupts the flow and meaning of a sentence. Too many of these interruptions will make your writing choppy and hard to follow, as in the following example.

  Headhunting (often called an executive search) is the practice of seeking out (sometimes through advertising, sometimes through more direct approaches to individuals) senior, specialized employees (when no one with sufficient expertise is available within an organization) for business.

Rewritten with only one parenthetical comment, the paragraph reads much more smoothly.

Headhunting (as executive searches are often called) is the practice of seeking out specialized senior employees for business firms when no one with sufficient expertise is available within an organization. Headhunters may advertise these positions or approach prospective candidates directly.

Using Other Punctuation with Parentheses

- If the parenthetical remark is a sentence within another sentence, the parenthetical sentence does not begin with a capital or end with a period.

   The baby was sleeping (at least his eyes were closed) when I peeked into the room.

- If the parenthetical remark is a complete sentence that is not part of another sentence, capitalize the first word and put the end punctuation inside the closing parenthesis.

   After weeks of dull, cloudy weather, the first snowflakes began to fall on Christmas Eve. (The children had been convinced that Christmas wouldn't be Christmas without snow.)

- If the parenthetical construction within a sentence requires a question mark or exclamation mark, that punctuation goes inside the closing parenthesis.

   It is important for students to learn how to think (who can deny that necessity?), but they also need facts and information to think about.

Brackets

Use brackets in the following ways.

- To enclose explanatory material inserted into a quotation. These square brackets tell your reader that the material was not part of the original quotation.

   In the essay "Grace before Meat," Charles Lamb says, "I hate a man who swallows it [his food], affecting not to know what he is eating. I suspect his taste in higher matters."

Note: The punctuation of the original sentence (the comma after *it*) goes outside the material enclosed in brackets.

- To show that you have changed a word (usually a verb or a pronoun) in a direct quotation so that it will fit grammatically with your sentence

    Old King Cole [is] a merry old soul / And a merry old soul [is] he.

- With the word *sic* (Latin for *thus*) to indicate that an error in spelling, grammar, or fact is part of the original quotation

    The newspaper headline read "Affects [sic] of cutbacks not yet known."

22e Quotation Marks

The main purpose of **quotation marks** is to acknowledge that you have used someone else's words. Use quotation marks in the following situations.

- Whenever you quote more than three consecutive words from any printed material. (For how to document your sources, see Appendix B, Documentation.)

    According to the article, many primatologists and psychologists believe that "chimpanzees have the capacity for self-awareness, self-consciousness, and self-knowledge."

- When you include comments made by someone you have interviewed. (For how to document interviews in a research paper, see Appendix B, Documentation.)

    According to Sharon Bush, records clerk in the registrar's office, "The completion rate for this course averages about 30 percent."

- When you include dialogue in a personal narrative or a short story. Indent the words of each speaker as you would indent separate paragraphs.

    "Do you have any plans to publish your autobiography?" the critic asked the novelist.
    "Actually, I was saving the best till last," remarked the author. "I might even arrange to have it published posthumously."
    "The sooner, the better," replied the critic.

Note: Remember that quotation marks set off direct speech. Don't use them with indirect speech.

22e

Quotation Marks

DIRECT SPEECH	The clerk asked the customer, "Will you pay cash, or shall I charge this purchase to your account?"

INDIRECT SPEECH   The clerk asked the customer whether she wanted to pay cash or charge the purchase to her account.

- Use single quotation marks to indicate a quotation within a quotation.

    The witness testified, "I was present when the accused said, 'She'll pay for what she did to me!'"

Other Uses of Quotation Marks

- Put quotation marks around the titles of short works that have not been published separately, such as titles of chapters, short stories, articles, and most poems.

    His favourite Poe story is "The Fall of the House of Usher."

- When you want to draw your reader's attention to a word used in a special way, you can either underline the word to indicate that it is italicized (see Italics and Underlining, 22f) or put quotation marks around it.

    It's quite acceptable to begin a sentence with "because."

- Avoid using either quotation marks or italics merely to draw attention to slang or irony.

NOT   My sister has become a real "couch potato."

NOT   Our "paperboy" is at least fifty years old.

Exercise 22.11

Quotation marks

Use quotation marks appropriately in the following sentences. If the sentence is correct, write **C**.

1. Two negatives make a positive, explained Ludwig. However, two positives don't make a negative.

    Yeah, right! replied Noam.

2. Heather said that she would pick Katie up from work and save Mother the trip.

3. According to an old Russian proverb, When money talks, the truth keeps silent.

4. I wish you would stop saying like and basically in every sentence. That habit drives me crazy, you know.

5. Virginia Woolf's essay The Death of the Moth is a thoughtful meditation on the nature of the life force.

Using Other Punctuation with Quotation Marks

When you close a quotation, should the end punctuation go inside or outside the quotation marks? Follow these guidelines.

- As a general rule, commas and periods go inside quotation marks; colons and semicolons go outside.

> Staring in disgust at the cans of escargots in the specialty section of the grocery store, Mr. Johnson remarked to his wife, "Let's can all the snails from the garden. We'll make a fortune." [Period is inside quotation marks.]

> Facing Mr. Waters squarely, William replied, "That, sir, is not your concern"; he then walked resolutely out of the room. [Semicolon is outside the quotation marks.]

- When a quotation is a question or an exclamation, the question or exclamation mark goes inside the quotation marks.

> "Where are the snows of yesteryear?" she asked pensively.

> "Get out of my way!" the enraged customer bellowed as he pushed through the crowd.

- When the entire sentence containing the quotation is a question or an exclamation, the question or exclamation mark goes outside the quotation marks.

> What does it mean to say "A stitch in time saves nine"?

> The Great China Circus is now truly "the greatest show on Earth"!

- When a quotation ends a sentence, whatever punctuation is inside the quotation mark also ends the entire sentence. Don't add any other punctuation.

> Jane listened with growing horror as the voice from the attic screamed, "Please let me out!"

22e

Quotation Marks

Exercise 22.12

Use quotation marks appropriately in the following sentences. Be sure to punctuate each sentence correctly. If the sentence is correct, write **C**.

1. No, I won't move my car shouted the irate driver.
2. Aunt Eva is fond of saying that no one is responsible for making another person happy.

3. Was it Archimedes who said Give me a firm place to stand, and I will move the earth

4. The term portmanteau word refers to a word combining the sounds and meanings of two other words. For example, the word smog is a blending of the words smoke and fog

5. In today's English class we explored the attitudes to war expressed in Wilfred Owen's poem Dulce et Decorum Est and Randall Jarrell's poem The Death of the Ball Turret Gunner

Exercise 22.13

Use quotation marks and other punctuation appropriately in the following sentences.

1. What did Mother mean when she said The acorn never falls far from the oak tree

2. If fifty million people say a foolish thing noted Anatole France it is still a foolish thing

3. Hearing the familiar bell, the children ran into the street yelling We all scream for ice cream

4. The words chimpanzee, gorilla, and zebra all came into English from African languages.

5. Sitting alone in the darkened room, Steve morosely hummed the tune to Sam Cooke's Sad Mood

22f

Italics and Underlining

22f Italics and Underlining

Use **italic** script in typeset and word-processed material, or underlining in handwritten or typed material, for each of the following cases.

- For the titles of books, newspapers, magazines, pamphlets, plays, films, television and radio series, works of art, albums or long musical compositions

  The city library has purchased two sets of *The Canadian Encyclopedia.*

  The police drama *Homicide: Life on the Streets* steadily gained popularity during its first few years.

- For the names of airplanes, ships, trains, and spacecraft

  Do not underline *the* or abbreviations that come before the name.

  > Captain James Cook commanded the H.M.S. *Resolution* on his second Pacific voyage.

- For foreign words and phrases that have not been accepted as English terms

  Examples of these expressions include the following:

  > *bon vivant* (a person who enjoys food and drink)
  > *casus belli* (an event that brings about war)
  > *tête à tête* (an intimate conversation between two people)
  > *weltanschauung* (a comprehensive concept of the universe and the relationship of humans to it)

- For words referred to as words, letters referred to as letters, and numerals referred to as numerals

  > The one word on the test that I couldn't define was *dipsomaniac*.

  > Don't forget to cross your *t*'s.

  > Is this an *8* or a *3*?

- For emphasis and clarity

  > I asked *who* you are, not *how* you are.

  > Late papers will *not* be accepted.

Note: Be cautious whenever you are tempted to use italics for emphasis. Like exclamation marks, italics lose their effectiveness if overused.

22g Hyphens

Hyphens are used as part of some compound words (*father-in-law*, *trade-in*). Other compound words are written as one word (*hairbrush, stepmother*) or as two words (*lawn bowling, token payment*). Because there is no pattern for forming compound words, and because compound words are constantly changing, your best source of current information is an up-to-date dictionary. You may find that dictionaries disagree on compound forms. Choose one spelling and use it consistently.

Use a hyphen in the following ways:

- With two-word numbers from twenty-one to ninety-nine

  > There are **ninety-nine** bottles of beer on the wall.

- With numbers used as adjectives

  Is the tank three-quarters full?

  Atsuko, a thirty-four-year-old musician, made her television debut last night.

- With the prefixes *self* (*self-satisfied*), *ex* (*ex-husband*), and *all* (*all-purpose*); with prefixes that come before proper nouns (*anti-Catholic*); and with the suffix *elect* (*minister-elect*).

- To avoid an awkward combination of letters or to prevent misunderstanding: *re-cover* (cover again)

- To indicate that two or more prefixes or words share a common root

  Both pre- and post-natal classes are available.

  This course covers eighteenth- and nineteeth-century drama.

- To join two or more words that function as a single adjective conveying a single concept: *well-written essay, reddish-brown hair*

Note 1: If these constructions come after the noun, they are **not** hyphenated.

  The essay is well written.
  Her hair is reddish brown.

Note 2: If the group of words contains an *ly* adverb, do **not** hyphenate: *poorly conceived plan, frequently used reference book.*

Hyphenating Words at the End of Lines

Hyphens

It's best to avoid dividing words at the end of a line if possible. Occasionally, however, you may not be able to squeeze all the letters on the line you are writing. Here are the guidelines to follow:

- Always hyphenate a word between syllables. The first part of the word must contain at least three letters. Try to divide the word in two approximately equal parts that convey the sense of the whole word (*butter-fly* not *but-terfly*).

- When a double consonant occurs at the end because you have added a suffix (*ing, ed*), divide between the two consonants (*let-ting* not *lett-ing*). If the root word ends in a double consonant, divide between the root word and the suffix (*bill-ing* not *bil-ling*).

- Include a single-letter syllable with the first part of the word (*regu-late* not *reg-ulate*).

- Do **not** hyphenate one-syllable words or words of five or fewer letters (regardless of the number of syllables). If possible, avoid hyphenating words of six letters.

- Do **not** hyphenate figures ($21.36, 123 000), dates (Dec. 10, 1926), abbreviations (UNICEF), or proper names (Albert Einstein, Calgary).

- Do **not** hyphenate the last word of more than two consecutive lines.

- Do **not** hyphenate the last word in a paragraph or the last word on a page.

Exercise 22.14

Add, change, or take out hyphens as necessary in the following sentences.

1. This neutral carpet can serve as an allpurpose floor-covering in any room.
2. You are looking particularly selfsatisfied after winning the job over twenty three equally-qualified candidates.
3. If you want to use gender neutral terms, use "workers" rather than "work-men" and "humanity" rather than "man-kind."
4. The ninety year old woman made her first parachute jump on the week-end.
5. Julia's ex boyfriend returned all the compact-discs she had given him as presents.

Exercise 22.15

How would you hyphenate each of the following words if it appeared at the end of a line? If the word should not be hyphenated, write **C**.

1. iconoclast
2. crybaby
3. wrapping
4. faded
5. CUSO
6. railroad
7. thrilling
8. jimjams
9. memorize
10. radio

22g

Hyphens

22h Apostrophes

Because plurals, possessives, and contractions using *s* sound the same, your ear is not a reliable guide for when and how to use an **apostrophe**. Instead, you need to know which of these forms you intend to create so that you can use the apostrophe appropriately. Remember, too, that if you're unsure of how to use an apostrophe, you are as likely to put it in the wrong place as to omit it in the right place.

- A **plural noun**, which is usually formed by adding *s* or *es*, indicates that more than one person, place, or thing is being discussed. Do not add an apostrophe when you wish to indicate a plural. Be especially careful with proper nouns.

PLURAL   All the **Joneses** congratulate you on keeping up with them. [The plural of *Jones* is formed by adding *es*.]

POSSESSIVE   The **Joneses'** car is in the garage. [The apostrophe indicates that the car belongs to the Joneses.]

- A **contraction** indicates that one or more letters have been omitted. The sense of the sentence will indicate whether the apostrophe signals possession or a contraction.

CONTRACTION   Your **report's** already three weeks late. [*report's = report is*]

POSSESSIVE   Your **report's** recommendations are out of line with current department policy. [The apostrophe indicates that the recommendations belong to the report.]

- **Possessive pronouns** (*yours, hers, its, ours, theirs*) do not take apostrophes. Only nouns and indefinite pronouns (*someone, something, somebody, everyone, everything, everybody, no one, nothing, nobody, anything, anybody*) take an apostrophe to show possession.

NOT   These problems are **their's** to solve.

BUT   These problems are **theirs** to solve.

- *Its* is a possessive; *it's* is a contraction.

POSSESSIVE   The dog buried **its** bone in the garden.

CONTRACTION   **It's** a serious problem.

22h

Apostrophes

Guidelines for Making Nouns and Indefinite Pronouns Possessive

- To make an indefinite pronoun possessive, add *'s*.

  This is **nobody's** business.

  Everyone's assignments have been marked.

- To make a singular noun that does not end with *s* possessive, add *'s*.

  The **child's** bike lay abandoned on the driveway.

  The **horse's** saddle is hanging on a nail in the barn.

- To make a singular noun that ends with *s* or *ss* possessive, add *'s* if the word is one syllable. Add only an apostrophe if the noun is more than one syllable.

  James's gloves are lying on the hall table.

  The **boss's** instructions are on her desk.

  The next **witness'** testimony is crucial to the defence.

  The **actress'** hopes were raised by the screen test.

- To make a plural noun that ends with *s* possessive, add only an apostrophe.

  All **students'** marks will be posted by the main office.

  There will be a meeting of the **girls'** hockey team on Wednesday.

- To make a plural noun that does not end with *s* possessive, add *'s*.

  Men's suits are on sale this week.

  The **children's** story hour has been cancelled.

- To make a compound noun possessive, add *'s* to the last word.

  Mario borrowed his **father-in-law's** lawn mower over the weekend.

- To indicate that two or more people own one thing (joint possession), add *'s* to the last name.

  Carmen and Roberta's restaurant opened last month.

- To indicate that two or more people own things separately (separate possession), make all the names possessive.

  Ralph's and **Howard's** cars are in for repairs.

22h

Apostrophes

Note: Possessive nouns do not always refer to people. They can also refer to animals or objects.

  The **sun's** rays are very strong today.

Today's news is better.

This **society's** children have special needs.

Exercise 22.16

Add all necessary apostrophes to the following sentences.

1. Helens and Stephanies projects both won honourable mentions at this years science fair.

2. Several patrons cars were vandalized in the mall parking lot.

3. Nobodys pecan pie is as good as yours.

4. Mens and womens cross trainers are advertised in the stores flyer.

5. Annes sister-in-laws mail was delivered to the wrong address three days in a row.

Other Uses of the Apostrophe

- To form the plural of letters, add 's. Italicize or underline the letter but not the s.

    Pay particular attention to the long *o*'s in this poem.

- To form the plural of words referred to as words, add 's. Italicize or underline the word but not the s.

    There are five *a lot*'s in this one paragraph.

- To form the plural of abbreviations, add 's.

    She has two **M.A.'s**, one in English and one in history.

- You have a choice in forming the plural of numerals and dates. Add 's or s alone.

    His family emigrated from Scotland in the **1920's** [1920s].

    What are the chances of rolling nothing but **2's** [2s] in a dice game?

Exercise 22.17

Add all necessary apostrophes to the following sentences.

1. For some reason, I can never remember that *vacuum* has two *us* and only one *c*.

2. Its important to respond to your hostess invitation promptly and courteously.

3. Lester and Marys puppy chewed up three pairs of shoes in less than a week.

4. Justins parents cottage is badly in need of a new roof.

5. Someones pen was left on the desk.

6. I need to buy some apples and bananas for the childrens lunches.

7. Short pauses in your oral presentation are perfectly acceptable. Dont fill the space with *ums* and *uhs*.

8. Janet paid a months rent in advance before moving into her apartment.

9. Wont you have more tea and another of Grandmother Mildreds ginger snap cookies?

10. The books cover has been torn in half.

22i *Abbreviations*

Abbreviations are appropriate in scientific and technical writing and in footnotes and bibliographies. In most other kinds of writing, use abbreviations sparingly. If you wish to abbreviate a term that you intend to use repeatedly, write the term out in full the first time you use it, and then use the abbreviation.

> American Sign Language (ASL) is the first language of many deaf children. Because ASL has a different grammatical structure from English, deaf children who use ASL must learn English as a second language.

The following guidelines cover the appropriate uses of abbreviations in nontechnical writing.

Names of Dates and Times

- Write out the names of months and holidays.

> **Hanukkah** comes in the darkest part of December.

- Use *a.m.* (*ante meridiem*) to refer to exact times before noon and *p.m.* (*post meridiem*) to refer to exact times after noon. Note that these abbreviations are not capitalized.

> The meeting began at 9:07 a.m. and concluded at 5:31 p.m.

- Use *BC* (Before Christ) to refer to dates before the birth of Christ. Put *BC* after the date. Use *AD* (*anno Domini*) to refer to dates after the birth of Christ. Put *AD* before the date. Stop using *AD* when you can assume that your reader knows that the event did not take place before the birth of Christ, usually for any date after AD 500.

> Julius Caesar, who unified the Roman Empire under his dictatorship, was assassinated in **44 BC.**

> Hadrian's Wall, completed in **AD 123**, was constructed to prevent northern tribes from invading Roman Britain.

If you prefer, use BCE (Before the Common Era) and CE (Common Era). Both of these abbreviations follow the year.

Units of Measurement

Write out metric words such as *gram, metre*, and *kilometre* when you use them without numerals.

> Speed limits are now given in kilometres per hour.

Abbreviate these words when you use them with a numeral. Don't put a period after the abbreviation.

> Combine 10 g flour with 1 l milk.

Scientific and Technical Terms

Some commonly known scientific and technical terms are usually abbreviated.

> DNA (deoxyribonucleic acid)
>
> DDT (dichlorodiphenyltrichloroethane)
>
> AIDS (Acquired Immune Deficiency Syndrome)

Common Latin Terms

Although it's useful to know the following Latin abbreviations, it's usually better to omit them or replace them with English equivalents. If you use them, note where the periods go.

> **e.g.** *exempli gratia* (for example)
>
> **i.e.** *id est* (that is)
>
> **etc.** *et cetera* (and so forth)

Be especially careful with *etc.* Using it at the end of a list suggests that you have run out of ideas. Instead, use the phrase *such as* or an equivalent expression.

> NOT   The Niagara region grows apples, peaches, pears, **etc.**

The Niagara region grows fruits **such as** apples, peaches, and pears.

The Ampersand (&)

Never use this symbol in general writing. Use the ampersand only when you are copying the name of an organization or following APA documentation style.

> He works the night shift at the local **A&W**.
>
> Maccoby, E.E. **&** Jacklin, C.N. (1974) . . .

22j Capitalization

All proper nouns are capitalized. A proper noun names a specific person, place, or thing.

> Meet me at the main entrance of **The Bay**.

Use capitalization in the following way:

- For kinship terms such as mother, father, brother, sister when they are part of a name (as in *Mother Teresa, Grandfather McGregor*) or when they are used as a substitute for the proper name. Do not capitalize kinship terms preceded by a possessive adjective (*my, our, your, her, his, their*).

  > Is **Baba Kostash** going to the dance?
  >
  > Is **Grandfather** going to the dance?
  >
  > We are going with our father and mother.

- For titles used as part of a person's name

  > I have a meeting with **Professor Qureshi** this afternoon.
  >
  > I get along well with two of my **professors** this term.

- For the names of directions (*north, south, east, west*) when they are part of a proper name or a place name in themselves

  > It has always been his ambition to travel to the **North**.
  >
  > The house faces **north**. [*North* names a direction, not a place.]

- For the names of planets, stars, and other heavenly bodies. Do not capitalize *sun* and *moon*. Do not capitalize *earth* when it is modified by *the*.

  > The astronauts saw **Earth** from their spaceship.
  >
  > Unless we act now, all the waters of **the earth** will be polluted.

- For the names of institutions, organizations, political parties, and branches of government. Do not capitalize words such as *party*, *college*, or *university* unless you are using the term as a shortened version of the full name.

> Faryl has a **university** degree in biology.
>
> Tim will complete his final year at **Capilano College** this spring.

- For nationalities, languages, religious groups, religions, sacred and religious names.

> Canadian, Cree, Protestant, Taoism, the Koran, the Bible

- For days of the week, the months, holidays, events. Do not capitalize the names of seasons.

> Monday, January, New Year's Eve, the Middle Ages, summer, winter, spring, fall

- For the names of specific courses. Do not capitalize the names of general subjects, except languages.

> **Psychology** 101, **Chemistry** 400
>
> I studied **English, French, drama, math,** and **sociology** in my first year of university.

Other Occasions for Capitalization

- Capitalize the first word in a quotation if the quotation is a complete sentence. If the quotation is not a complete sentence, do not capitalize the first word.

> The instructor turned to me and said, "Please give me your views on the opening scene in *Macbeth*."
>
> Susan remarked that she would rather be "poor and healthy" than "rich and sick."

- Capitalize the first, last, and all important words in the titles of books, short stories, plays, poems, articles, newspapers, magazines, movies, and musical compositions.

> *The Day the Earth Stood Still*   *Pride and Prejudice*
> *Empire of the Sun*   *Of Mice and Men*

22k

Numbers

22k Numbers

Numerals are appropriate and preferred in scientific and technical writing. In general writing, however, certain conventions determine the use of numerals or words to express numbers.

Use numerals in nontechnical writing in the following cases:

- *To provide a series of numbers*

> In 1986, **250** children were involved in the school lunch program. By 1987, the number had increased to **300** children. Last year, **350** children were eating lunch at school.

- **To express a number that would take more than two words to spell out**

  Last year the shelter for battered women helped **259** women and their children.

- **To express exact times of the day and with a.m. and p.m.**

  We'll begin the meeting at **9:15** sharp.

  The plane from Toronto will arrive at **8:03 a.m.**

- **To express exact sums of money**

  This wonderful car can be yours for only **$2999.99**.

- **To express dates.** Years are always expressed in numerals; centuries should be written out.

  The events between **1939** and **1945** affected the rest of the **twentieth century**.

You can use *st, nd, rd, th* with numerals in dates if you do not give the year, but these abbreviations are not essential.

  The concert is scheduled for August 20th [or August 20].

- **To express addresses**

  2939 107 Street; #976, 10098 Elm Street; P.O. Box 12

- **To express percentages and decimals**

  29%, 87 percent, 3.9 cm

- **To express page, line, verse, act, and scene numbers in literary works.** See Appendix B, Documentation for more information.

  Act 3, Scene 2, lines 23–38 **or** 3.2.23–28

  John 1:1–5; 1 & 2 Corinthians

Use words in place of numerals in these two instances:

- **For numbers that can be spelled out in one or two words**

  At least **fifty** people were invited to the party.

- **To express round numbers used with money, times of the day, and measurements**

  Every day she gets up at **five o'clock** to do her homework.

  I used to be able to buy a huge bag of candy for **ten cents**.

  The man loitered in the alley about **two metres** from the parked car.

22k

Numbers

- ## *When you begin a sentence with a number*

    Thirty percent of first-year students need some form of financial assistance.

Note: Use a combination of words and numerals to prevent confusion.

NOT   He ordered **2 10 cm** pieces of wood.

BUT   He ordered **two 10 cm** pieces of wood.

Exercise 22.18

Correct all errors in the use of numerals or words to express numbers in the following sentences. If the sentence is correct, write **C**.

1. He bought 4 250-page packages of binder paper at the beginning of the term.

2. 15 percent of those polled responded that they were still undecided about how they would vote in the election.

3. At least 20 customers have returned the sheets because they were labelled the wrong size.

4. Including the PST and GST, the chocolate bar costs $1.14.

5. Some sports analysts say that Wayne Gretzky was at his peak playing with the Edmonton Oilers in the nineteen eighties. Gretzky retired from professional hockey in nineteen ninety-nine.

22l *Commonly Misused Words*

221

Commonly Misused Words

Here is a list of frequently misspelled or misused words and expressions.

A Lot

A lot is an informal expression meaning *many, much,* or *a great deal of.* Avoid *a lot* in most writing. When you use it, spell it as two words.

    I have **a lot** of work to do this weekend.

Affect/Effect

Affect is usually a verb.

    Her mood was **affected** by the cold weather and the isolation.

Effect is usually a noun.

Extreme cold and isolation have an **effect** on most people's nerves.

All Right

All right should be spelled as two words. *Alright* is incorrect and should not be used.

"**All right**," the coach agreed reluctantly, "you can miss the practice Thursday afternoon."

Allude/Elude

Use *allude* when you mean *refer to*, as in an allusion to the Bible or to Shakespeare.

In his opening comments, the guest speaker **alluded** to Hamlet's indecision.

Use *elude* when you mean to *avoid* or *escape*.

The wary old wolf managed to **elude** the hunter.

Allusion/Illusion

An **allusion** is a reference, often to literature, the Bible, or an historical event or figure.

The commander clarified his attitude toward wars of conquest with an **allusion** to the exploits of Alexander the Great.

An **illusion** can be something that deceives a person by producing a false impression. An illusion can also refer to the state of mind in the person who is deceived.

The mirror in the fun house gave viewers the **illusion** that they had just grown a metre taller.

Mirrie clung to the **illusion** that Dennis would always love her.

Among/Between

Use *between* when you are referring to two things.

Divide the candy **between** the twins.

Use *among* when you are referring to more than two.

Share the food **among** all the refugees at the shelter.

Amount/Number

Use *amount* to refer to things considered as a mass (*a large amount of work, a small amount of money*). Use *number* to refer to things that can be counted (*a large number of people, a small number of desks*).

A large **amount** of money is missing.

A large **number** of bills were stolen.

Bored with

Use *bored with* (never *bored of*) to mean *wearied with dullness*.

She is **bored with** her courses this year.

Cite/Site/Sight

Cite is a verb meaning to quote from a source (usually an authority) to support an argument or to acknowledge a source of information.

Frederick **cited** recent statistics on the decline of fish stocks.

Site is a noun meaning a place.

This is the **site** of the original fort.

Sight can be a noun or a verb referring either to the sense of vision or to something remarkable to look at.

Jack recovered his **sight** after cataract surgery.

At last the weary hikers **sighted** the hostel.

The final seconds of the fireworks were an amazing **sight**.

Defer/Differ

Use *defer to* when you mean *to give respect to* or *to yield to*.

I'll **defer** to the experts in this area.

Use *differ from* when you mean *to be unalike*.

Your interpretation of the new tax laws **differs from** mine.

Disinterested/Uninterested

Use *disinterested* when you mean *impartial*.

The two sides in the dispute sought the advice of a **disinterested** third party.

Use *uninterested* when you mean *not interested*.

Jacob was completely **uninterested** in hockey.

Elusive/Illusory

Use *elusive* when you want to describe something that is good at escaping or difficult to express or define.

> The **elusive** silver wolf disappeared into the dark forest.

> The practical implications of the employment equity policy remained **elusive**.

Use *illusory* when you want to describe something that is false or unreal.

> Given the decline in sales, plans to expand the business are **illusory**.

Hanged/Hung

Use *hanged* as the past tense of the verb *to hang* when you are referring to a person.

> The convict **was hanged** at dawn.

Use *hung* when you are referring to objects.

> Her latest painting **was hung** in the city gallery.

Hopefully

Hopefully is an adverb meaning *full of hope*. It is used correctly in this sentence: *The sales representative knocked hopefully at the door.*

Do not use *hopefully* to mean *I hope* or *perhaps*.

NOT   Hopefully, we'll be able to meet next week.

BUT   Perhaps [or I hope] we'll be able to meet next week.

It's/Its

It's is the contraction for *it is*.

> **It's** about time you got here.

Its is the possessive form of *it*.

> The dog jealously guarded **its** new toy.

Don't put an apostrophe in *its* unless you mean *it is*.

Lead/Led

The past tense of the verb *to lead* is *led*.

> Yesterday he **led** the band in the Earth Day parade.

Commonly Misused Words

Less/Fewer

Use *less* with mass nouns (*less unemployment, less hunger*) and *fewer* with countable nouns (*fewer courses, fewer assignments*).

I'm having **fewer problems** this year.

I'm having **less difficulty** this year.

Lie/Lay

The principal parts of the verb *to lie* (to recline) are *lie, lay, lying,* and *lain*.

The principal parts of the verb *to lay* (to place) are *lay, laid, laying,* and *laid*.

Be careful not to confuse these verbs.

NOT	She **lays** on the chesterfield all afternoon.
BUT	She **lies** on the chesterfield all afternoon.
NOT	He **laid** in the sun for half an hour.
BUT	He **lay** in the sun for half an hour.

Like/As

Use *like* as a preposition. Use *as* to introduce a clause.

She was witty and informal, **like** any good master of ceremonies.

She was witty and informal, **as** any good master of ceremonies should be.

221

*Commonly
Misused
Words*

Loose/Lose

Loose is usually an adjective or adverb (*loose change, loose clothing, let loose*).

Occasionally *loose* is used as a verb meaning *to set free* (*He loosed the dog on the intruder*). Don't confuse *loose* with *lose* (to misplace).

He often **loses** his way when he is in a strange city.

I can only give you a **loose** translation of that phrase.

Principal/Principle

Principal means *main* or *chief*.

My **principal** objection to the new plan is the cost.

Principle means *rule* or *belief*.

What are the main **principles** underlying the pro-life position on abortion?

Take Part in/Partake of

To *take part in* something is *to join* or *to participate*. To *partake of* is *to have a share of something* (usually a meal).

Hamlet refused to **take part in** the wedding festivities.

Would you be willing to **partake of** our simple meal?

Their/There/They're

Their is the possessive form of *they* (*their house, their mortgage*).

There is an adverb (*Put the plant over there*) or an expletive (*There were many more problems to be solved*).

They're is a contraction for *they are* (*They're going south for a week*).

Then/Than

Then is an adverb meaning *at that time*.

Our expectations were higher **then**.

Than is a conjunction usually found after comparative adjectives and adverbs.

In the past, our expectations were higher **than** they are now.

Your/You're

Your is the possessive form of *you* (*your book, your problem*).

You're is a contraction for *you are* (*You're late again.*)

221

Commonly Misused Words

Exercise 22.19

Correct all the usage errors in the following sentences. Some sentences have more than one error.

1. Archaeologists have uncovered what they believe is the principle residence of Colonel John Butler in Niagara-on-the-Lake. Butler lead his Loyalist Rangers in numerous raids into New York State during the American War of Independence.

2. Its true that your now taller then your father, but you still weigh considerably less.

3. During a chinook some people suffer from headaches or depression; others are not effected at all.

4. Louis Riel was hung at Regina on November 7, 1885.

5. "Help, I'm loosing my balance!" yelled Jack.
"Are you alright?" Jill called after him as he tumbled down the hill.

6. Rip is over their laying under the maple tree, apparently disinterested in everything around him.

7. By the middle of the movie, a lot of the patrons were bored of the trite plot and one-dimensional characters. In fact, a considerable amount of people had already left the theatre.

8. Like I said before, I usually trust my own judgment, but this time I'll differ to your greater experience.

9. Mother divided the candy equally between all the children.

10. Hopefully, we will be able to catch David Copperfield's special on television. He is a master of allusion.

221

*Commonly
Misused
Words*

Reference Works

- The classic *Elements of Style* by Strunk and White
  www.columbia.edu/acis/bartleby/strunk

- *Webster's Dictionary*
  c.gp.cs.cmu.edu:5103/prog/webster

- *Roget's Thesaurus*
  humanities.uchicago.edu/forms_unrest/ROGET. html

- University of Maine Writing Center Online Resources for Writers, including several translation dictionaries
  www.umaine.edu/~wcenter

- Carnegie-Mellon Online Reference Works
  www.cs.cmu.edu/Web/references.html

- University of Toronto Library
  utll.library.utoronto.ca/www/writing/advise.html

Writing Centre Handouts

- The Online Writing Centre at Purdue offers handouts on a variety of writing-related topics. This site provides links to approximately fifty other online writing sites.
  owl.english.purdue.edu/owls/writing-labs.html

- These are handouts written since 1993 by consultants at the Undergraduate Writing Center at U.T. Austin—they include information on apostrophes, documenting sources, non-sexist language, reading literature, and wordiness.
  www.utexas.edu/depts/uwc/.html/handout.html

Grammar Guides

- An Elementary Grammar—from The English Institute in the U.K.
  www.hiway.co.uk/~ei/intro.html

- From the University of Ottawa—Hypergrammar is an online grammar handbook.
  www.uottawa.ca/academic/arts/writcent/hypergrammar.html

- Grammar and Style Notes by Jack Lynch at Rutgers University—alphabetical listing
  andromeda.rutgers.edu/~jlynch/Writing

*Commonly
Misused
Words*

General Writing Resources

- If you log on to **www.altavista.com** and type "online writing" in the SEARCH box, you will find dozens of sites for online writing resources.

APPENDICES

Appendix A

Quotations

A1 Using Direct Quotations

Although you will often need to cite sources of information in any paper you are writing, you don't always need to quote your sources directly. In fact, you shouldn't include quotations unless the exact wording seems important. For this reason, you're more likely to use direct quotations in literature essays than in essays for the sciences and social sciences.

It takes skill and practice to use direct quotations effectively. Follow the guidelines below. The examples come from Jane Austen's novel *Pride and Prejudice* (Oxford: Oxford UP, 1970).

Use Your Own Words

Make all the major points in your own words and use brief quotations to support them. Do not rely on the quotation to make the point for you; your reader may interpret the quotation quite differently from the way you do. Often you can shorten a quotation by expressing most of it in your own words and quoting only the crucial part.

Weak Example

Charlotte's extremely practical approach to the central problem in *Pride and Prejudice*—how to catch a suitable man—is clear in the following comment:

> If a woman conceals her affection with the same skill from the object of it, she may lose the opportunity of fixing him; and it will then be but poor consolation to believe the rest of the world equally in the dark. There is so much of gratitude or vanity in almost every attachment, that it is not safe to leave any to itself. We can all begin freely—a slight preference is natural enough; but there are very few of us who have heart enough to be really in love without encouragement. In nine cases out of ten, a woman had better shew more affection than she feels (17).

Strong Example

Charlotte's extremely practical approach to the central question in *Pride and Prejudice*—how to catch a suitable man—is clearly set out in her comment that a woman should not be too cautious in showing a man that she likes him. Charlotte acknowledges that there is some risk of embarrassment, but this risk is preferable to losing him. After all, as Charlotte points out, "there are very few of us who have heart enough to be really in love without encouragement. In nine cases out of ten, a woman had better shew more affection than she feels" (17).

Use Quotations in Context

Do not take quotations out of context and use them to mean something other than what the writer intended, as in this example.

Original Text

"The movie was entertaining, but it simplified the more interesting complexities of the novel."

Misleading Extract

"The movie was entertaining . . . interesting complexities . . . "

Establish the Context for the Reader

Introduce each quotation with a sentence that makes its context clear. Be sure to identify the speaker and the circumstances of the comment.

Weak Example

"It is a truth universally acknowledged, that a single man in possession of a good fortune, must be in want of a wife" (1). This quotation is a good example of Jane Austen's irony because single women, not single men, need to marry.

Strong Example

The irony of the opening sentence of *Pride and Prejudice* introduces the central concern of the novel—the economic necessity for women to marry: "It is a truth universally acknowledged, that a single man in possession of a good fortune, must be in want of a wife" (1).

Introduce Quotations Separately

Do not string several quotations together; introduce each one separately.

Weak Example

Mr. Bennet's lack of proper concern for the welfare of his family can be seen in his remarks to Elizabeth when she asks him to stop her wild younger sister, Lydia, from going to Brighton:

> "Lydia will never be easy till she has exposed herself in some public place or another . . ." (204).
> "We shall have no peace at Longbourne if Lydia does not go to Brighton" (205).
> "At any rate, she cannot grow by many degrees worse, without authorizing us to lock her up for the rest of her life" (205).

Strong Example

Mr. Bennet's lack of concern for the welfare of his family can be seen in his remarks to Elizabeth when she asks him to stop her wild younger sister, Lydia, from going to Brighton. Well aware that "Lydia will never be easy till she has exposed herself in some public place or another" (204), Mr. Bennet places the temporary quiet gained by Lydia's absence ahead of his family's reputation, arguing that "We shall have no peace at Longbourne if Lydia does not go to Brighton" (205). Undeterred by these excuses, Elizabeth reminds her father that Lydia's uncontrolled behaviour is likely to disgrace the whole family. But Mr. Bennet has already given up. He rationalizes his unwillingness to expend the time and energy necessary to deal with a rebellious, boy-crazy sixteen-year-old by saying that "At any rate, she cannot grow by many degrees worse, without authorizing us to lock her up for the rest of her life" (205).

Link Quotations Grammatically to the Previous Sentence

- Be sure each quotation fits grammatically with the sentence that introduces it.

Weak Example

When Elizabeth criticizes Darcy for being proud, she forgets Mary's distinction "Pride relates more to our opinion of ourselves, vanity to what we would have others think of us" (*Pride and Prejudice*, 16).

Strong Example

In condemning Darcy as proud, Elizabeth ignores the distinction between pride and vanity made by her sister, Mary, who points out that "Pride relates more to our opinion of ourselves, vanity to what we would have others think of us" (16).

A2 Quotation Format

Integrating Short Quotations

If the quotation is short (not more than five lines of prose or three lines of poetry), incorporate the quotation into your paragraph.

- Do not change the capitalization in the quotation.

- Put the page reference in parentheses after the quotation, followed by the end punctuation for the sentence.

- If the quotation is obviously incomplete, do not put an ellipsis (three spaced periods) before or after it.

  Elizabeth's pride in her own intelligence is obvious in her remark that she would "never ridicule what is wise and good" (50).

- If you are quoting poetry, use a slash, with a space before and after it, to indicate line divisions. Put the line reference in parentheses after the quotation.

  Near the beginning of *Paradise Lost*, Milton asks God to help him in this great task: "what in me is dark / Illumine; what is low, raise and support" (Book I, 23–24).

- If you are quoting from a play with act, scene, and line numbers, give these in your reference.

Claudius realizes that Hamlet is not really mad: "Love! His affections do not that way tend, / Nor what he spake, though it lacked form a little, / Was not like madness" (3.1.156–158).

Integrating Longer Quotations

Use a long quotation only when you want to make detailed comments on the passage.

- Indent one inch from the left- and right-hand margins.

- Double-space the quotation.

- Do not use quotation marks unless the quotation is dialogue.

- Put the reference in parentheses on the last line of the quotation.

Claudius is intelligent enough to realize that although he can escape justice on earth, there is still a final reckoning to contend with:

> In the corrupted currents of this world
>
> Offence's gilded hand may shove by justice,
>
> And oft 'tis seen the wicked prize itself
>
> Buys out the law. But 'tis not so above.
>
> There is no shuffling; there the action lies
>
> In his true nature, and we ourselves compelled,
>
> Even to the teeth and forehead of our faults,
>
> To give in evidence. (3.3.57–64)

Punctuation with Quotations

1. Put the punctuation at the end of the sentence after the parenthetic page reference. See the examples above.

2. If the quotation is short (not more than one sentence) and the sentence introducing the quotation ends with *that*, do not use a comma before the quotation.

In his despairing cry that "Frailty, thy name is woman" (1.2.146), Hamlet extends his disillusionment with his mother to all women.

3. Use a comma between your introductory comment and the quotation if the comma fits with the structure of the whole sentence.

To his treacherous friends Rosencrantz and Guildenstern, Hamlet remarks, "I am but mad north-north-west; when the wind is southerly, I know a hawk from a handsaw" (2.2.344-345).

4. Use a colon if the sentence introducing the quotation is grammatically complete and the quotation is also a complete sentence.

Convinced at first that the ghost is that of his father, Hamlet begins to doubt: "The spirit that I have seen / May be a devil . . . and perhaps / Out of my weakness and my melancholy / . . . abuses me to damn me" (2.2.610-615).

Appendix B

Documentation

B1 What to Document

Whenever you use facts or ideas from other sources in a research paper or any other kind of writing, you must clearly indicate what you have borrowed. Use parenthetical references (called in-text citations) to acknowledge your sources within your paper. Use a list of references at the end of your paper to provide more complete bibliographical information.

Documenting your sources is important for two reasons. First, it enables your reader to check statements that you have made or to look up more information on your subject. Second, it ensures that you do not take credit for information that is not your own (see Documenting Sources, 14d). For these reasons, knowing what to document is just as important as knowing how to do it.

You **don't** need to give the source of commonly known pieces of information, such as the fact that the earth is the third planet from the sun, or the source of familiar quotations, such as St. Paul's statement that it is "better to marry than to burn" or Hamlet's "to be or not to be" soliloquy, when you use them as allusions.

You **do** need to give the source of all facts, ideas, and opinions that you have taken from written sources *whether or not* you have quoted directly. Be especially careful to acknowledge the source of statistics. Don't make the mistake of thinking that you avoid having to acknowledge the source of your information if you change the wording slightly. Failure to cite your references in this situation is still plagiarism.

There are two main systems of documentation. The Modern Language Association of America (MLA) is the accepted authority for documentation in the humanities (for example, English, history, or philosophy). The American Psychological Association (APA) is the accepted authority for documentation in education, the social sciences (for example, psychology, sociology, or anthropology), and many fields in the physical sciences.

B2 MLA System: In-Text Citations

Guidelines

Place the name(s) of the author(s) and the page number(s) in parentheses immediately after the quoted or paraphrased material (Austen 17).

- Omit the author if the introduction to the quotation makes this information clear (17).

- If you will be referring to more than one work by the same author, give a shortened version of the title and then the page reference (Austen, *Sense* 17).

Sample Citations

The following examples demonstrate in-text citations for particular references.

- ***Quotation from primary text (author previously identified)***

For novels, short stories, and essays, give the page number (without *p.* or *pp.*) in parentheses after the quotation.

> By the time she reaches seventeen, Anne has become what Marilla wanted: "All I want is that you should behave like other little girls and not make yourself ridiculous" (89).

For short poems, give the line numbers in parentheses after the quotation. If you set off the quotation, type a space between the end of the quotation and the reference.

> John Donne begins "The Sun Rising" by complaining that the sun has awakened him:
>
> > Busy old fool, unruly sun,
> > Why dost thou thus,
> > Through windows, and through curtains, call on us?
> > Must to thy motions lovers' seasons run? (1–4)

For plays written in verse, give the act, scene, and line(s) in Arabic numerals (unless your instructor prefers Roman numerals).

> The image of the state as "an unweeded garden / That grows to seed" (*Hamlet* 1.2.135-36) appears throughout Shakespeare's plays.

- ***Quotation from a critic***

  As James L. Johnson points out, "Tom's world is one in which 'adventure' replaces 'experience'" (51).

- ***Reference without a quotation***

  Tom is not changed by his encounters with Muff Potter, Dr. Robinson, and Injun Joe, even though encounters such as these would ordinarily affect how one sees the world (Johnson 51).

B3 MLA System: List of Works Cited

Guidelines

At the end of your paper, on a separate sheet entitled Works Cited, present a list of references. In most cases, your list of Works Cited should include only the works you have actually cited in your paper. If you consulted a reference, but did not cite it in your work, do not include it on the list.

- Make sure you include every work you refer to in a form your readers can find. If you have cited an essay in an edited collection, for instance, the bibliographical entry should appear under the author's name, not under the name of the editor.

- List the entries alphabetically according to the author's last name. If a work has more than one author, keep the names in the order they are given and alphabetize according to the first name in the list.

- If the author is not given, alphabetize according to the first word in the title (not *The*, *A* or *An*).

Double-space within the entry and triple-space between entries. The first line of each entry should start at the left-hand margin. Indent subsequent lines by five spaces. Do not number bibliographical entries.

In the following examples, note both the order of information and the punctuation. For a model of the MLA system of documentation, see the sample research essay, "*Tom Sawyer* and *Anne of Green Gables*: Two Models of Heroism" (14f).

Sample Citations

Print Publications

• *Article*

last name	first name	title of article	name of periodical
↓	↓	↓	↓
Fetterley,	Judith.	"The Sanctioned Rebel."	*Studies in the Novel*

	volume +	year	inclusive page numbers
	↓	↓	↓
	3	(1971):	293–304.

If each issue in the volume starts with page one, give the issue number as well: 3.1 (1971).

• *Book*

last name	first name	title	place	publisher	date
↓	↓	↓	↓	↓	↓
Davies,	Robertson.	*The Cunning Man.*	New York:	Viking,	1995.

Note 1: If the city of publication is not well known or could be confused with another city of the same name, add the abbreviation for the province, state, or country (Paris, TX). If several places are listed, give only the first.

Note 2: Give only a short form of the publisher's name (McClelland, not McClelland and Stewart Inc.).

• *Part of a book*

Put the editor's name (if applicable) after the title and the inclusive page numbers of the part you are citing at the end.

Cohen, Leonard. "Suzanne Takes You Down." *The HBJ Anthology of Literature*. Eds. Jon C. Stott, Raymond E. Jones, and Rick Bowers. Toronto: Harcourt, 1993. 632–33.

Whitley, John S. "Kids' Stuff: Mark Twain's Boys." *Mark Twain: A Sumptuous Variety*. Ed. Robert Giddings. London: Vision Press, 1985. 57–76.

Atwood, Margaret. "Uglypuss." *Bluebeard's Egg*. Toronto: Seal, 1984. 67–93.

• *Subsequent work by the same author*

Type ten hyphens in place of the author's name. Continue as for the appropriate entry.

——————. "Unearthing Suite." *Bluebeard's Egg*. Toronto: Seal, 1984. 240–58.

• *Multiple authors or editors*

Invert the order of the first name only.

Bowles, Samuel, and Herbert Gintis. *Schooling in Capitalist America*. New York: Basic, 1976.

When there are more than three names, use only the first name and *et al.*

Gettleman, Marvin E. et al., eds. *El Salvador: Central America in the New Cold War*. New York: Grove, 1981.

• *Encyclopedia*

If the article is signed, the author's name comes first; if not, the title of the article comes first. If the encyclopedia is well known, omit the place of publication and the publisher, but include the edition (if given) and the year. If the work is arranged alphabetically, omit the volume number and the page number.

"Biological Effects of Radiation." *Encyclopaedia Britannica*, 1974 ed.

Electronic Publications

The format for citing material you access either through a portable electronic database (such as a CD-ROM) or through an online database (such as the Internet) does not differ much from other citations. You include everything you would give for the print version of your source, but you also need some additional information.

1. *The publication medium*—This information is important because versions of the same material published in various media (CD-ROM, diskette, magnetic tape) may not be identical.

2. *The name of the vendor*—This is required if the information provider has released different versions of the data to more than one vendor.

3. *The date of the electronic publication*—For an online database, indicate both the date of its publication and the date you looked at it, since material online may be changed or updated frequently.

You may not be able to find some of the required information. Cite what is available.

• *CD-ROMs and other portable databases*

Portable databases are electronic media that you can carry around, such as CD-ROMs, diskettes, and magnetic tapes.

1. *Periodically published databases on CD-ROM*—Many periodicals (scholarly journals, magazines, and newspapers) and reference works such as annual bibliographies are now available on CD-ROM as well as in print versions. Begin your entry by following the guidelines for citing the print version. Then give the title of the database, the publication medium, the name of the vendor (if relevant), and the electronic publication date.

Feaver, William. "Michelangelo." *Art News* 94 (1995): 137–38.

database	**medium**	**vendor**	**electronic pub. date**
↓	↓	↓	↓
Art Index.	CD-ROM.	SilverPlatter.	1995.

2. *Books on CD-ROM*—Cite these publications as you would the print version, but add the medium of publication.

                           medium
                            ↓

  The Oxford English Dictionary. 2nd ed. CD-ROM. Oxford UP, 1992.

3. *Publications on diskette or magnetic tape*—Cite these publications as you would books, but add the medium of publication.

Kriya Systems Inc. *Typing Tutor III with Letter Invaders for the IBM PC.* Diskette. New York: Simon and Schuster, 1984.

• *Online Databases*

Online databases are available only through computer services (such as Dialog, CompuServe, Prodigy) or networks (such as the Internet). Give all the information you would for the appropriate print version. Then add the name of the database, the publication medium (*Online*), the name of the computer service or network, and the date you accessed the material.

Schiff-Zamano, Roberta. "The Re/membering of Female Power in *Lady Oracle.*" *Canadian Literature* 112 (1987): 32–38. *MLA Bibliography 1963–1989.* Online. Dialog. 8 Aug. 1995.

↑	↑	↑	↑
database	**medium**	**network**	**date accessed**

For further information, see Joseph Gibaldi, *MLA Handbook for Writers of Research Papers*, 4th ed. New York: The Modern Language Association of America, 1995.

Other Material

• *Film or video recordings*

Include the title, the director, the distributor, and the date. Add any other information that is relevant to the discussion (such as the names of the principal actors or the costume designer) just before the distributor and the date.

> *Anne of Green Gables.* Dir. Kevin Sullivan. Perf. Megan Follows and Colleen Dewhurst. Sullivan Films, 1986.

If, instead of the film itself, you are citing the work of a director, actor, or screenwriter, begin your entry with that person's name. For videocassettes and similar recordings, give the original release date and put the medium (videocassette, filmstrip) before the name of the distributor.

• *Interview*

Give the names of the person interviewed, the type of interview (personal, telephone, e-mail), and the date.

> Brandt, Di. Personal interview. 3 Feb. 1996.

B4 APA System: In-Text Citations

Guidelines

- As with the MLA system, place parenthetical references to your sources immediately after quoted or paraphrased material.

- When you paraphrase an idea, give only the author's last name and the year of publication at the end of your sentence. (Note that in the APA system, name and date are separated by a comma.)

  Japanese and Chinese immigrants have the lowest rate of alcoholism of any ethnic group, while Inuit and native Indian populations have the highest (Peele, 1986).

- If you include the author's name in the sentence introducing the reference, put the year of publication immediately after the author's name.

  In another study, McMahon and Davidson (1986) report that while depression and alcoholism are associated, it is not necessarily the depression that comes first.

- If you are quoting directly, put the page number after the year in the parenthetical citation, with *p.* or *pp.* For electronic text, paragraph numbers may be used in place of page numbers.

  (McMahon and Davidson, 1986, p. 45)

- If you are citing a work that is discussed in another work, name the original work; then cite the source you consulted and give the date for that source.

  Singh's study (as cited in Robertson, 1995) . . .

  . . . (Singh, as cited in Robertson, 1995).

- If you are repeating the same source in the same paragraph, omit the year of publication and include only the author's name in parentheses.

- If you will be referring to more than one work written in the same year by the same person, include a shortened version of the title in the reference.

Sample Citations

- ***Multiple authors***

If the work has two authors, cite both names every time you refer to the work. If the work has fewer than six authors, cite all the authors in your first in-text citation. In subsequent references, include only the surname of the first author followed by *et al.* and the year. If the work has more than six authors, cite only the surname of the first followed by *et al.* and the date in all in-text citations.

- ***No author***

Give a short version of the title in your in-text citation.

- ***Corporate authors***

Spell out the name of corporate authors in every in-text citation (National Film Board, 1996).

- ***Newspaper articles***

If the author's name is given, put the name, the date, and the year in parentheses.

(Talbot, Aug. 6, 1995).

If the author's name is not given, use a short version of the title.

("Hiroshima Remembered," Aug. 6, 1995).

B5 APA System: Bibliographical References

Guidelines

At the end of your paper, on a separate sheet entitled *References*, present a list of all the works you have cited. Alphabetize according to the authors' last names, in the order in which they appear in the publication. If a work has no author, alphabetize by the title. Government and corporate publications are alphabetized by the name of the corporate author.

Double-space within the reference and double-space between references. Begin the first line of each reference at the left margin; indent subsequent lines 5 to 7 spaces. (In articles submitted for publication, the first line is indented and subsequent lines start at the margin.)

Capitalize only the first word of the title and of the subtitle of books and articles. Do not put quotation marks around the titles of articles.

Sample Citations

Print Publications

• *Article*

Do not use *p.* or *pp.* for page numbers of journal articles, but do use them for magazine and newspaper articles.

name	initial	date	title of article
↓	↓	↓	↓
Baumeister, R.	(1990).		Suicide as an escape from the self.

title of journal	volume	issue	inclusive pages
↓	↓	↓	↓
Psychological Review,	*97*	(1),	90–113.

• *Book*

name	initial	date	title	place of publication	publisher
↓	↙	↙	↓	↓	↙
Katz, J.	(1991).		*Seductions of crime.*	New York:	Basic Books.

• *Part of a book*

name initial date   title of article or chapter
  ↓   ↓   ↓   ↓
Adam, K. (1994). Suicidal behavior and attachment. In M.B.

      editor(s)   title of book
        ↓   ↓
Sperling & W.H. Berman (Eds.), *Attachment in adults*

  inclusive page nos. place publisher
       ↓   ↓   ↓
  (pp. 275–298).   New York: Guilford.

• *Subsequent work by the same author*

If you have used more than one source by the same author, arrange the works by year of publication, starting with the earliest. Arrange two or more works by the same author in the same year alphabetically by the title (disregard *A, An,* or *The*).

> Bowlby, J. (1977). The making and breaking of affectional bonds. *British Journal of Psychiatry, 130,* 201–210.
>
> Bowlby, J. (1980). Attachment and loss. Vol. 3, *Loss, sadness, and depression.* New York: Basic Books.

• *Multiple authors*

Give last names followed by initials for all authors, in the order in which they appear in the publication. Use a comma and an ampersand to join the last two authors in the entry.

> Bowles, S., & Gintis, H. (1976). *Schooling in capitalist America.* New York: Basic Books.

• *Encyclopedia entry*

If no author is given, begin with the title of the entry.

> Dinosaurs. (1993). *Collier's Encyclopedia.* New York: Collier.

Electronic Publications

• *CD-ROMs and other portable databases*

1. If there is a print version that's the same as the electronic version, cite the print version.

2. If there is no print equivalent, give the author, date, and title as for print versions.

3. Put the type of medium (CD-ROM, electronic data tape, computer program) in square brackets after the title.

4. If you are citing a bibliographic database, give the location and name of the producer and distributor.

5. When giving retrieval information, do not end with a period. Stray punctuation will interfere with retrieval.

For materials published periodically on CD-ROM, follow this format:

Beck, C., & Stewart, S. (1996). Attention span in five-year-olds

medium	**availability**
↓	↓

[CD-ROM]. *Memory & Cognition*, *24*, 379–394. Abstract from :

distributor	**retrieval information**
↓	↓
SilverPlatter	File: PsycLIT Item: 83-42075

Books on CD-ROM are cited as follows:

Statistics Canada. (1992). 1991 *Census Profiles* [CD-ROM].

Dictionary of organic compounds (Version 3.2) [CD-ROM]. (1995). Head Software International (Producer). Chapman & Hall (Distributor).

Often, publications on diskette or magnetic tape do not give an author. In such cases, begin with the title. Do not underline titles of computer languages, programs, or software.

Typing tutor III with letter invaders for the IBM PC [computer software]. (1984). Kriya Systems (Producer). New York: Simon and Schuster (Distributor).

- *Online databases*

1. Give the author, date, and title as for a print version. If the material is revised regularly, give the most recent update instead of the date of publication. If you can't determine a date, give the date you accessed the material.

2. Put the medium in square brackets immediately after the title: [Online], [Online serial].

3. Instead of the location and name of a publisher, provide an availability statement that would allow your reader to retrieve the material, such as the computer network, the

directory, and the file name: Available FTP: 137.122.136.1
Directory: pub/harnad File: psyc.93.2.33.memory.14.beck

Note: Do not end an availability statement with a period. Stray punctuation will interfere with retrieval.

Beck, C., & Stewart, S. (1996). Attention span in five-year-olds

medium
↓
[Online]. *Memory & Cognition, 24*, 379–94. Abstract from :

network   **retrieval information**
↓   ↓
SilverPlatter   File: PsycLIT Item: 83-42075

Other Material

- ***Films, videotapes, audiotapes, slides, charts, works of art***

Give the titles of the originator and primary contributors in parentheses after the name, and the medium of publication in square brackets after the title.

originator   **and/or primary contributors**
↓   ↓
Kilbourne, J. (Writer), & Lazarus, M. (Producer & Director).

medium
↓
(1987). *Still killing us softly* [Videorecording].

- ***Interview***

In APA documentation, personal communications—letters, interviews, e-mail—are cited parenthetically in the text and not given in the list of references.

For a model of the APA system of citations and references, see the sample research essay, "What Is Psychology?" (14g).

For more information and references not covered here, consult the *Publication Manual of the American Psychological Association*, 4th ed. (Washington: Amer. Psychological Assn., 1994).

- A version of *Online! A Reference Guide to Using Internet Sources* by Andrew Harnack and Eugene Kleppinger is available at this address:

  www.smpcollege.com/online-4styles~help>

Appendix C

Format
Conventions

C1 Format: Essays and Other Writing Assignments

The presentation of any writing assignment creates your reader's first impression and ensures that your ideas are clearly communicated. Take time to proofread and format your paper properly, using the following guidelines.

• Typing

Strive to produce a clean, professional-looking paper. Most instructors prefer papers to be typed and some insist on it (publishers accept only typed material).

Make sure the print is legible. If you are planning to print the final copy on a dot-matrix printer, check that your instructor will accept it (some people find dot-matrix printouts hard to read). Use a standard 12 cpi font. Avoid fonts and typographical devices that create a cluttered look.

If you are allowed to submit handwritten papers, use blue or black ink.

Even if someone types for you, you are responsible for any errors. Proofread and make neat corrections in ink before you hand the paper in.

• Paper

White 8 1/2 in. x 11 in. paper is standard. If you are handwriting, use lined paper of approximately the same size. Write or type on only one side of the page. Use plain white computer paper.

• Spacing

Always type double-spaced to allow room for comments. Many readers prefer handwritten work to be double-spaced for the same reason. Others prefer handwriting single-spaced on wide-lined paper.

• *Margins*

Leave a margin of 4 cm (1 1/2 in.) on the top and left of your manuscript. Leave a 2.5 cm (1 in.) margin on the bottom and right. Besides making your text more readable, adequate margins give room for comments.

• *Title*

Your title should make the subject of your paper and the assignment you have chosen clear to your reader. The title of an essay is often a short form of the thesis. Or it may suggest the subject and arouse interest. Never use labels such as "Essay #1" or "Personal Essay."

• *Title page*

Place the title of your paper in the centre of the page. Write it or type it in normal-size letters and do not put quotation marks around it or underline it. In the bottom right-hand corner on separate lines, put your name, the name of the course, and the date. You may also want to include your instructor's name (spelled correctly) and the section number of the course. See the title page of the sample research paper below, for an example.

• *Pagination*

Do not number either the title page or the first page of your paper. Begin numbering on the second page (2). Place page numbers in the centre of the top margin or in the upper right-hand corner. (Some instructors ask that you include the title or your name before the page number in case pages become separated.)

• *Bibliography*

End your paper with your list of References or Works Cited, if required. Be sure to number these pages.

• *Fastening*

Use a staple or paper clip to fasten the pages. (Some instructors and editors object to staples; all object to straight pins and other hazardous devices.)

• *Copies*

Keep a copy of your paper in case the original is lost.

C2 Sample Title Page

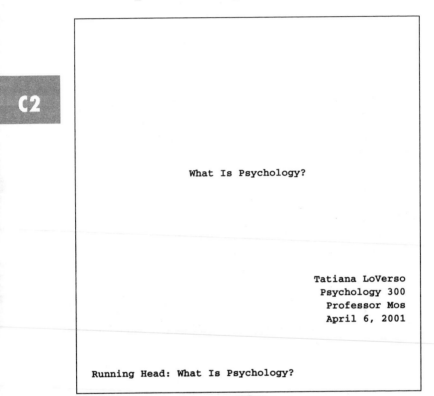

What Is Psychology?

Tatiana LoVerso
Psychology 300
Professor Mos
April 6, 2001

Running Head: What Is Psychology?

C3 Format: Business Letters

Like other kinds of writing, business letters have their own conventions that raise certain expectations in a reader. By adhering to these conventions, you create a favourable first impression—one suggesting that you know what you are doing and should be taken seriously. Even if your handwriting is perfectly legible, type all business correspondence.

Here is the standard format for business letters. Every business letter should have the first six components.

1. *Your address and the date*
Place this information in the upper right or left corner, single-spaced. If you are using letterhead stationery that includes the

address, type the date below it. Do not include your name with your address.

123 Juniper Drive
Thompson, MN R7N 2K8
April 26, 2001

2. *Your correspondent's name and address*
Place this information on the left margin, single-spaced. It should include everything you would type on the envelope.

C3

3. *The salutation (Dear . . .), followed by a colon*
If you do not know the name of the person to whom you are writing, use the title of the individual or department (*Dear Editor* or *Attention: Customer Relations Department*) or the name of the organization (*Dear Starbuck's*).

4. *The body of the letter*
Your business letter will normally consist of at least two short paragraphs. Business letters are seldom more than one page. If you need a second sheet, place the page number at the top. Never use the back of a page.

5. *The complimentary closing*
Use *Yours truly* for more formal letters and *Yours sincerely* or *Sincerely* for less formal letters. Capitalize the first word of the closing. Place a comma at the end.

6. *Your signature*
Type your name below the signature.

7. *Enclosures*
Draw your reader's attention to any enclosures, such as a brochure or a cheque, by typing either *Enclosure* or *Enc.* beside the left margin after the signature. Indicate more than one enclosure like this: *Enc. 2.* Name an especially important enclosure in this way: *Enc.: contract.*

8. *Copies forwarded*
Use the notation *c* or *copy*, followed by either a colon or a period, to indicate that copies of the letter are being sent to other people:

c: Mrs. Elizabeth Nelson
copy: Dr. F. D. Schmidt

C4 Sample Business Letter

In the following business letter, the numbers correspond to the eight components discussed above.

Centre for Applied Language Studies
Carleton University   (1)
Ottawa, ON K18 6B6

October 30, 1998

Dr. Samuel Lieberman
English Department
Mount Saint Vincent University   (2)
Halifax, NS B3M 2J6

Dear Dr. Lieberman: (3)

Thank you for responding so fully and promptly to
our questionnaire on computer-assisted learning
programs for second-language English students. Your
detailed critique of several popular software packages was especially useful.

    Please find enclosed our latest issue of   (4)
Carleton Papers in Applied Language Studies. We
would be especially interested in your response to
self-assessment as a guide to placing second language students.

    I am looking forward to talking with you again at
our summer retreat in July. Don't forget to bring
your fishing tackle.

    Sincerely, (5)

Black (6)

Alison Black

Enc. *Carleton Papers*   (7)
c: R. B. McKim, Editor, *Carleton Papers*   (8)

C5 Format: Memorandums

Memorandums, or memos, are the usual form of communication between members of the same organization. Follow the guidelines for letter writing to organize the content of your memorandum. The format conventions are illustrated below.

C6 Sample Memorandum

DATE: July 23, 2001

TO: Susan Schnell, Franchise Manager [name
            and title of the person to whom the memo-
            randum is sent]

FROM: Luigi Amodio [name of the writer]

SUBJECT: Bunk Bed Safety [precise statement of the
            main focus]

Last week I received a letter from the Consumers'
Advocates of Sarnia reporting complaints about the
safety of children's bunk beds. These complaints
included concerns about ladders that became
detached from the bed frames and bunks that were
not securely bolted together.

The most serious problems, however, occurred when
sleeping children were caught between the guard
rail and the mattress. The enclosed safety guidelines from Consumers' Advocates clearly show how a
child can suffocate.

Please use these guidelines to check your stock
and warn all sales personnel of the dangers posed
by the models listed in the second enclosure. Sales
staff should alert prospective buyers of the risks
bunk beds may pose to children under six years of
age.

Enc. 1.: safety guidelines

Enc. 2.: list of bunk bed models

Luigi Amodio

Luigi Amodio

Appendix D

Writing Essay
and Short-Answer
Examinations

D1

D1 Preparing for Examinations

You can help to prepare for essay examinations by taking these
steps.

- Review the overall purpose and direction of the course. If the
  instructor emphasized the acquisition of one or more skills,
  such as the ability to analyze a piece of writing, review the
  terms and procedures appropriate to those skills.

  If the instructor emphasized the acquisition of a body of
  knowledge, such as the nature of a particular historical period or
  different theories of human behaviour, decide which three or
  four units of material seem most important and learn this material
  thoroughly.

- Outline the relevant chapters of textbooks or your notes, set
  yourself a question about each unit, and practise writing out
  the answer. Writing the information will help you remember
  it better than merely reading it over.

- Make notes about similarities and differences among events,
  theories, works of literature. Comparison questions are frequently set on exams because they cover more material and
  emphasize important concepts in the course.

- Memorize key names, dates, facts, and so forth. The more
  specific information you give, the better your answer will be,
  as long as the information is relevant.

D2 Tips on Writing Exams

1. Look over the whole exam paper and decide how much time to spend on each section. If one section of the exam is worth 60 percent, for instance, plan to spend 60 percent of the available time on it.

2. If you have a choice of questions or essay topics, first note any restrictions (such as not writing twice on the same subject or work) and then select accordingly.

3. Answer easier questions first. That will give you confidence. It will also allow your mind to work subconsciously on the harder questions before you tackle them.

4. Read the directions for each question carefully. Often they will suggest a focus for your response and provide directions on how to develop it. In the topic *What was Nixon's "southern strategy" and what was its impact on the policies pursued by his government?* the key terms are *southern strategy* and *policies*. To develop your answer, you would need to use both definition and causal analysis.

D2

D3 Writing an Essay Exam

1. Read the essay topics carefully. Make sure you understand exactly what is required.

2. Plan your essay before you start writing. It's a waste of time to write out a complete rough draft and then attempt to revise and copy it. Begin by brainstorming on your topic (for more on brainstorming and other invention techniques, see Chapter 2, Gathering Material). Once you have some ideas on paper, you can work out an outline. Be sure that each part of your outline is directly relevant to your essay topic. (For more information on outlining, see Making an Outline, 3b).

3. Stick to the essay topic. Writing a focus statement or giving your essay a title will help you to stay on track.

4. Place your thesis at the end of your introduction; use topic sentences at the beginning of paragraphs to develop the points made in your thesis; and write a conclusion that summarizes what you've said.

5. Develop your ideas fully within the essay and include details and examples to support them. State your ideas clearly and precisely even if that means simplifying your normal style. Exams must often be marked very quickly. Ideas buried in elaborate sentence patterns may be overlooked.

6. Proofread carefully. Check for errors in grammar, spelling, and punctuation. These mistakes can make a negative impression on your reader.

D4 Responding to Short-Answer Questions

The most common types of short-answer questions ask you to analyze (6d), define (6c), or make brief comparisons (6b). We will focus on the types of answers expected for identification questions.

Answering Identification Questions

Identification questions generally consist of individual items or brief quotations. Answer as many of the standard questions (*who, what, when, where, why, and how*) as are relevant. Superior answers include 1) specific rather than general information about the item itself; and 2) a clear explanation of why the item is important. That importance might cover, for example, the item's causes, its effects, its role in a larger context, or its relation to the theme of a literary work.

Sample History Exam Question

Question: Briefly identify the following: *War Measures Act*

Superior Answer

The *War Measures Act*, passed in 1914, gave the federal Cabinet emergency powers to govern by decree during "war, invasion or insurrection." The Act was invoked during both world wars to justify regulations that limited the freedom of Canadians, including the internment of 20 000 Japanese Canadians during the Second World War. The *War Measures Act* has been invoked only once during peacetime. Prime Minister Trudeau, declaring a state of "apprehended insurrection," invoked the Act during the October Crisis of 1970 in response to the kidnappings of British trade commissioner James Cross and Québec Minister of Labour and Immigration Pierre

Laporte by the FLQ. Regulations promulgated under the Act banned the FLQ and permitted more than 450 people to be arrested or detained without charge. Although government officials defended these measures as necessary to combat terrorism, Québec nationalists and civil libertarians accused the federal government of unwarranted infringement of civil liberties. Opposition to this use of the *War Measures Act* contributed to the popularity of the separatist Parti Québécois, which won the Québec provincial election in 1976.

Weak Answer

The *War Measures Act* allowed the government to use emergency powers during both world wars. It became well known when Prime Minister Trudeau used the *War Measures Act* against terrorists in the October Crisis. A lot of people thought Trudeau was justified at the time, but later it seemed that he might have used the Act for political purposes. There has recently been a movement to limit the powers given to the government under the Act.

D4

In comparison with the superior answer, the weak answer contains few specific facts and no discussion of the effects of the *War Measures Act*.

Sample Literature Exam Question

Question: Briefly identify the following: the black box.

Superior Answer

In Shirley Jackson's short story "The Lottery," the black box contains slips of paper drawn by villagers to determine who will be stoned to death in the annual ritual. The box's colour symbolizes death. The shabby condition of the box and casual treatment it receives during the rest of the year reinforce the theme of the story: that the force of habit and the authority of tradition can lead seemingly ordinary people into barbaric acts of violence.

Weak Answer

The person to be stoned is chosen by drawing from the black box in the story "The Lottery." After Bill Hutchison draws his family's name, each member of the family has to draw again. The wife gets the X. Her little boy is given small stones to help in the killing of his mother.

The superior answer correctly identifies the author and title of the story, and explains the literal and symbolic functions of the black box and its relation to the theme. The weak answer, in contrast, omits the name of the author and merely tells what happens in the story. Summarizing the plot shows that you have read the material; it does not show that you are able to analyze what you read.

Appendix E

Glossary of
Grammatical Terms

Active Voice

A construction in which the subject performs the action of the verb.

Lightning **struck** the enormous tree.

In the passive voice, the sentence would read:

The enormous tree **was struck** by lightning.

Adjective

A word that modifies a noun or pronoun. An adjective can express quality (*red* balloon, *large* house, *young* child) or quantity (*one* apple, *many* peaches, *few* pears). Other words or grammatical constructions can also function as adjectives, including present and past participles (*skating* party, *torn* shirt) and subordinate clauses (the woman *who is chairing the meeting*).

Adjectives change form to show degrees of comparison—positive, comparative, superlative (*clean, cleaner, cleanest*).

Adverb

A word that modifies or describes a verb (run *quickly*), an adjective (*extremely* heavy), or another adverb (eat *very* slowly). Adverbs usually answer the questions *how, when, where,* or *why.* (They whispered *how*? / They whispered *quietly*.)

Phrases (walked *into a room*) and clauses (He couldn't speak *because he was angry*) can also function as adverbs.

Adverbs change form to show degrees of comparison—positive, comparative, superlative (*quickly, more quickly, most quickly*).

Antecedent

The noun to which a pronoun refers. The antecedent usually, but not always, comes before the pronoun.

The **dancers** [antecedent] are rehearsing **their** [pronoun] routine.

Appositive

An explanatory word or phrase that follows a noun or pronoun.

Martha, **my closest friend**, is visiting from Halifax.

Auxiliary Verb

A verb that helps to form the tense or voice of another verb (*have been* practising, *should have* phoned, *was* consulted).

Case

The form of a noun or pronoun that shows its relationship to other words in a sentence.

Possessive case [nouns and indefinite pronouns]: **Bill's** car, **nobody's** business.

Subject case [personal pronouns]: **She** and **I** left early.

Object case [personal pronouns]: Give the message to **him** or **me**.

Clause

A group of words containing a subject and a verb. **Main clauses** can stand on their own as grammatically complete sentences.

He didn't finish dinner.

Subordinate clauses, sometimes called dependent clauses often begin with subordinate conjunctions such as *because, although, while, since, as, when.*

Because he was in a hurry, he didn't finish dinner.

Other subordinate clauses begin with relative pronouns such as *who, which,* and *that.* These subordinate clauses function as adjectives or nouns.

The man **who didn't finish dinner** is in a bad mood. [adjective clause]

She wished **that the ordeal would end**. [noun clause]

Comma Splice

A sentence structure error in which main clauses have been joined by a comma alone, or by a comma and a conjunctive adverb.

The party is over, everyone has gone home.

The party is over, **therefore** everyone must go home.

Complex Sentence

A sentence containing one main clause and one or more subordinate clauses. See *Clause.*

If we can't fit everyone in the car, we'll take the bus.

E1

Compound Sentence

A sentence containing two or more main clauses. See *Clause*.

We can't fit everyone in the car, so we'll take the bus.

Compound-Complex Sentence

A sentence containing two or more main clauses and one or more subordinate clauses.

Before the storm broke, Mary put away the lawn chairs and Shistri closed the windows.

Conjunction

A word or phrase that joins words, phrases, or clauses. See *Conjunctive Adverb, Coordinate Conjunction, Correlative (Paired) Conjunction,* and *Subordinate Conjunction.*

Conjunctive Adverb

An adverb used with a semicolon to join main clauses in a compound or compound-complex sentence. Common conjunctive adverbs include *therefore, however, nevertheless, otherwise, thus, furthermore, moreover.*

I must hurry; **otherwise**, I'll be late for class.

Coordinate Conjunction

A word used to join ideas of equal importance expressed in the same grammatical form. The coordinate conjunctions are *and, but, or, nor, for, yet, so.*

He was down **but** not out.

The weather was good, **but** the facilities were terrible.

Coordination

The stylistic technique of using coordinate and correlative conjunctions to join ideas of equal importance. See *Coordinate Conjunction* and *Correlative (Paired) Conjunctions.*

The battery is dead **and** all four tires are flat.

Neither the fridge **nor** the stove is working.

Correlative (Paired) Conjunctions

A pair of conjunctions used to join ideas of equal importance expressed in the same grammatical form. The correlative conjunctions are *either/or, neither/nor, both/and, not only/but also.*

Not only are these apples expensive **but** they are **also** of poor quality.

These apples are **both** expensive **and** of poor quality.

Dangling Modifier

A modifying phrase that is not logically connected to any other word in the sentence.

Turning green, the pedestrians crossed the street.

Definite Article

The word *the*, which specifies the noun it is describing: *the* book, *the* baby, *the* opportunity of a lifetime.

Fragment

A phrase or subordinate clause punctuated as if it were a complete sentence.

And last, but not least.

Although it seemed like a good idea at the time.

Fused Sentence (also called *Run-on Sentence*)

The error of writing two main clauses as if they were one, with no punctuation between them.

It's cold today my ears are freezing.

Indefinite Article

The words *a* and *an*, which do not specify the nouns they describe: *a* book, *a* breakthrough, *an* amazing feat.

Infinitive

To + a verb: *to run, to walk, to think.* See *Split Infinitive.*

Interjection

A word or phrase thrown into a sentence to express emotion.

"Oh great, we're going on a picnic!"

For Pete's sake, I knew that already.

Some interjections can stand on their own as complete sentences.

"Wow!" "Ouch!" "Hurray!"

Misplaced Modifier

A modifying word, phrase, or clause that has been put in the wrong place in the sentence.

Lying in the driveway, Mr. Jones drove over the bicycle.

Mixed Construction
(also called an *Awkward Sentence*)

The error of mixing incompatible grammatical units.

An example of this is when she daydreams constantly.

The more he learns, **he doesn't seem to remember much.**

Modifier

A word, phrase, or clause that changes or qualifies the meaning of a noun, pronoun, or verb.

Restrictive modifiers provide essential information and are not enclosed in commas.

Teenagers **who take drugs** need help.

Nonrestrictive modifiers provide additional information and are enclosed with commas.

Susan, **who has been taking drugs for several years**, needs help.

Mood

The form of the verb that shows whether the speaker is stating a fact (indicative mood: He *wants* some food), giving a command or making a request (imperative mood: *Give* him some food), or suggesting a possibility or condition (subjunctive mood: If we *were to give* him some food).

Noun

A word that names a person, place, thing, quality, idea, or activity. A **common noun** is not capitalized and refers to any one of a class: *woman, cat, city, school.* A **proper noun** is capitalized and refers to a particular person, animal, place, thing: *Linda, Fluffy, Guelph, Westlane Elementary School.* A **collective noun**, such as *herd, flock, family, community, band, tribe,* is singular when the group is acting as a unit and plural when the group members are acting as individuals.

The band is on an extended trip.

The band are unpacking their instruments.

Object

A word, phrase, or clause that receives the action of the verb or that is governed by a preposition.

Stephen lent me his pen. [*Me* is the indirect object of the verb *lent; pen* is the direct object.]

She has already left for work. [*Work* is the object of the preposition *for.*]

Parallel Structure

A construction in which ideas of equal importance are expressed in the same grammatical form.

His analysis is **precise, thorough**, and **perceptive**. [parallel adjectives]

What he says and **what he means** are completely different. [parallel clauses]

Participle

A verb form that can function as a verb or as an adjective. Present participles are formed by adding *ing* to the present tense. Past participles of regular verbs are formed by adding *ed* to the present tense.

When combined with an auxiliary verb, participles become the main verb in a verb phrase (*is laughing, has been dancing, could have finished*).

As adjectives, participles can modify nouns and pronouns (*smiling* face, *running* water, *chipped* tooth, *sworn* testimony; *frowning*, he addressed the assembly).

Parts of Speech

Types of words, such as nouns, verbs, and adverbs. See *Adjective, Adverb, Conjunction, Interjection, Noun, Preposition, Pronoun, Verb.*

Passive Voice

A construction in which the subject is acted upon by the verb.

The water **was tested** for contaminants by the researchers.

In the active voice, this sentence would read:

The researchers **tested** the water for contaminants.

Preposition

Prepositions include such words as *by, between, beside, to, of,* and *with.* A preposition, its object (usually a noun or a pronoun), and any words that describe the object make up a prepositional phrase (*toward the deserted beach*). These phrases can function as adjectives (the man *with the red beard*) or as adverbs (walked *down the road*, tired *of waiting*).

Pronoun

A word that substitutes for a noun.

Indefinite pronouns *everybody, everyone, everything, somebody, someone, something, nobody, no one, one, nothing, anybody, anyone, anything, either, neither, each, both, few, several, all*

Personal subject pronouns *I, we, you, he, she, it, they*
Personal object pronouns *me, us, you, him, her, it, them*
Possessive pronouns *my, mine, our, ours, your, yours, his, her, hers, its, their, theirs*
Reflexive/Intensive pronouns *myself, ourselves, yourself, yourselves, himself, herself, itself, themselves*
Relative pronouns *who, whom, which, that, what, whoever, whomever, whichever*

Pronoun Agreement

The principle of matching singular pronouns with singular nouns and pronouns, and plural pronouns with plural nouns and pronouns.

The **committee** forwarded **its** recommendations.

Everyone has made **his or her** views known to the nominating committee.

Pronoun Reference

The principle that every pronoun should clearly refer to a specific noun. See *Antecedent*.

Tom told Hussein that **he** had won the scholarship. [pronoun reference unclear]

Tom told Hussein, "**You** won the scholarship." [pronoun reference clear]

Pronoun Shift

The error of shifting abruptly and with no logical reason from the expected personal pronoun.

I didn't like working in the complaints department because **you** were always dealing with dissatisfied customers.

Split Infinitive

A form of misplaced modifier in which an adverb is placed between *to* and the verb.

to **quickly** run

Subject

The word or group of words that interact with a verb to establish the basic meaning of a sentence or clause. Subjects are nouns, pronouns, or constructions that function as nouns.

Costs are rising.

To argue with him is a waste of time.

Cleaning the garage is not my idea of a pleasant way to spend the weekend.

Subject–Verb Agreement

The principle of matching singular subjects with singular verbs and plural subjects with plural verbs.

He has his work cut out for him.

They have their work cut out for them.

Subordinate Conjunction

A word used to begin a subordinate clause—a clause that expresses an idea of subordinate or secondary importance. Subordinate conjunctions include words such as *although, because, before, since, while, when, if, until*. See *Clause*.

Subordination

The stylistic technique of expressing less important ideas in subordinate clauses and phrases.

Although I am angry with you, I am still willing to listen to your side of the story.

Tense

The form of the verb that shows its time (past, present, future).

Tense Shift

The error of shifting abruptly and with no obvious reason from one verb tense to another.

Hamlet **was** angry when he **confronts** his mother.

Verb

A word that indicates action (*run, jump, breathe*), sensation (*feel, taste, smell*), possession (*have, own*), or existence (*are, were, seem, become*). A verb phrase consists of a main verb (a past or present participle) and one or more auxiliary verbs. For more information on verb phrases, see *Participle* and *Auxiliary Verb*. For more information on verbs, see *Tense, Mood, Active Voice, Passive Voice*, and *Subject–Verb Agreement*.

E1

Appendix F

Answer Keys

Chapter 18

Exercise 18.1

1. you must not falsify data or ignore contradictory evidence.
2. Clarence cut the questioning short
3. Kathryn wound up for the pitch.
4. Govind admired his handiwork
5. Hans noticed a large blue stain

Exercise 18.2

1. I dreaded the monthly special on quarter chicken legs.
2. The packages were poorly sealed.
3. The juices leaked all over the conveyor belt and all over my hands
4. I sanitized the belt and my hands with antibacterial cleanser after each order.
5. my dog would practically knock me to the ground in his efforts to "kiss" me hello.

Exercise 18.3

Because sentences containing comma splices can be corrected in a number of ways, these sentences suggest only one of a number of possible revisions.

1. A loud crackling sound alerted Gerta to the fact that she had left the foil cover on the dish; both the meal and the microwave oven were ruined.
2. Alicia offered to replace my shift; when I called to confirm the arrangement, however, she had changed her mind.
3. As we waited in line, we heard Jason's unmistakable braying laugh. We hoped he wouldn't see us before we could disappear into the darkened theatre.

4. Tina groaned in dismay at the error message; then she pulled out the massive user guide and started her search for help.

5. Neither team chose Maria, so she took her ball and went home.

Exercise 18.4

Technology is presented as much less powerful in *Dr. Jekyll and Mr. Hyde* than in *The Fly*. **While** Dr. Jekyll remains recognizably human as Mr. Hyde, Seth Brundle becomes completely non-human by the end of *The Fly*. Of course, Dr. Jekyll remains human-looking partly because special effects were more limited in the 1930s. Thus there are only minor changes in his appearance when he becomes Mr. Hyde: his hair is longer, his eyes are brighter and darker, and his jaw is larger to accommodate his bigger teeth. The focus in this movie is less on the power of science than on the evil part of Dr. Jekyll's nature when it is acted out by Mr. Hyde. Science is much more threatening in *The Fly* **because** it has the power to change not only a man's appearance but his species as well. In fact, the focus in *The Fly* is almost entirely on the horrifying changes taking place in Seth Brundle's appearance. By the end of the film, he is spitting teeth into a sink and accidentally tearing off parts of his face. His inner organs are now mostly outside his skeleton. This, the film is telling us, is what happens to scientists who do not know how to control the technology they have created. They can turn the machine on, but they cannot predict what it will do or stop it once it has started.

Exercise 18.5

1. Marvinder shifted slowly and repeatedly between forward and reverse; she was therefore able to gain traction and move the car out of the mud.

2. Beatrice checked e-mail three times a day because she didn't want to miss any messages.

3. Watch where you're going, or you'll walk into the wall.

4. Without thinking, Delmar opened the side door and was startled by a shrieking siren. He had forgotten to deactivate the alarm.

5. Washing four loads of shirts this morning was a chore; even more daunting is the prospect of all that ironing.

Exercise 18.6

The contrasting endings of the two films reveal very clearly the difference fifty years have made in people's attitudes toward scientific technology. In the earlier film, Mr. Hyde becomes Dr. Jekyll again as soon as the potion wears off, **but** in the later film Seth Brundle can do nothing to stop his transformation into a fly once the computer has locked him into its program. In *Dr. Jekyll and Mr. Hyde*, the focus is more on the character and intentions of the scientist than on the technology he **employs. The** implication in this film is that we have nothing to fear from science as long as it is in the hands of the right people. In *The Fly*, on the other hand, the technology is so powerful that the character and intentions of the people who use it are much less important. In this film, scientists create machines with minds of their **own; moreover,** these machines are indifferent to the wishes and best interests of their creators. In the 1930s scientists could control their creations, **so** they were responsible for them. In the 1980s no one could be sure what would happen when high-tech machinery was set into motion.

Exercise 18.7

1. Wendell **drove** around in circles, unable to find his date's house in the maze-like neighbourhood.
2. According to *The Hitchhiker's Guide to the Galaxy*, forty-two is the answer to the meaning of life, the universe, and everything.
3. After getting up to change channels himself because the remote control battery was **dead, Brad** sank back exhausted onto the couch.
4. Lydia **is** the last person I expected to quit school.
5. **The driver was** angry at the parking attendant for writing up a ticket because the meter had expired.

F1

Exercise 18.8

1. **He was** always quick to judge others, but he bridled at even the mildest criticism.
2. **C**
3. The fans **cheered** wildly as the defenceman raced down the ice.
4. **C**
5. **She is** a woman with fierce pride and a determined spirit.
6. The reason for the fire **was** a pot of hot oil left burning on the stove.
7. **C**
8. **She tore** open the envelope and nervously **removed** the transcript of her final grades.
9. Although I could detect movement inside, no one **answered** my knock.
10. Because he didn't phone in or show up for work, **Garry lost his job**.

Exercise 18.9

Marsha slammed the car into the parking spot, jumped out, and raced across the lot. **She prayed** she wasn't too late. The usual crises that morning **had delayed** her escape from the house. Darren's little tirade— he would not eat peanut butter sandwiches for lunch two days in a row— had taken a good five minutes. Krista's venting—why did Marsha keep buying her such stupid clothes for school?—**lasted** another ten. The clock read 8:30 as Marsha shoved in her card for imprinting. **It was official;** she was on time. Marsha couldn't afford to keep losing a quarter-hour's pay as penalty for punching in late. She opened the supervisor's memo and looked over the day's orders. "(1) Dust all the shelves from top to bottom. Don't miss any shelves," the list began. "(2) Put the new price labels on the shelves. Be sure to use the correct prices." *Yes, the correct prices,* Marsha thought. Well, maybe she could do something right today. Marsha picked up the duster **and set to work**.

Exercise 18.10

1. Robert can either work and save money for college or take out a student loan.
2. The more I try to convince him otherwise, the more determined he is to dye his hair green.
3. The Bennetts' house is smaller than their neighbour's.
4. My car needs new paint, new tires, and a new transmission.
5. **C**
6. The store went out of business because of inferior merchandise, high prices, and poor customer service.
7. I haven't decided whether to study or whether to go skiing during reading week.
8. Gina is both a skilled pianist and a talented baseball player.
9. Before becoming actors, some famous stars worked in other fields. For example, Harrison Ford was a master carpenter, and Michelle Pfeiffer was a cashier.
10. **C**

Exercise 18.11

The flu symptoms started with a minor sore throat that slowly evolved into searing pain with every swallow. Tiredness progressed to exhaustion, a slight flush transmuted into a burning fever and drenching perspiration, and general discomfort metamorphosed into total misery. All my major joints and most of my major muscles ached profoundly. To make matters worse, the pain of past injuries returned to torment me. The scar on my left thumb, the result of stitches needed to close a gash caused by the slip of a paring knife, hurt as intensely as a fresh wound. My right hamstring, which I'd pulled years ago in a skiing accident, throbbed mercilessly. Several knuckles, mashed last summer when I misjudged the distance to the end of the swimming pool, stiffened in agony. With this flu virus I was doubly cursed. All I could do was gulp down aspirins, lie in bed, and pray for an end to the pains, both present and past.

Exercise 18.12

1. Because their home was badly damaged by fire, the Wongs have been living in a rented house.

   Or

   The Wongs have been living in a rented house since their home was badly damaged by fire.

2. Although Gina used the proper amount of bromine and shocked the pool regularly with chlorine, the pool sides were still covered with algae.

3. The pilot light in the basement fireplace frequently goes out when snow blocks the outside vent.

4. Because Todd forgot to include his charitable receipts in his income tax return, his refund was delayed.

5. If you want to buy a computer, call Roman, who is an expert on the best buys.

6. Although Craig isn't doing well in physics, he doesn't seem particularly concerned.

7. When I entered the building and heard the final bell, I knew I was late for class.

8. Even though Marina hates the taste of ketchup, she likes ketchup-flavoured potato chips.

9. Because I couldn't hear what he was saying, I asked him to speak up.

10. Everyone has been complaining about the heat since the air conditioner broke down.

Exercise 18.13

1. Geraldine asked her brother Ben how much longer he would be in the shower.

2. Because my dog ate my computer disk, my paper is late.

3. Portaging is carrying a boat overland between navigable lakes or rivers.

4. In his letter Darrin explained why he resigned his position.

5. The reason we cut our vacation short is that it rained for a solid week.

6. Without more donations, the shelter will have to close.

7. Looking at his bank statement, Domenic wondered how he had spent so much money in only a month.

8. Mary shows her thoughtfulness when she cuts the lawn for her elderly neighbours.

9. The theatre program lists all the actors in the play.

10. The next day Frank finally thought of a snappy comeback to Vincent's insulting remark.

Chapter 19

Exercise 19.1

1. seriously
2. runs well
3. fewer players
4. really interested
5. do so well

Exercise 19.2

1. most lively
2. considerably better
3. went well
4. fewer social occasions
5. is empty
6. C
7. as honestly
8. really tired
9. C
10. less happy

Exercise 19.3

1. Soak the shirt with the spaghetti sauce stain in cold water.

2. Sonia could run almost ten full circuits around the field.

3. The students examined the jar of tapeworms preserved in formaldehyde.

4. I promise not to judge you unfairly.

5. Standing by the band, I had difficulty hearing the conversation.

Exercise 19.4

1. The singer's fans could hardly wait . . .

2. You can eat properly cooked hamburger . . .

3. I want to consider all my options thoroughly . . .

4. **C**

5. Seeing the accident ahead, Tran pulled the car to the side of the road and got out to investigate.

6. Eating our lunch on the patio, we enjoyed . . .

7. . . . you ate only half the pizza.

8. With his mouth full of toothpaste, Jim heard . . .

9. On the hall table there is a family picture . . .

10. **C**

Exercise 19.5

1. P   3. P   5. A

2. A   4. P

Exercise 19.6

1. Walking into the room, I saw a strange sight.

   Or

   When I walked into the room, a strange sight caught my eye.

2. While George was in high school, his father was promoted and the family moved to Vancouver.

3. Because Maurice was exhausted by a heavy work schedule, the doctor recommended a complete rest.

4. To make a perfect omelette, you require the freshest ingredients.

5. After pleading earnestly, Theresa was happy when her parents extended her curfew to midnight.

Exercise 19.7

1. To have a chance at winning the lottery, you must first buy a ticket.

2. **C**

3. Driven by arrogance and greed, Joe soon alienated his friends.

4. After working so hard on the committee, Bernard definitely deserves our gratitude.

5. **C**

6. While I was reading Stephen King's *Cujo*, my dog began barking in the backyard.

7. **C**

8. While Hank was driving on the highway, his car engine suddenly seized.

9. As I stared intently at the small print, spots began to swim before my eyes.

10. To build a better mousetrap, you need the proper tools.

F2

Exercise 19.8

When the morning radio announcer reported that snow was moving in rapidly from the country and had already reached the city limits, Karen went to the window in anticipation. Soon the first flakes filtered down and clung to bare tree branches, bushes, and the few hardy annuals in the front flower bed that had survived the last frost. The snow that reached the lawn, driveway, and road melted immediately. *Oh, I hope some of it stays,* thought Karen. *The first snow makes everything look so much cleaner and fresher.*

The snow had been falling only a few hours, but already the world was transformed. Karen looked out at the road and yard, which had merged into one smooth, pristine expanse. "Exquisite," she sighed. She pushed away thoughts of tomorrow and work; she wanted merely to enjoy the beauty of the snow, the warmth of the fireplace, and the cozy security of her family room. Wishing there were more days like this, she went back to her novel.

As she stood again at the window in late afternoon, Karen could barely see through the dense whiteness. Turning on the radio, she heard reports of numerous cars in ditches and two injury accidents downtown. City crews were struggling to clear major arteries, while most side streets remained impassable. Motorists were advised to avoid area highways because of white-out conditions. "Well, folks," the announcer continued, "with no end to the snow in sight, it looks as though we're going to have a few more days like this."

Chapter 20

Exercise 20.1

1. should have done
2. have worn
3. lies
4. had known
5. The reason is
6. rang
7. has not written
8. **C**
9. saw
10. **C**

Exercise 20.2

As a child, Vanessa expresses her imaginative concerns in the stories of "spectacular heroism" that she composes in her head to counteract the boredom of Sunday School lessons. Essentially she **rejects** any ties between her fictional world and the reality she experiences growing up in a little prairie town. Although she acknowledges Manawaka in her tale of the infant swept away in its christening robe by the flooding Wachakwa River, she **transforms** this muddy little river into an agent of the grotesque. Beyond this, Manawaka seems hardly worthy of literary note. For Vanessa, the "ordinary considerations" of life **are** completely divorced from the dramatic considerations of art. Thus she abandons her heroic epic, "The Pillars of the Nation," when she **learns** that Grandfather Connor, with his boring stories of the past, is himself one of those pillars.

Exercise 20.3

1. The light changed to amber before Oliver reached the intersection.
2. **C** [The agent opening the pool is unknown or unimportant.]
3. Burt completely misunderstood my directions.
4. **C** [The agent adjourning the meeting is unimportant.]
5. Marietta spilled the milk, but she made no effort to wipe it up.
6. **C** [The agent shutting down the site is unknown.]
7. **C** [if you want to emphasize Marcia's feelings]
8. After we trimmed and raked the lawn, we weeded the front flower bed.
9. Before setting out to write my exam, I searched for my good luck pen, but I couldn't find it anywhere.
10. **C** [The sentence emphasizes the late delivery.]

Exercise 20.4

1. sisters/are	6. goldfish/makes
2. team/has	7. **C**
3. Neither/is	8. jury/has
4. **C**	9. Each/has
5. Fear/is	10. Nothing/seems

Chapter 21

Exercise 21.1

1. manager/his or her [**Or** all managers/their]
2. immigrant/he or she [**Or** new immigrants/they]
3. day-care worker/his or her [**Or** day-care workers/their]
4. actor/he or she [**Or** actors/they]
5. customer service representative/his or her [**Or** customer service representatives/their]

Exercise 21.2

1. supervisor/his **or** supervisor/her [**Better:** Neither the supervisor nor the employees/their]
2. **C**
3. herd/its/its
4. committee/its
5. Matt/Richard/his
6. government/its
7. group/its [**Or** the hotel]
8. **C** [class acting as individuals]
9. family/its [family acting as unit]
10. Pierre/Antoine/his

Exercise 21.3

1. Everyone/his or her
2. **C**
3. Each/his or her
4. Neither/his/he
5. **C**

Exercise 21.4 Pronoun Agreement Review

1. writer/his or her [**Or** writers/their]
2. Neither/his
3. **C**
4. No one/his or her
5. **C**
6. Stacey/Veronica/her
7. addict/his or her [**Or** addicts/their]
8. **C**
9. army/its
10. Everyone/his or her
11. **C**
12. Sandra/Brianne/her
13. Neither/his
14. winner/his or her
15. who/his [*Who* is singular because it refers to *man*.]

Exercise 21.5 Pronoun Agreement Review

Psychologists say that altruism, which the dictionary defines as an "unselfish concern for the welfare of others," is actually a form of selfishness. In essence, altruists are motivated as much by self-interest as by interest in others. For example, altruists genuinely enjoy helping their neighbour build a fence. Altruists feel needed when they offer advice to family and friends. Altruists gain comfort themselves by comforting others in sorrow or pain. In short, being good makes an altruist feel good. This description is not meant to disparage altruism, of course. Someone for whom virtue truly is a reward is a decent and worthy person, and the world deserves more of his or her kind.

Exercise 21.6

1. We workers
2. He and I
3. than she
4. whom to contact
5. or me
6. or him
7. Adrilla and I
8. Michael, Stephen, and he
9. that she and her sister
10. **C**

Exercise 21.7

1. anyone's
2. Whose
3. yours
4. Theirs
5. its

Exercise 21.8 Review of Pronoun Case and Possessive Pronouns

1. Nigel or me
2. he and his brothers
3. than I that you and she
4. their furniture
5. whose limousine
6. hers
7. Between you and me
8. **C**
9. Dave and I
10. her boyfriend and she

Exercise 21.9

This past spring my sister Adele and **I** decided to throw a surprise anniversary party for Aunt Charlotte and Uncle Ted, my mother's brother. Swearing our parents to secrecy, we enlisted **their** help in making up a guest list. That simple request marked the beginning of a heated debate about **who** was and **who** was not in the family's good graces. Mother vetoed her sister Gerta because Gerta hadn't stopped by or even phoned to say hello the last time she was in town. In fact, Mother said that **she** and Gerta hadn't spoken since. Father agreed that Gerta was a pain and that he wanted both **her** and Mother's sister Lucille off the list. Father had never been able to stomach Lucille's constant yackety-yack about those boring Caribbean cruises **she** and Uncle Dan took every winter.

"And just **whose** brother never shuts up about his glorious high school football career, as though anyone cares about what happened thirty years ago?" rejoined Mother.

I remained silent, but my sister, always more forthright than I, jumped in with, "Let's not fight. An anniversary is a time of celebration, of loving and caring and sharing. Why can't we all just get along?"

"Good grief," said Mother as she glared at both my sister and **me**, "what greeting card have you been reading? Between you and **me**, **ours** is not the most functional of families. A special occasion is a time when we can stick it to annoying relatives by leaving them out." With those parting words, Mother went to make supper, and Father to walk the dog.

"Okay," I said to Adele, "**it's** obviously up to **us** two to send out the invitations ourselves. It will be a surprise party all right. Everyone will get a big surprise when they see who's there."

"Right," Adele replied. "Now, I know you like Cousin Carol, but I have a few thoughts on that matter."

Exercise 21.10

1. Experts say

2. when you know your behaviour upsets her?

3. when Nicole told her, "You [or I] didn't get the job."

4. but my efforts

5. the service representative said

6. but at the time Giselle didn't know what had caused the problem.

7. The pie crust is tough because Raul added too much water to the dough and beat it mercilessly.

8. but these qualities don't bother his friends.

9. His actions greatly surprised me.

10. Mr. Carlsen ruined the lawn by applying too much weed killer and overwatering the grass.

Exercise 21.11

Benevolence is certainly a desirable quality, but **being benevolent** doesn't give us the right to force our goodwill on others. In performing our good deed or random act of kindness for the day, we must guard against making assumptions about what **other people** need. The fact that we may be too warm, for instance, doesn't mean that we have to turn up the car air conditioner and adjust the vent to blow directly into a **passenger's face**. The fact that we may love creamed rutabagas shouldn't compel us to urge third helpings on a dinner guest. And the fact that we know how to live our lives doesn't justify our constantly advising **family and friends** on how to live theirs. There are times to help other people and times to respect their independence and their ability to help themselves.

Exercise 21.12

1. because I never know
2. Even when they are knowledgeable and competent,
3. **C**
4. The owners claim that they can hear
5. because he doesn't want to lose a tooth that can be saved.

Exercise 21.13

You can write this paragraph in either the third person (applicants/the applicant) or the second person (you). Both versions are shown below.

    For Canadians, working in The Bahamas is not simply a matter of finding a job, packing a swimsuit, and heading south. Anyone seeking employment in The Bahamas must meet a number of requirements before he or she is considered for a work permit. [OR: If you are seeking employment in The Bahamas, you must meet a number of requirements before you are considered for a work permit.] One important requirement is verification from the [your] prospective employer that the position was first advertised in The Bahamas but that no suitable candidate was found. The employer will usually handle this detail. The applicant arranges [you arrange] for the remaining documentation. For example, an applicant [you] must hold a valid passport. Applying for a passport involves submitting an application form along with two passport-size photographs. One photo and the form must be signed by a professional, such as a medical doctor or school principal, who acts as a guarantor. In addition to the passport, applicants [you] must complete an Immigration Form I. In this form the applicant provides [you provide] information on passport number and date of expiry, all education and work experience, the job applied for, and expected salary. Applicants [you] must also attach two signed, passport-size photographs to this form and enclose the following: police certificate showing no record of conviction for the past five years, a valid medical certificate issued no earlier than thirty days before completion of the form, references from two previous employers, and copies of any results of public examinations described in the section on education. The applicant [you] must have this form signed and dated by a Notary Public. Applicants [you] will not receive permission to work in The Bahamas until they [you] have submitted the Immigration Form I and all of the supporting documentation.

Chapter 22

Exercise 22.1

1. two suitcases, called a cab, and headed for the airport.
2. eye of newt, toe of frog, wool of bat, and tongue of dog.
3. to put the armoire in the master bedroom, the console in the hall, and the pine desk in the study.
4. bread, cheese, cold cuts, fruit, and sodas
5. the meat was underdone, the vegetables were soggy, and the wine was sour.

Exercise 22.2

1. now, for
2. the wall, and David
3. editor, yet
4. colour, or the house
5. produce, but

Exercise 22.3

1. For example, pizza/groups, but
2. in Calgary,
3. on the tile floor, he
4. High above, the planes
5. No, I don't remember

Exercise 22.4

1. fever, isn't it?
2. **C**
3. However, I always counter, "Look before you leap."
4. no man, if you catch my drift.
5. the savage breast, not the savage beast.

Exercise 22.5

1. Thank you, Mr. Sutherland,
2. **C**
3. Punch Dickins, who won the Distinguished Flying Cross in World War I,
4. python, which hasn't eaten in a month,
5. promised us, however, that

Exercise 22.6 Comma Review

1. Winnipeg, Manitoba?
2. turkey sandwiches, turkey casserole, and turkey croquettes
3. has expired, Mr. Fortino, is not
4. microwave sounded, Ted
5. **C** [no commas]
6. Whenever we go camping, Father always says, "If you don't fish where the fish are, you'll be having hot dogs for supper."
7. opened the window, took a deep breath, and composed
8. The one novel that I didn't read was the basis for the essay question on the English exam. [no commas]
9. Lucy Maud Montgomery, the author of *Anne of Green Gables*, was born in Clifton, Prince Edward Island, on November 30, 1874.
10. Well, you
11. perspective, I
12. Yes, we do
13. Howard would bring the food, Cliff would bring the drinks, and you
14. deep drifts, and icicles
15. Taxes, of course, are
16. Even during the day, light
17. Mr. Ramondo said, "We're a few bricks short of a load, but I
18. **C** [no commas]
19. dark, stormy night I like nothing better than
20. to study engineering because she discovered that

Exercise 22.7

1. astronaut; he
2. jeans; however,
3. door; but, fortunately,
4. family; Erica
5. night; as a result,

Exercise 22.8

1. interpretation, he [semicolon replaced with a comma]
2. use; otherwise,
3. stop, patiently waiting [semicolon replaced with a comma]
4. **C**
5. local band;/comedy act; and

Exercise 22.9

1. choices: "When choosing
2. term: Basic Calculus,
3. convinced—I say this without reservation—that Luke
4. suspects—Winken, Blinken, or Nod—knew
5. companion: he

Exercise 22.10

1. escape: all [**Or:** escape—all]
2. **C**
3. Mrs. Christie—you met her last week at the Doyles' party—will
4. furniture—all
5. state: he

Exercise 22.11

1. "Two negatives make a positive," explained Ludwig. "However, two positives don't make a negative."
   "Yeah, right!" replied Noam.
2. **C**
3. proverb, "When money talks, the truth keeps silent."
4. "like" and "basically" [**Or** *like* and *basically*]
5. "The Death of the Moth"

Exercise 22.12

1. "No, I won't move my car!" shouted the irate driver.
2. **C**
3. said, "Give me a firm place to stand, and I will move the earth"?
4. The term "portmanteau word" refers to a word combining the sounds and meanings of two other words. For example, the word "smog" is a blending of the words "smoke" and "fog." [period goes inside the quotation marks]

   Or *portmanteau word/smog/smoke/fog.*
5. "Dulce et Decorum Est" and Randall Jarrell's poem "The Death of the Ball Turret Gunner." [period goes inside the quotation marks]

Exercise 22.13

1. said, "The acorn never falls far from the oak tree"?
2. "If fifty million people say a foolish thing," noted Anatole France, "it is still a foolish thing."
3 yelling, "We all scream for ice cream!"
4. "chimpanzee"/"gorilla"/"zebra" [**Or** *chimpanzee/gorilla/zebra*]
5. Sam Cooke's "Sad Mood."

Exercise 22.14

1. all-purpose floor covering
2. self-satisfied/twenty-three/equally qualified
3. "workmen"/"mankind"
4. ninety-year-old/weekend
5. ex-boyfriend/compact disks

Exercise 22.15

1. icono-clast
2. cry-baby
3. wrap-ping
4. **C** [no hyphen]
5. **C** [no hyphen]
6. rail-road
7. thrill-ing
8. jim-jams
9. memo-rize
10. **C** [no hyphen]

Exercise 22.16

1. Helen's/Stephanie's/year's
2. patrons'
3. Nobody's
4. Men's/women's/store's
5. Anne's/sister-in-law's

Exercise 22.17

1. *u*'s
2. It's/hostess'
3. Mary's
4. Justin's/parents'
5. Someone's
6. children's
7. Don't/*um*'s/*uh*'s.
8. month's
9. Won't/Mildred's
10. book's

Exercise 22.18

1. four 250-page
2. Fifteen percent
3. twenty
4. **C**
5. 1980s or 1980's/1999

Exercise 22.19

1. Archaeologists have uncovered what they believe is the **principal** residence of Colonel John Butler in Niagara-on-the-Lake. Butler **led** his Loyalist Rangers in numerous raids into New York State during the American War of Independence.

2. **It's** true that **you're** now taller **than** your father, but you still weigh considerably less.

3. During a chinook some people suffer from headaches or depression; others are not **affected** at all.

4. Louis Riel was **hanged** at Regina on November 7, 1885.

5. "Help, I'm **losing** my balance!" yelled Jack.
   "Are you **all right**?" Jill called after him as he tumbled down the hill.

6. Rip is over **there lying** under the maple tree, apparently **uninterested** in everything around him.

7. By the middle of the movie, **many** of the patrons were **bored with** the trite plot and one-dimensional characters. In fact, a considerable **number** of people had already left the theatre.

8. **As** I said before, I usually trust my own judgment, but this time I'll **defer** to your greater experience.

9. Mother divided the candy equally **among** all the children.

10. **I hope** we will be able to catch David Copperfield's special on television. He is a master of **illusion**.

F5

382

Index

Boldface italicized terms are included in the Glossary of Grammatical Terms (Appendix E).